S0-BRV-110

ANNEXATION, PREFERENTIAL TRADE, AND RECIPROCITY

ST. MARY'S COLLEGE OF MARYLAND
ST. MARY'S CITY, MARYLAND

46364

ANNEXATION, PREFERENTIAL TRADE AND RECIPROCITY

AN OUTLINE OF THE CANADIAN ANNEXATION MOVEMENT OF 1849—50, WITH SPECIAL REFERENCE TO THE QUESTIONS OF PREFERENTIAL TRADE AND RECIPROCITY

BY

CEPHAS D. ALLIN, M.A., LL.B.

Assistant Professor of Political Science, University of Minnesota

AND

GEORGE M. JONES, B.A.

English and History Master, Humberside Collegiate Institute, Toronto

GREENWOOD PRESS, PUBLISHERS
WESTPORT, CONNECTICUT

Originally published in 1912
by The Musson Book Company, Ltd.,
Toronto and London

First Greenwood Reprinting 1971

Library of Congress Catalogue Card Number 79-114453

SBN 8371-4706-9

Printed in the United States of America

PREFACE

ALTHOUGH the United States has exercised a most important influence on the course of Canadian history, but little attention has been paid by historians and political scientists to the mutual relations of the two countries. The question of the incorporation of the British American colonies in the American union has been a recurrent subject for political consideration since the War of Independence. In Canada, from time to time, it has become a vital political issue. But almost all the discussions of the question have been marked by the most bitter partisan feelings. The simple facts of history have sometimes been suppressed, and ofttimes misrepresented, or gravely distorted for political purposes. Even the biographers and historians, in some cases, have been tempted to accept their facts, and their judgments in respect to the same, from the opinions of interested politicians or the views of a partisan press.

In this monograph, the writers have attempted to deal with one phase, and that perhaps the most important one, of the annexation movement in Canada. They have endeavoured to discover the origin of the political and economic discontent of 1849, to trace out

v

the development of the agitation, to show the extent of its ramifications and its effect upon political parties, and to explain, in part at least, the divers reasons for the failure of the movement. A few paragraphs have been added in regard to the condition of affairs in the maritime provinces, and as to the state of public opinion in England and the United States. In order that the reader may better appreciate the spirit of the movement, the authors have thought it best to allow, as far as possible, the chief participants in these stirring events to tell their own contradictory stories, rather than themselves to set forth an independent interpretation of the historical facts. A study of the facts presented, it is believed, will serve to remove any preconception as to the superior quality of Canadian fealty, or as to the immunity of any political party from the insidious virus of disloyalty during protracted periods of economic distress and social and political unrest ; but, at the same time, it will bear the most convincing testimony to the self-sacrificing loyalty of the great body of the Canadian people under the most trying circumstances, and to their firm attachment to the polity and free institutions of the motherland.

CONTENTS

CHAPTER I

THE ORIGIN OF THE MOVEMENT

CHAPTER II

THE SPIRIT OF DISCONTENT

CHAPTER III

THE MANIFESTO AND THE COUNTER MANIFESTOS

CHAPTER IV

THE MOVEMENT IN LOWER CANADA

CHAPTER V

THE MOVEMENT IN UPPER CANADA

CHAPTER VI

THE DECLINE OF THE MOVEMENT

CHAPTER VII

THE COLLAPSE OF THE MOVEMENT

CHAPTER I

THE ORIGIN OF THE MOVEMENT

The revolt of 1837—The grant of responsible government—The Rebellion Losses Bill—Bitterness of the Tory Party—Imperial preferential trade—Canadian Corn Act, 1843—Adoption of Free Trade—Protests of Canadian Boards of Trade—Fiscal freedom of the Colonies—Abolition of English preference—Economic distress—The question of reciprocity—Representation of Lord Elgin—The Navigation Laws—Petition for repeal of Laws—Memorial of Montreal Board of Trade—Address of Liberal Free Traders—Whig Government proposes abrogation of Laws—Opposition of Tory Party—Repeal of the Navigation Laws—Movement for American reciprocity—The Dix Bill—Enactment of Reciprocity Bill by the Canadian Parliament—English opinion in regard to the Colonies—The Liberal Imperialists—The Manchester School—Influence of the new tenets in Canada—Opinion of Lord Elgin regarding annexation sentiment.

THE long and apparently fruitless struggle of the Upper Canada Reformers against the exclusive political privileges of the Family Compact drove the extreme wing of the party under Mackenzie into an alliance with Papineau, the fiery leader of the French Canadian Radicals, who, under the guise of a constitutional agitation for popular elective institutions, was marshalling the simple habitants into battle array against the racial ascendency of the English minority. Out of this alliance of the ultra-democratic parties in the two provinces developed the revolt of 1837. The constitutional outcome of the rebellion was a complete reorganization of the government of the Colonies under the Act of Union, 1840. The political results were equally far-reaching and important : the re-establishment of the personal authority of the Governors, the rehabilitation of the Tory Party—the stalwart defenders of British institutions—and the temporary demoralization of the Reformers. Torn by internal dissensions and discredited by the rebellion, the Reform Party scarcely dared for a time to oppose the haughty supremacy of the Government.[1]

Fortunately for colonial Liberalism, a gradual change was taking place in the views of English statesmen in respect to colonial policy. The leaders of the Whig Party began to realize that the Liberal principles of the British Constitution could no longer be restricted to the motherland, but must be extended to the colonies as well. The several Colonial Secretaries were not averse to satisfying the demands of colonial Liberals for a wider measure of local autonomy ; but, for a time, they each and all were firmly possessed of the idea that the exclusive political responsibility of the Governor to the Colonial Office was essential to the permanence of the imperial connection. To surrender the control of the Colonial Executives to the Colonial Legislatures would necessarily involve, in their opinion, the grant of independence. This fundamental postulate of colonial policy was admirably stated by Lord John Russell, one of the most liberal and sympathetic of British statesmen, in a speech in the House of Commons in 1837. " Responsible government in the Colonies," he declared, " was incompatible with the relations which ought to exist between the mother country and the colony. Those relations required that Her Majesty should be represented in the colony, not by ministers, but by a Governor sent out by the Sovereign and responsible to the Parliament of Great Britain. Otherwise Great Britain would have in the Canadas all the inconveniences of colonies without any of their advantages."

The rebellion of 1837 opened the eyes of the English

---

[1] It should be added, however, that the first shortlived ministry after the Union was a coalition one, of which Baldwin was a member.

Government to the gravity of the situation in Canada, and to the necessity of introducing some constitutional reforms. The special mission of Lord Durham produced the celebrated report which is justly regarded as the most important constitutional document in the history of Canada. In this report his lordship recommended that " the responsibility to the united legislatures of all officers of the Government, except the Governor and his Secretary, should be secured by every means known to the British Constitution." But Her Majesty's advisers were scarcely prepared as yet to grant such an extension of responsible government as was contemplated by Lord Durham. However, an important step was taken in that direction in a despatch of Lord John Russell, in 1839, in respect to the tenure of office of colonial officials. An even more important concession was made in the instructions which were given to Lord Sydenham for his guidance in the conduct of the local administration.

In addressing the first Parliament of the united provinces in 1841, his lordship declared : " The Governor-General has received Her Majesty's commands to administer the government of the provinces in accordance with the well-understood wishes and interests of the people, and to pay to their feelings, as expressed through their representatives, the deference that is justly due to them." But the fair promise of a more liberal administration was cut short by the death of the popular Governor, and the nomination two years later of a successor of altogether different type and principles. Sir Charles Melcalfe quickly quarrelled with his Liberal constitutional advisers over the question of the appointment of officials, forced their resignations, and threw himself on the side of the Tories in the ensuing elections. Thanks to the strenuous efforts of the Governor, who fought the campaign on the old loyalty cry, the Tory Party was restored to power with a very small majority. As a result of the victory, Sir Charles was enabled to re-establish the former régime of the personal ascendency of the Governor. He was in fact his own Prime Minister. Fortunately for the Governor, a Tory Government was in power in England, and he was able to count upon the whole-hearted support of the Colonial Office throughout his administration.

The restoration of the Whigs to office promised brighter things for colonial Liberalism. Several of the leaders of the Whig Party together with their Radical supporters were inoculated with the liberal principles of the Manchester School. The appointment of Lord Elgin as Governor-General in 1847 practically committed the Whig Ministry in advance to the application of British constitutional principles in Canada. At the provincial general elections the following year Lord Elgin assumed a strictly impartial attitude ; and, as a result of the withdrawal of the accustomed influence of the Governor, the Tory Ministry went down to a crushing defeat. His Excellency at once called upon the Reformers to form a government. A union of the French and English sections of the party resulted in the formation of a strong Coalition Ministry under the joint leadership of Lafontaine and Baldwin. The goal of the Reformers was at last attained. To their own chosen leaders was entrusted by a sympathetic Governor the responsibility of directing the affairs of the colony according to the Liberal principles of the British Constitution.

Their defeat at the general election was a bitter pill for the Tory Party. They had been so long accustomed to regard themselves as the only loyal party, and as such entitled to enjoy the exclusive favour of the Governor, that they could not readily become reconciled to seeing their unpatriotic opponents in office.[1] To make matters worse, with the loss of power they had also lost the political patronage with which the leaders of the party had fostered their own loyalty and rewarded that of their supporters. Their defeat

[1] *Letters and Journals of Lord Elgin*, p. 71.

appeared to them in the light of a dangerous revolution, as an overthrow in fact of a natural and established order of things. It was necessary to find some explanation for their undoing, some vent for their righteous indignation. Unfortunately for the history of Canada, a simple explanation was at hand, namely, French domination. At the general election in 1848, the Tories had failed to carry a single French-Canadian seat. Back of the Lafontaine-Baldwin ministry was marshalled the almost united strength of the French members and population. As a natural consequence, a strong feeling of resentment against the alien race spread throughout the ranks of the Tory Party in Upper Canada.

The rumoured intention of the Government to introduce a Bill to compensate those who had suffered losses in the recent rebellion fanned this resentment into a flame. The introduction of the Bill shortly after set the whole heather afire with anger and indignation. The entire Tory press attacked the proposition in the most reckless inflammatory manner. Mingled with violent denunciations of the Government and tirades against French ascendency were heard some low mutterings of annexation sentiment. The prophecy of Lord Durham had indeed come true ; some of the English minority of Quebec were prepared, if necessary, to sacrifice their allegiance in the hope of retaining their nationality. In Montreal, the bitterness of the English Tories exceeded all bounds. Several of the leading papers openly preached disloyalty, and some of them even resorted to threats of violence. *The Montreal Courier*, one of the leading Tory papers, rashly exclaimed : " A civil war is an evil, but it is not the worst of evils, and we say without hesitation that it would be better for the British people of Canada to have a twelve months' fighting, if it would take so long, and lose five thousand lives, than submit for ten years longer to the misgovernment induced by French domination." [1]

[1] *Montreal Courier*, quoted from *The Examiner*, April 4, 1849.

An equally dangerous and seditious utterance of one of the Montreal papers was regarded by Lord Elgin as sufficiently important and symptomatic of the attitude of the Tory extremists to warrant the serious attention of the Colonial Secretary. "The obvious intent of the majority, composed of Frenchmen aided by treacherous British Canadians, is," it declared, "to force French institutions still further upon the British minority in Lower Canada. The intention is obvious, as we have said, and we are glad that it is openly shown. We trust that the party of the Government will succeed in every one of their obnoxious measures. When French tyranny becomes insufferable, we shall find our Cromwell. Sheffield in the olden times used to be famous for its keen and well-tempered whettles ; well, they make bayonets there now just as sharp and well-tempered. When we can stand tyranny no longer, it will be seen whether good bayonets in Saxon hands will not be more than a match for a race and a majority." [1] On the streets of the city the question of annexation was freely discussed. The state of public opinion among the Montreal Tories was thus summed up by the local correspondent of *The Toronto Patriot*. "The only on-dit of the day worthy of credit refers to the undercurrent leaning of the Anglo-Saxons here towards an annexation with their brethren of the United States, unjustly and untruly attributed to them by Lord Durham in his time, but true as the gospel now." [2]

In Upper Canada the feelings of the Tories were scarcely less bitter and exasperated. In the month of March, *The Kingston Argus* announced that a petition to Her Majesty to allow the province to be annexed to the United States was being circulated in that city. [3] Articles appeared in several of the staunchest Tory papers, such as *The Toronto Colonist* and *The*

[1] Despatch of Elgin to Grey, April 30, 1849.
[2] *The Patriot*, quoted from *The Examiner*, March 14, 1849.
[3] *The Kingston Argus*, March 3, 1849.

Hamilton Spectator, containing scarcely veiled suggestions of annexation. A correspondent of the Hamilton paper declared : " Rather than be trodden upon by French licentiousness . . . let us seek an alliance with at least a kindred race, whose republican views are at least not so rampant. The sad alternative is painful to the loyal heart, but it is decidedly the least of impending evils." A few days later *The Spectator* warned the English authorities of the danger of separation. The Tories, it asserted, would never revolt, but neither would they submit to French domination. When they became dissatisfied with existing conditions, it would not be necessary for them to rebel, for the imperial tie would be severed without opposition. But in any case the responsibility for the final destiny of Canada remained with the English Government.[1] *The Colonist* likewise declared that the intolerable political conditions of the time would inevitably strengthen the demand for annexation among the commercial community.[2]

Political feeling ran almost equally high in the legislative halls. In the course of the debate on the Rebellion Losses Bill, Colonel Gugy frankly stated, in reply to a pointed question from across the House, that, " if this Bill, as passed, be assented to by Her Majesty, it will have the effect of absolving Her Majesty's colonial subjects from their oath of allegiance." The speeches of some of the other Tory members were scarcely less incendiary, if not as seditious, in character.

Some of the Tory fury was undoubtedly inspired by a genuine fear of French domination, but it is nevertheless true that much of the agitation was worked up for purely political ends in the hope of embarrassing the Ministry, and, if possible, of intimidating the Governor into vetoing the Bill.[3] A few of the Tory

---

[1] *The Spectator*, April 7, 1849.
[2] *The Colonist*, July 3, 1849.
[3] *Letters and Journals of Lord Elgin*, p. 75.

papers, realizing the dangerous course upon which the agitation was starting, endeavoured to check the seditious utterances of their contemporaries. " What," asked *The Quebec Gazette*, " would the Tories, and descendants of the United Empire Loyalists, gain as a political party by annexation? They cannot sincerely wish for it. They may, however, by talking of annexation for the purpose of intimidating the Governor, destroy their own reputation for consistent loyalty, ruin the character and credit of the country abroad, and retard its prosperity by preventing the influx of British capital and population." *The Toronto Patriot*, likewise, scented the danger, and called its fellow Tories severely to task for their foolish talk of annexation for purely party purposes.

The Ministerial Party and press did all in their power to minimize the importance and significance of the growing agitation. Their favourite weapon of political warfare was to asperse the motives of their opponents by accusing the latter of stirring up a spirit of disaffection for selfish, political purposes. *The Toronto Globe*, in particular, scored the opposition in merciless fashion. " The Canadian Tories have not been a year out of office, and they are at the rebellion point. . . . Withdraw the supplies, and the Tory soon lets you know that it was not the man or his principles which he loved, but the solid pudding which he could administer." [1] The lesser Reform journals throughout the province faithfully followed the lead of the chief party organ.

A somewhat similar view of the situation was taken by the English Government, which staunchly supported the policy of the Governor-General and his advisers throughout the political crisis. In a caustic editorial, *The London Times*, the mouthpiece of the Whig Ministry, tersely summed up the state of Canadian affairs. " We continue of the opinion, therefore, that at present it is quite unnecessary that

[1] *The Globe*, March 3, 1849,

we should throw ourselves into an agony of indignation at the conduct of the Canadian Cabinet. The
province, of course, is in terrible excitement. Sir
Allan MacNab is now out of office, and has nothing
to do ; so to satisfy a mind of more than ordinary
energy, he has taken to agitation, and is lashing the
whole colony into foam."

When it became apparent that the Government was
determined to force the Rebellion Losses Bill through
Parliament, the Tories turned to the Governor-General,
and besought him either to veto the Bill, or reserve
it for the consideration of the Crown. Indignation
meetings were held in all parts of the country, and
petitions and resolutions protesting against the passage
of the Bill came pouring in to the Governor-General
from all sides. But all this agitation was of no avail.
His Excellency determined to accept the advice of his
ministers ; and, in accordance with the true principles of responsible government, to which he was
pledged on his appointment, duly attached his signature to the Bill. At once a furious storm of Tory passion
broke loose. A wild mob insulted the Governor-
General, stoned his carriage, and completely disgraced
the country by burning the Parliament buildings.

The Tory leaders resolved to carry the fight over
to England. Sir Allan MacNab and a colleague
accordingly set out for Westminster, in the hope of
inducing the English Government to veto the Bill,
and to recall Lord Elgin. The attitude of the extreme
section of the party in respect to the mission was
decidedly menacing towards the home Government.
They declared, in effect, that, if the British Ministry
did not comply with their demands, so much the worse
for the British connection. But unfortunately for
the Tory Party, they did not properly appreciate the
change which had taken place in the views of Whig
statesmen in respect to colonial policy. Despite the
able championship of Mr. Gladstone, and the staunch
support of the Tories in the British Parliament, the

mission of Sir Allan was altogether fruitless. The Whig Ministry stoutly defended the course of the Governor-General, and refused in any way to intervene in what they properly considered a purely domestic controversy between the two political parties.

But an even more insidious source of political discontent was working as a canker upon the loyalty of the Canadian people. The whole province, and particularly the Montreal district, was passing through a period of severe commercial adversity. The trade of many foreign states and of the motherland was, at the time, in a generally depressed condition, the effect of which was unmistakably felt in all the colonies ; but owing to local circumstances, largely arising out of the change in England's commercial policy, Canada was plunged into a slough of financial distress from which she did not seem able to extricate herself.

The early commercial policy of England, as of other European nations, had been based upon the strictest mercantilistic principles. The primary object of colonization was to gain a monopoly of trade. Imperial commerce was reserved, as far as possible, as an exclusive field for British traders and manufacturers. In time, the narrow policy of monopoly gave way to a more enlightened system of preferential trade,[1] but the old spirit of commercial privilege still reigned supreme. "The principle," said Earl Grey, "of placing the trade with the colonies on a different footing from that of other countries had been maintained up to the year 1846, and was generally regarded as one of unquestioned propriety and wisdom."[2] Although the colonies were chiefly prized as valuable markets for English exploitation, nevertheless the fiscal policy of the parliament at Westminster was not so selfish and one-sided as to exclude the colonies from certain reciprocal advantages in the markets of the homeland. The principle of a mutual preference between England

---

[1] Shortt, *Imperial Preferential Trade*, p. 30.
[2] Lord Grey, *Colonial Policy*, vol. i. p. 7.

and the colonies served, it was thought, the twofold purpose of promoting inter-imperial trade, and of strengthening at the same time the loyalty of British subjects throughout the dependencies.

The preferential duties of the colonies in favour of the motherland were moderate in amount, and did not impose much of a burden upon either England or the colonies on account of the essential difference in their economic status. England was not a food-exporting nation, and the colonies as yet had scarcely entered upon the industrial stage of their existence. The preference was of little advantage to England in respect to European nations, since, by reason of her superior industrial organization, she could manufacture much more cheaply than any of her competitors. On the other hand, the colonial preference in the English market was of the greatest importance to the colonists, as their products were excluded from the markets of other nations by high protective tariffs. As a natural consequence, the export trade of the colonies was almost entirely restricted to Great Britain.

The principal products of Canada, especially corn and timber, enjoyed a substantial preference in England over similar products from foreign countries. In order to encourage the production of colonial corn, Lord Stanley, Secretary of State for the Colonies, introduced into parliament, and in the face of the strong opposition of the Whig Party [1] secured the passage of, the Canadian Corn Act of 1843, by which, in consideration of the imposition by Canada of a duty on American corn, Canadian wheat and flour were admitted into England at about one-fifth of the rate levied upon similar products when imported from other countries. The leaders of the Liberal party warned the Government that the inevitable consequences of the Act would be to build up a few favoured industries in the colonies upon the unstable basis of a temporary commercial advantage. But the warning fell on unheeding ears.

[1] Egerton, *British Colonial Policy*, p. 331.

The Ministry were resolved to entrench the waning policy of protection behind the barrier of an imperial preference.

The people of Canada were equally heedless of the growing antagonism of the English free traders to any form of colonial preference. In their eager desire to take advantage of the manifest benefits accruing from the Act, they overlooked the danger of a reversal of policy in case of the advent of a free-trade government to office. The immediate results of the Act were beneficial alike to the agricultural and commercial interests of the province. Since the preferential tariff extended not only to Canadian-grown corn, but likewise to American wheat, if made into flour in Canadian mills, it gave a tremendous impetus to the milling industry throughout the province, and especially along the border. Large amounts of capital were quickly invested in various subsidiary undertakings, such as ship-building and transportation.[1] An active policy of improving the internal waterways of the country by the construction of canals and the deepening of the natural highways to the sea was set in motion with every prospect of diverting a large proportion of the trade of the Western States through the mouth of the St. Lawrence. Numerous warehouses were erected at strategic points along the inland highways for storing and forwarding the agricultural products of the country to the English market. The harbours on the lower St. Lawrence were filled with English ships, and the merchants of Montreal reaped a rich harvest from the transatlantic trade which centred in that city. As a natural result of this abnormal development, a dangerous boom in real estate and a wild speculation in wheat broke out in the business community. But the day of reckoning was at hand. The Canadian public had recklessly discounted the future in their intense pursuit of the almighty dollar ; they

[1] Lucas, *Historical Geography of the British Colonies*, vol. v, p. 195.

had foolishly left the changing sentiment of the British nation out of their calculations.

For a time the fiscal policy of successive English ministers had been weak and vacillating.[1] But the doctrines of Adam Smith were taking a firm hold upon the minds of the wide-awake manufacturers of the home land, who saw in their economic superiority a splendid opportunity of capturing the markets of the world under conditions of free trade with outside nations. At the same time the high duty on foreign corn, though somewhat relieved by the colonial preference, was proving a heavy burden upon the poor working classes of the English cities. The famine in Ireland gave the *coup de grâce* to the policy of protection. But, however beneficial the abolition of the Corn Laws was to the English public, it proved, for the time being at least, disastrous to the interests of the colonies. The free-trade policy of the homeland dealt the trade and industries of Canada an almost fatal blow. In truth, the statesmen at Westminster, in endeavouring to relieve the prevailing distress at home, practically disregarded the dependent commercial conditions of the colonies, for which their legislation was largely responsible. They overlooked the fact that it was the commercial policy of England, and not that of Canada, which had rendered the interests of the latter almost entirely dependent upon the British tariff and the maintenance of an imperial preference. The Whig statesmen of the day were Little Englanders at heart ; they were much more interested in the promotion of English trade at home and in foreign countries, than concerned about the preservation of the vested interests of the colonies.

With the adoption of the free-trade policy in England, the whole system of imperial preferential trade had to go.[2] The practice of granting English goods a preference in colonial markets, as well as the reciprocal

[1] Egerton, *British Colonial Policy*, p. 331.
[2] *Ibid.*, p. 328.

advantage extended to colonial products in England,
was incompatible with the new commercial tenet of
international free trade.   England, it was felt, could
not consistently seek an open market in foreign countries
on terms of equality with the native producers and
manufacturers, if she herself maintained, or encouraged
the colonies to maintain, discriminating tariffs against
the products of foreign states, and in favour of imperial
traders, whether English or colonial.   Accordingly,
in 1846, the Colonial Legislatures were empowered by
the British Possessions Act [1] to repeal any or all tariff
Acts imposed on them by the Imperial Parliament,
including the various discriminatory duties by which
a preference had been hitherto granted to British ships
and products.   The speech from the throne at the
opening of parliament, the following year, invited the
colonies to rid themselves of the obnoxious system of
differential duties, with a view to the benefit of colonial
consumers, and the general furtherance of an enlightened international policy.   Instead of longer
seeking to develop inter-imperial trade by preferential
duties, the English Government now sought to foster
international free trade by their abolition.

The mercantile community in Canada were quick to
perceive the destructive effect which the adoption of
the policy of free trade would have upon colonial trade
and industry.   Scarcely had Sir Robert Peel made his
celebrated announcement in the House of Commons,
when a letter of protest was addressed to *The London
Times* by Mr. Isaac Buchanan, a prominent Tory
politician, who was at the time on a visit to London.
In this communication,[2] he predicted that the withdrawal of the colonial preference would involve, on
the part of England, national bankruptcy and the
downfall of the monarchy, and on the part of Canada
the repeal of the Canadian preferential tariff and the
inevitable severance of the imperial tie.   The over-

[1] 9 & 10 Vict. c. 4.
[2] *The London Times*, February 6, 1846.

burdened people of England would soon begin to object most strenuously to the expense of administering distant dependencies which were no longer of any commercial advantage to the mother country. On the other hand, " Any hint from England of a desire for separation will be cheerfully responded to by the people of Canada, who will be writhing under the feeling that England has dishonourably broken the promise of protection to Canadian wheat and lumber made by every ministry from the timber panic of 1806 downward ; and will have got their eyes open to the fact that, as there remains no longer any but the slightest bond of interest between Canada and the mother country, no reason can be given why Canadians should risk their lives and property in defending nothing, or should allow Canada to be any longer used as a battlefield of European and American squabbles." As soon as the details of Peel's proposals reached Canada, measures were at once taken by the leading commercial bodies of the province to fight the proposals. Memorials were drawn up to the Secretary of State for the Colonies by the Boards of Trade at Montreal, Toronto, and Quebec, setting forth the serious injury which the withdrawal of the colonial preference would inflict upon the principal industries of the province.[1]

At a meeting of the Toronto Board of Trade, Mr. Workman, the President of that body, made a vigorous protest against the proposed legislation of the home Government. He had been informed that some of their fellow citizens, " from whom he had not expected such sentiments, had declared that there was nothing left for Canada but annexation. He implored those gentlemen to be very careful in the promulgation of their opinions or apprehensions."[2] The language of the Solicitor-General of the Crown conveyed an even more solemn warning of the danger of separation. " He did hope, however, that the commercial

[1] *Colonial Correspondence*, 1846.
[2] Hansard, vol. 86, p. 556.

class would maturely weigh all the consequences which must result from the substitution of the United States markets for those of the mother country. It would be impossible but that such a change in our commercial relations would very soon bring about a change in all our other relations. Our interests would cease to be identified with the interests of the parent state ; our mental associations would assume new forms ; our customs and laws, aye, and our institutions too, would be assimilated to those of the people with whom we cultivated mercantile relations. There was a time . . . when he believed that patriotism had no connection with self-interest ; but he had lived long enough to change his opinion on that subject ; and he did think that loyalty had some relation to pecuniary considerations. If, however, by a course of imperial policy, over which the people of Canada can exert no possible control, they are forced into a new sphere of social and political attraction, they are not the culpable party." [1]

The memorial of the Quebec Board of Trade also proceeded to point out the serious political consequences of a change of fiscal policy on the relation of Canada to the homeland. "That the question no doubt will suggest itself to you, whether the natural effect of this seductive law will not gradually, silently, and imperceptibly to themselves, wean the inclinations of the subjects of Great Britain from their true allegiance to the parent state, and bias their minds in favour of a closer connection with a foreign country through which the transport of their merchandise and produce is encouraged, and a consequent more frequent intercourse with its inhabitants produced." [2] The situation of affairs, as it presented itself to a well-informed foreign critic, was admirably described in the columns of *The New York Herald.* " The intelligence from Canada is beginning to be of an extremely inter-

---

[1] Hansard, vol. 86, p. 557.
[2] *Ibid.*, vol. 86, p. 562; *Colonial Correspondence*, 1846; Porritt, *Fifty Years of Protection in Canada*, pp. 56–60.

esting character. On the receipt of the news of the proposed tariff of Sir Robert Peel, considerable dissatisfaction was manifested in Canada. They say, that to abolish the duties on grain produced in the western parts of the United States must materially affect the commercial interests of Canada, and facilitate its annexation to the United States. It does not require any great sagacity or foresightedness to arrive at this conclusion, nor to perceive that it will be the means of hastening the annexation—a measure which time and the moral effect of our laws and institutions must finally consummate." [1]

Notwithstanding the force of these warnings and representations, the British Government refused to alter its fiscal policy. The free-trade members of the House of Commons were not at all frightened by the threats of colonial separation which were borne to their ears from over the ocean. They placed little confidence in the good faith of these alarming rumours, the origin of which they ascribed to the selfish policy of the Canadian protectionists. The views of the Liberal members were admirably voiced by Mr. Roebuck, in reply to a speech of Lord Bentinck on the commercial policy of the Government in respect to Canada. "That very party, who had always pretended to such extraordinary loyalty and affection for the mother country, now, when they feared that some measure was to be adopted hurtful to their pecuniary interest, turned round, as he (Mr. Roebuck) had told them they would, and threatened them with annexation to America. It was not the people of Canada, whom they had deprived of all they held dear,—it was not the Lower Canadian French population who talked of annexation to America. It was the English, Scotch, and Irish merchants, who had embarked their capital in a favoured trade, supported as they believed by protective duties ; and who, the moment it was proposed to do justice to the people of the country by the adoption

[1] Hansard, vol. 86, p. 560.

of free trade, threatened this country with republicism and annexation." [1]

The era of modern colonial history dates from the acceptance of the principle of free trade as the basis of the fiscal policy of the motherland. [2] The political consequences of this change of policy were scarcely less revolutionary than the economic. By the Act of 1846, Great Britain virtually surrendered her control over the fiscal systems of the self-governing colonies, save in respect to the treaty-making power. The limited right which Canada had enjoyed of imposing customs duties for local revenue purposes, subject to the careful supervision of the Colonial Office, was now extended into a complete control over the assessment, collection, and distribution of all the revenues of the colony. The period of commercial tutelage was ended. Canada was advanced to the status of fiscal independence. She was free to adopt such commercial policies as she might see fit, in so far as such policies did not conflict with the international obligations of the motherland. [3]

The local legislature quickly took advantage of its newly acquired liberty to alter materially the fiscal policy of the province. The budget of 1847 abolished the system of differential duties, and adopted the principle of a uniform tariff upon a revenue-producing basis. Henceforth no distinction was made as to the source of importation ; the same duties were levied upon the products of the sister provinces, the motherland, and foreign states. Steps were subsequently taken for the improvement of the commercial relations of the province with the United States. A good beginning had already been made in this direction by the repeal of the discriminatory duties against the United

[1] Hansard, vol. 86, p. 570.
[2] Lewis, *Government of Dependencies*, Introduction by Lucas, p. xxxiii.
[3] Davidson, *Commercial Federation and Colonial Trade Policy*, p. 15.

States, and the reduction of the tariff on American manufactured goods from $12\frac{1}{2}$ to $7\frac{1}{2}$ per cent.[1]

But a general reciprocity treaty for the free admission of natural products was felt to be desirable, in order to put their relations upon a satisfactory basis. Negotiations were accordingly set on foot by the Secretary for the Colonies, at the instance of the Canadian Executive, with a view to inducing the Government at Washington to enter into a reciprocity arrangement. But the American Government was too much absorbed in the domestic concerns of the moment to give due consideration to the fiscal proposals of its northern neighbour. The Canadian people were quickly made to realize that fiscal independence, though of the greatest constitutional importance as a recognition of their new nationality, could not compensate them for the loss of the special advantages they had heretofore enjoyed in the English markets. The abolition of the preference on English goods in colonial ports was of small concern to the colonists, but the withdrawal of the corresponding preference to colonial goods in English markets struck a terrible blow at the prosperity of the British-American provinces. The grant of commercial freedom was of little use to a country whose financial, agricultural, and industrial interests were paralyzed by the arbitrary action of the Parliament at Westminster.

The fears of the Canadian Boards of Trade were fully confirmed. In one of his letters Lord Elgin feelingly spoke of " the downward progress of events ! " These are ominous words. But look at the facts. Property in most of the Canadian towns, and more especially in the capital, has fallen 50 per cent. in value within the last three years. Three-fourths of the commercial men are bankrupt, owing to Free Trade ; a large proportion of the exportable produce of Canada is obliged to seek a market in the States. It pays a duty of

[1] U.S. Ex. Doc. No. 64, 1st Session, 31st Congress ; Haynes, *The Reciprocity Treaty with Canada of* 1854, p. 12.

20 per cent. on the frontier. How long can such a state of things be expected to endure ?

" Depend upon it, our commercial embarrassments are our real difficulty. Political discontent, properly so called, there is none. I really believe no country in the world is more free from it. We have, indeed, national antipathies hearty and earnest enough. We suffer, too, from the inconvenience of having to work a system which is not yet thoroughly in gear. Reckless and unprincipled men take advantage of these circumstances to work into a fever every transient heat that affects the public mind. Nevertheless, I am confident I could carry Canada unscathed through all these evils of transition, and place the connection on a surer foundation than ever, if I could only tell the people of the province that, as regards the conditions of material prosperity, they would be raised to a level with their neighbours. But if this be not achieved, if free navigation and reciprocal trade with the Union be not secured for us, the worst, I fear, will come, and that at no distant day." [1]

Temporary insolvency was the price which Canadians paid for the triumph of English free trade.[2] Much of the capital of the country was tied up in the ruined industries which the protective policy of the motherland had called into existence. There was but a limited local market for the agricultural products of the province, and, in the neutralized market of England, the Canadian traders now found themselves exposed to the keen and merciless competition of their American neighbours, whose larger establishments and superior transportation facilities enabled them to undersell their less favoured competitors. Piteous were the complaints which arose from the millers and ship-owners of the province against the injustice of the policy of England in arbitrarily withdrawing the colonial preference, without at the same time securing for them

---

[1] *Letters and Journals of Lord Elgin*, p. 70.
[2] Goldwin Smith, *Canada and the Canadian Question*, p. 142.

an alternative market in foreign countries. The feelings of this important section of the community were well expressed by Mr. James R. Benson, a leading ship-owner of St. Catherine's, in a letter to William Hamilton Merritt, in which, after voicing the general dissatisfaction of the public since the passage of Peel's Act, he declared [1] : " If the former system of protection be not adopted by Great Britain, or she should not obtain for us the free admission of our produce into the United States market, I am well convinced that the result will be an alienation of the minds of the most loyal men in Canada from the mother country, and a desire to become a state of the Union ; it is already frequently asked if such was the case now, would our property become less valuable : the answer is undeniable." [2]

The question of finding a market for Canadian products became the most pressing problem before the country. With the loss of the English market the United States appeared to be the natural outlet for Canadian trade, but, unfortunately, that market was closed by a high protective tariff. The friendly attitude of the American Government fostered the hope in the minds of the Canadian public that a reciprocity arrangement might be effected with the United States for the free admission of certain raw materials of the two countries. For some time past, the subject of reciprocity had engaged the serious consideration of Mr. Hamilton Merritt, one of the most influential men of the Niagara District. As a result of his investigations, he was convinced that the only relief for the deplorable economic conditions of Upper Canada was to be found in a reciprocity agreement with the United States. Both in Parliament and through the press, he ably championed the cause of reciprocity. In a convincing letter to Lord Elgin upon this, his favourite

[1] April 20, 1848 ; *Canadian Archives*, 4995.
[2] See also a letter of Mr. J. Keefer, of Thorold, April 19, 1848, to Mr. Merritt ; *Canadian Archives*, 4995.

topic, he pointed out that the higher prices which prevailed across the border " would produce dissatisfaction and lead to an early separation from the mother country." [1]   The opinions of Mr. Merritt were shared by many members of the commercial community, as well as by the great bulk of the farming population of Canada West. In view of the growing depression, it was little wonder that many of the inhabitants lost faith in the future of the province and were prone to regard their country's fiscal freedom as a curse, rather than a blessing.

In a letter to the Colonial Secretary, Lord Elgin vividly described the " frightful amount of loss to individuals, and the great derangement of the colonial finances," which had resulted from the adoption of the policy of free trade.   " Peel's Bill of 1846 drives the whole of the produce down the New York channels of communication, destroying the revenue which Canada expected to derive from canal dues, and ruining at once mill-owners, forwarders, and merchants. The consequence is that private property is unsaleable in Canada, and not a shilling can be raised on the credit of the province. We are actually reduced to the disagreeable necessity of paying all public officers, from the Governor-General downwards, in debentures, which are not exchangeable at par. What makes it more serious is that all the prosperity of which Canada is thus robbed is transplanted to the other side of the lines, as if to make Canadians feel more bitterly how much kinder England is to the children who desert her than to those who remain faithful. For I care not whether you be a protectionist or a free trader, it is the inconsistency of imperial legislation, and not the adopting of one policy rather than another, which is the bane of the colonies. I believe that the conviction that they would be better off, if annexed, is almost universal among the commercial classes at present, and the peaceful condition of the province, under all

[1] *Canadian Archives*, 4995.

the circumstances of the time, is, I must confess, often a matter of great astonishment to myself." [1]

The position of Canadian traders was made much more difficult by the unjust operation of the Navigation Laws. The policy of the English Government was carried out with reckless disregard of the rights and interests of the colonies. The British Parliament, in withdrawing the colonial preference, had retained a monopoly of the colonial carrying trade for British ships. [2] The Navigation Acts had undoubtedly proved of some slight benefit to Canadian ships in admitting them into the exclusive privilege of the West Indian trade, but this small gain was more than offset by the loss of colonial merchants through the higher freight to and from England on colonial and English products. So much were the freights enhanced by the British shipping monopoly, that it was extremely doubtful if the excess charges did not equal, if not exceed, the benefits which the colonists derived from the preferential policy. Such at least was the opinion of some of the leading members of the Free Trade Association of Montreal, and a comparison of the rates from Montreal and New York respectively, to and from England, appeared to lend considerable support to this contention. [3] With the change in English policy, a twofold loss was inflicted on Canadian merchants. They continued to bear the burden of excess freights without the compensating advantage of English preference. Thanks to the Navigation Acts, they could no longer compete on even terms with their American competitors in the English markets. The colonies, in truth, were unjustly penalized in order to enhance the profits of English ship-owners.

The American Government was quick to take ad-

---

[1] *Letters and Journals of Lord Elgin*, p. 60.
[2] Lucas, *Historical Geography of the British Colonies*, vol. v. p. 196.
[3] See letter of a Montreal merchant quoted in *The Patriot*, January 9, 1850!

vantage of the changing fiscal conditions in Canada. Prior to the abolition of· the preferential duties in favour of English products, the merchants of Upper Canada had found it advantageous to draw their supplies from Montreal and Quebec rather than from New York, since the duties were from 25 to 30 per cent. higher on importations through, or from, the United States. The repeal of the discriminatory tariff in 1847 was speedily followed by the adoption by Congress of an Act permitting the carriage of foreign and Canadian goods through the United States in bond without the payment of duty.

The effect of these two measures was to throw a large part of the trade of the St. Lawrence merchants with the inhabitants of Upper Canada into the hands of the New York dealers, since the merchants of Toronto and the western districts now found it more advantageous to import and export their supplies through American ports, which, unlike the St. Lawrence, were open all the year round. It was indeed a great convenience to the merchants of Canada West to be able to secure their goods at short notice in New York, instead of having to order them, long in advance, through the wholesale houses of the Lower St. Lawrence. Moreover, as we have seen, the operation of the Navigation Acts placed the business men of Montreal at a still greater disadvantage, owing to the higher freight rates to colonial ports. New York accordingly became the distributing centre for the business of Western Canada, and the American traders reaped a splendid harvest at the expense of the unfortunate merchants on the Lower St. Lawrence. Loud and bitter were the remonstrances of the Montreal merchants against the differential operation of English and American legislation. They were suffering through no fault of their own ; but, on the contrary, were made to pay the penalty of the " inconsistency of imperial legislation." A vigorous demand arose for the abrogation of the Navigation Laws, coupled in some instances with a request for the restoration of the system of preferential duties in favour of the colonies.

The Provincial Legislature was alive to the danger of the situation, and lent a willing ear to the complaints of the St. Lawrence merchants. Although there was considerable difference of opinion among the members as to the wisdom of the free-trade policy of the motherland, there was general agreement as to the necessity for repealing the unjust discrimination of the Navigation Acts. A joint address was accordingly introduced by the Government into the Legislative Council and the Assembly, professing the loyalty of the people to the Crown, and praying Her Majesty's Government to repeal the Navigation Laws, and to throw open the St. Lawrence to the free navigation of all nations. In the Assembly, an amendment was moved on behalf of the Tory protectionist members to add a clause to the address in favour of the restoration of the system of protective duties in England. The House refused, however, to dictate the fiscal policy of the motherland, and, after an animated debate, the amendment was defeated by the decisive vote of 49 to 14.[1] The address was thereupon adopted without further opposition. In the Legislative Council the address was received with general favour, and carried without debate.

The complaints of the Canadian public aroused the English Government to a sense of its responsibility for the serious condition of affairs in that colony.[2] The speech of the Lords Commissioners at the opening of Parliament recommended the consideration of the Navigation Laws with a view to ascertaining whether any changes could be adopted which might promote the commercial and colonial interests of the empire. Steps were subsequently taken by the Ministry to remedy the grievance of the colonists ; but, owing to

---

[1] January 24, 1849.
[2] Lucas, *Historical Geography in the British Colonies*, vol. v. p. 196.

the lateness of the session, and the pressure of domestic concerns, the Government were reluctantly compelled to give up all expectation of passing a Bill for the alteration of the Navigation Laws that session. The President of the Board of Trade, however, promised that the question should be brought to the early consideration of the House at the next session, so that Parliament would be able to pass a well-matured measure.[1]

A rumour of the intention of the British Government not to proceed with the Bill for the amendment of the Navigation Laws soon crossed the Atlantic, and at once called forth a strong letter of protest from Lord Elgin to the Secretary for the Colonies.[2] The report, he stated, had produced a very painful feeling : "The Canadian farmer is a supplicant at present to the Imperial Legislature, not for favour, but for justice ; strong as is his affection for the mother country and her institutions, he cannot reconcile it to his sense of right that after being deprived of all protection for his products in her markets, he should be subjected to a hostile discriminatory duty in the guise of a law for the protection of navigation." His Excellency was confident that, " if the wise and generous policy lately adopted toward Canada be persevered in, the connection between the province and the motherland may yet be rendered profitable to both, in a far greater degree than has been the case heretofore." It would be dangerous, however, to Canadian interests, " if provisions are suffered to remain on the British statute book which would seem to bring the material interests of the colonists and the promptings of duty and affection into opposition."

With the withdrawal of the measure to free the St. Lawrence from the baneful restrictions of the Navigation Acts, the gloom of depression settled down more heavily upon the city of Montreal. The views

[1] August 10, 1848.
[2] June 15, 1848 ; Hansard, 1849, vol. 105, p. 71.

of the mercantile community of that city were ably voiced in a petition of the Board of Trade to the Queen at the close of 1848, which set forth : [1]

" That the abandonment by the mother country of her protective policy is producing important changes in the commercial relations of the colony, which, unless regulated or counteracted by wise legislation, may lead in the end to consequences which every loyal subject would deplore. That the most prominent of the changes referred to is a growing commercial inter-course with the United States, giving rise to an opinion which is daily gaining ground on both sides of the boundary line, that the interests of the two countries under the changed policy of the Imperial Govern-ment are germane to each other, and under that system must sooner or later be politically interwoven.

" That being deeply interested in the trade and pros-perity of this province, and, moreover, in common with the great mass of the population being devotedly attached to the institutions of Great Britain, and desiring to see the existing colonial connections which unite us perpetuated, your petitioners most respectfully take leave to lay before Your Majesty the following representations :

" 1. The result of a total cessation of the differential duty on grain in England will be to make New York the port of shipment for the great bulk of the produce of Canada.

" 2. The port which is found to be most eligible for the exports will also be found to be the best suited fer the imports of a country.

" 3. The bonding system introduced by the American Government must have the effect of attracting the merchants of Canada to New York for the purchase of supplies, . . . and thus the ruin of the trade of the St. Lawrence . . . cannot fail to be consummated. It would be superfluous for your petitioners to point out the injurious effect which could not but result from

---

[1] *Quebec Gazette*, January 8, 1849.

such a diversion of trade ; suffice it to say, it would create and cement ties of beneficial interest between Canada and the United States, and proportionally weaken the attachment which this colony entertains for the mother country.

"Your petitioners are indeed aware that it has been asserted by a class of political economists that the colonies are a source of pecuniary loss to England, and that she might profitably abandon them altogether ; but your petitioners have too much confidence in the wisdom of Your Majesty's Government to suppose that such sentiments are shared in by them, or that, even were the proposition to be true, they would draw the same precipitate conclusion from it.

"In nations there are interests infinitely transcending those of a mere pecuniary nature, and your petitioners would regard the integrity of the British dominions, the preservation of Britain's political power and influence as cheaply purchased by any pecuniary loss the colonies may occasion her. It is in this belief, and with the desire to avert the dismemberment of the empire, so far at least as Canada is concerned, that your petitioners at this time approach Your Majesty. They do not seek the restoration of the old system of protection ; on the contrary, they have no objection to the utmost freedom of trade compatible with the safety of the ties subsisting between the colony and the mother country ; but, having shown how that connection must be endangered when the measures of Sir Robert Peel take full effect, they will briefly point out those remedial measures which, in their opinion, would avert the evil, and continue to attach the province to England by the claims of interest, as well as of affection and duty. These measures, as far as imperial legislation is concerned, are :

"1st. The repeal of the Navigation Laws as they relate to Canada, and the throwing open the navigation of the St. Lawrence ; and

"2nd. The enactment of a moderate fixed duty, say

not less than five shillings per quarter on foreign wheat, colonial to be admitted free."

The memorial proceeded to set forth in detail the material benefits which such a policy would confer upon Canada, by the diversion of the trade of Upper Canada and the American West through the St. Lawrence. An alluring prospect was held out to the industrial interests of the motherland, that the increased revenue which would result from such an enlightened policy would enable the local legislature " to materially reduce, if not entirely repeal, the import duties on British manufactures." At the same time, the British public was confidently assured that the burden of the duty on wheat would not fall upon the English consumer, but would be borne by the unfortunate foreign producers. " A duty of this kind in favour of Canada would preserve the trade of the St. Lawrence, add to the revenue derivable from the St. Lawrence canals, diffuse universal satisfaction throughout the colony, and, what in the opinion of your petitioners is all-important, would continue to attach Canada to the mother country, thus perpetuating the present connection, and preserving inviolate the British dominions."

The language of the address was severely criticised by the Montreal free traders, as putting the loyalty of the colony on too low a plane. They professed the most self-righteous indignation that their allegiance to the sovereign should be placed upon a purely mercenary basis. Accordingly, a protest was prepared, which won the enthusiastic commendation of Earl Grey as " the most important document which had proceeded from a large commercial body since the famous London petition in favour of free trade." This protest, which was signed by many of the leading Liberals of the city,[1] set out by declaring : " We trust that the loyalty of the province depends upon something loftier than a mercenary motive," and then proceeded by a carefully

[1] Including Messrs. Holmes, M.P., Boyer, McDougal, Holton, Grass, and Workman.

constructed argument to draw the sound constitutional conclusion : " We conceive that all we have a right to ask of the mother-country is to repeal the Navigation Laws as far as they relate to Canada, and to throw open the St. Lawrence to the navigation of the vessels of all nations, from which measure, coupled with our own energy and enterprise, we feel confident of being able to secure all that the Council of the Board of Trade expect to acquire from the re-enactment of a tax upon the bread of the people of the United Kingdom."

But little reliance, however, could be placed upon the professions of loyalty of some of the Liberal free traders. In a private communication to their English correspondent, shortly after, the firm of Holmes, Young & Knapp, one of the members of which had taken a prominent part in drawing up the recent protest, declared : [1] " The feeling of annexation to the United States seems to be the most prevalent at present among our people ; could the measure be brought about peaceably and amicably, there is not a doubt but that three-quarters, if not nine-tenths, of the inhabitants would go for it. No country can expect to retain colonies under a free trade system, unless allied to each other by contiguity, or for the purpose of mutual protection. The commercial system of the United States now offers more advantages to the province than any other within view, but to avail ourselves of it is impossible without the question of annexation being involved." The Canadian public were generally disappointed at the non-concurrence of the United States in the scheme for reciprocal free trade, and, in the judgment of the writer, would not rest content until they had secured the free admission of their native products into the American market. There was, however, " but one way to bring it about, and that way was annexation."

The majority of the mercantile community, together with most of the Montreal papers, supported the views

[1] See speech of Lord Stanley in the House of Lords, May 8, 1849.

of the Board of Trade, rather than the more reasonable judgment of the Liberal minority. The prevailing opinion of the business public found expression in a leading article of *The Montreal Gazette* (Tory), which declared : [1] " We consider annexation as the last issue on the board and only to be thought of after England has determined to persevere in treating Canada as a foreign nation, instead of as an integral part of the empire. We shall resist it so long as we see a chance of our affairs being placed on a proper footing without it. . . . But the die is in the hands of England."

True to its promise, the English Ministry brought down a measure for the amendment of the Navigation Laws, soon after the opening of the session in 1849. In moving for a committee of the whole House to consider the resolution of the Government, the Hon. H. Labouchere, President of the Board of Trade, stated [2] that, in the opinion of the Executive, since the protection which the colonies had hitherto enjoyed in the markets of the mother country has been withdrawn, " it would be the height of intolerable injustice to maintain those restrictions (of the Navigation Laws) upon their trade which prevent them from enjoying the advantages of foreigners—an injustice which I think absolutely incompatible with the continued connection between the most important of the colonies and the mother country." By the surrender of her shipping monopoly, England would confer " a boon of incalculable value " on the North American colonies, and "rivet them by ties of gratitude to the motherland " in the most effective manner. Parliament should not further delay to remove this colonial grievance. " They ought to be sensible of the patience and good feeling which the people of Canada had shown under the most trying circumstances ; they should ill repay that patience and good-feeling, if they did not embrace the earliest opportunity to show

[1] May 8, 1849.
[2] November 14, 1849 ; Hansard, 1849, vol. 102, p. 682.

themselves anxious to set right a system so impolitic and unjust, which destroys the trade of the North American colonies, which destroys the trade of the inhabitants of the United States of America for no earthly object, which directs the trade from Canada to the United States of America without effecting any benefit in return, which injures the revenue of Canada by preventing the full use and employment of those canals which have been made there at so great an outlay, but which are now completely useless and unproductive, and must remain so as long as the Navigation Laws continue in force."

At the very outset, the proposals of the Executive met with the strongest opposition on the part of the Conservative Party. The members of the opposition, however, were too busy defending the last surviving tenets of the mercantile system to devote much attention to the interests and desires of the colonies. Mr. Herries was the only speaker to consider at length the colonial aspect of the question. He charged the Government with a callous indifference to the sufferings of the colonists; they had driven the Colonies to the point of exasperation, and had finally consummated their ruin by the withdrawal of colonial protection. The relaxation of the Navigation Laws, he contended, would not suffice to repair the mischief which the free-trade policy had inflicted upon the colonies.

The battle was renewed upon the second reading of the Bill. Save for an interesting pronouncement of Mr. Robinson on the subject of imperial relations, and a few scattered references to the state of colonial opinion, the debate was strictly confined to the consideration of the effect of the abrogation of the Navigation Laws upon the commerce and naval supremacy of England. The remarks of Mr. Robinson set forth in the clearest light the mercantilistic theory of the Tory Party in respect to the colonies. "He was satisfied that the ultimate aim of the United States was the possession of the entire American continent.

In fact, the measures of the Government had so disgusted the colonies, that in their public meetings now they were discussing whether it would not be better for them to unite themselves to the American Republic than to remain a dependency of this country. He was not quite clear himself whether that would not be the best thing for them to do. Sure he was of this, that, so far as England was concerned, it would be better for her to give them up than to persevere in their recent ruinous policy. When they had given up their colonial trade, what had they to do with colonies except to maintain expensive governments and a large military force? They were, in fact, abandoning them in maintaining the doctrine that their own subjects had no more claim upon them than the citizens of any other country."

The dogmas of Adam Smith were, however, in the ascendency ; and notwithstanding the vigorous opposition of the Tory Party, the second reading of the Bill was carried by a majority of fifty-six : Ayes 266, Noes 210.

In the House of Lords, the policy of the Government was defended by the Colonial Secretary in a speech of exceptional power.[1] " It must be agreed on all hands," he declared, " that it is the want of steadiness and consistency in our legislation which has inflicted this injury upon Canada ; and therefore we are bound, upon the plainest principles of common sense and justice, to relieve that colony from the consequences of our own conduct." He contended that, in the light of what had passed, it would be most unjust to tell the Canadians that their produce should not only be exposed to unrestricted competition in the English market, but that they should also be made to suffer the disadvantages of a monopoly, as compared with their rivals, in conveying that produce to this country. This Parliament, therefore, must do one of two things, unless they wished to set justice utterly

[1] May 8, 1849.

at defiance ; they were bound either to retrace their
steps, and to restore to Canada the protection of which
they had deprived her, or else to give her the advantage
of the fullest competition in bringing her produce here.
If the present Bill were rejected in the face of the
opinion of the Governor and the overwhelming sentiment of the colonists, he believed that they would
give a most serious shock to the security of the British
power in the North American colonies.

" They all knew, and, he believed, would all acknowledge that the connection between this country and
the North American colonies could not be maintained
on any other ground than that of perfect equality, and
by this country possessing the confidence and affection
of the people of those provinces.   It was not possible,
nor, if it were possible, would it be desirable that the
possession of Canada and the other provinces of
North America—for in this matter they should all be
considered as one—should be maintained on any other
terms.   In the midst of the colonial agitation, no
doubt impudent and violent men would sometimes be
found to talk of a union with the United States.   In
the United States, too, some persons had talked of
the same thing, or, as they termed it, of a nullification
of the connection between this country and the North
American colonies.   But still, in the midst of all their
party disputes and violence, he had no doubt but
that they were sincerely attached to this country, and
that they were becoming daily more sensible of the
benefits which they derived from belonging to the
British Crown."   But he was not prepared to say
that this feeling would be continued, if so gross an
act of injustice should be committed as that of the
rejection of this measure.   On the contrary, he believed
that if their Lordships threw out the Bill, they would
part with their best security for the attachment of
these colonies to the British Crown.

" It was the opinion of many who had watched the
current of political opinion and events in the world

for the last few years, that the connection of these provinces with the mother country was drawing rapidly to a close, and that they would become an independent people at a very early day. If this were so, and this country should lose the present opportunity of doing with a feeling of good grace an act of favour to these colonies, they might put it out of their power to secure to themselves even the benefits which would arise from the maintenance of friendly relations with them, when they should become an independent power." He believed, however, that the colonies should be retained on higher grounds than the mere material advantages which were to be derived from their possession. On the contrary he considered " the maintenance of our North American provinces to be an essential element of our national strength," and on imperial grounds boldly justified the adoption of the present principles of the Government " as an important and necessary step for the security of the Colonial Empire." The two Houses, he concluded, should take warning, from their unfortunate experience with the United States, of the danger of attempting to limit the commercial activities of the colonies.

Lord Stanley, the leader of the Conservative Party in the Upper House, warned the Colonial Secretary that, by abandoning all attempts at controlling the dominant majority in the Canadian Parliament, he might lay " the foundations of deep-rooted discontent, disaffection, and disloyalty in the minds of a hitherto loyal and contented people." He scornfully referred to the spurious Patriotism of Messrs. Holmes, Young and Co., who were privately spreading the doctrine of annexation while openly professing the most devoted loyalty to the Crown. The affairs of Canada were indeed in a serious condition. " The conclusion was inevitable, that a connection with that country (the United States) could alone give all the privileges which they (the Canadians) desired ; and that loyalty must indeed be powerful which continued undiminished

under circumstances of so great trial." The debate
was very bitterly contested on both sides of the House,
but the remaining speakers quite disregarded the
colonial aspect of the question and the probable effect
of the Government's proposals upon the relations of
the colonies to the motherland. Upon a division
being taken, the Bill was carried by the narrow majority
of 10 : Contents, 173 ; Non-Contents, 163. On
June 26 Her Majesty duly signified her assent to the
Bill.

Unfortunately the passage of the Bill was too long
delayed to be of material service that season to the
merchants on the St. Lawrence. More than half of
the season of navigation was over before they learned
of the opening of colonial ports to the ships of all
nations. For the time being, therefore, the anxiously
awaited boon was of very little value. Moreover the
condition of business in Montreal was so stagnant
that trade and shipping shunned the city. The docks
of the city were deserted, and the warehouses filled with
unsold goods.

For some time past the thoughts of the commercial
community had been directed to the United States,
by the impending change in the fiscal policy of the
motherland. In 1846,[1] an address was voted by the
Canadian Parliament to Her Majesty, praying that in
the event of a modification in the law regulating the
admission of foreign grain into the British market,
due regard should be had to the interests of Canada ;
and, as a measure which would be greatly conducive
to that end, Her Majesty was respectfully requested
to cause the necessary steps to be taken for opening
up negotiations with the Government of the United
States for the admission of Canadian products into the
ports of that country on the same terms that American
products were admitted into the ports of Great Britain
and Canada. To this request Her Majesty was pleased

---

[1] May 12, 1846 ; Haynes, *The Reciprocity Treaty with Canada of*
1854, p. 11 (Amer. Econ. Assoc., November, 1892).

to accede, and the Governor-General was authorised to assure the Canadian Assembly that the earliest opportunity would be taken to press upon the United States the subject of an " equality of trade " between the two countries.[1]

Accordingly, towards the end of the year, the British ambassador at Washington brought the matter to the attention of Mr. Walker, the Secretary of the Treasury, who submitted the whole question to the President and his advisers. The views of the American Government " were favourable to the principle of a reciprocal relaxation of commercial intercourse between Canada and the United States." As the speediest way of bringing about so desirable an object, it was judged most expedient to introduce into Congress a Bill for the free exchange of certain agricultural and natural produce upon terms of reciprocity on the part of Canada. A Bill was drawn up by Mr. Grinnel, an influential member of the Committee on Commerce, and its adoption was strongly recommended by the Secretary of the Treasury in a communication to that committee. The Bill passed through the House of Representatives without opposition, but owing to the great pressure of other business was not voted upon by the Senate.[2]

Since the repeal of the Canadian differential duties, the attention of many American traders in the New England and Eastern States had turned to the possible development of a valuable market for American products in Canada. Already a considerable commerce had grown up between New York and the western district of Upper Canada, thanks to their propinquity, the beneficial operation of the bonding privileges, and the system of drawbacks of the United States tariff. The results of this limited freedom of exchange had

---

[1] Porritt, *Fifty Years of Protection in Canada*, p. 85 ; Haynes, *The Reciprocity Treaty with Canada of* 1854, p. 12.

[2] *Ex. Doc.*, No. 64, 1st Session, 31st Congress ; Porritt, *Fifty Years of Protection in Canada*, p. 89.

proved so satisfactory to some of the northern traders that an agitation had arisen in certain quarters for a more liberal commercial arrangement with Canada.

The fiscal policy of the President was well adapted to promote the interests of the border states. Early in the following session another attempt was made by the Administration to comply with the wishes of the Canadian people, as expressed by the British ambassador.[1] To this end a Bill was introduced into Congress by Senator Dix of New York, providing for a limited free trade across the boundary in respect to certain agricultural products, the growth of the respective countries. In the course of an able advocacy of the measure, the Senator was led to consider the state of Canadian opinion upon the question, and the relation between the kindred subjects of reciprocity and annexation. "I know personally," he declared,[2] "many of the prominent men in Canada. I know that they are strongly opposed to separation from the mother country. They desire union with England first, independence next, and annexation with the United States last of all. They desire a free exchange of products with us, because they believe that the existing restrictions upon our commerce are prejudicial to both countries; and they desire nothing more. What the feeling is with the great body of people in Canada I have no means of knowing. That they desire free intercourse with us there is no doubt.

"For myself, I have hitherto spoken freely upon this subject. I would neither be forward in courting the annexation of adjacent states, nor backward in acceding to it. I would neither make overtures, nor repel them, without good cause. I believe that we are large enough for all the purposes of security and strength; but I do not fear further extension, nor would I decline it, when circumstances render it convenient to ourselves or others.

---

[1] Porritt, *Fifty Years of Protection in Canada*, pp. 90–94.
[2] *Congressional Globe*, 2nd Session, 30th Congress, p. 331.

" Mr. President, this consideration has been urged, and urged directly, as an objection to commercial freedom between the United States and Canada. I have recently heard it from the anti-Liberal party in Canada, who are for new restrictions upon our commerce. They are in favour of the existing restrictions, as well as new ones, upon the ground that free intercourse may lead to a political union between Canada and the United States. . . .

" Whether this view is just or not, I do not believe that the result is to be defeated in either of the modes proposed—by a continuation of existing restrictions, or by the imposition of new ones. I believe the tendency of such measures will be to hasten and to consummate the very end they are intended to defeat."

Reciprocity, he pointed out, had been recommended on several occasions by the Treasury Department, as a measure well calculated to promote the mutual interests of the two countries. He warned the Southern senators, who were opposing the Bill, that unless the existing commercial restrictions were removed, they might hasten the desire for annexation among the Canadian people. But, notwithstanding the support of the President, the Bill again failed to pass owing to a variety of causes—the lateness of the session, the insistent demand of the manufacturing interests for the addition of certain finished products to the list of free exchanges, and, more particularly, the stubborn opposition of the Southern members, who regarded the Bill with a jealous suspicion as a quasi-annexation measure, which might in the end adversely affect the maintenance of slavery by the incorporation of new free states in the Union.

At the same time, the Canadian Legislature was dealing with a similar proposal. A resolution was introduced into the Assembly by Mr. Hamilton Merritt,[1] at the instance of the Ministry, in favour of an agreement with the United States for the exchange of certain

[1] February 2, 1849.

natural products.   The resolution was strongly opposed
by the protectionist members of the House, who endeavoured to secure a postponement of the question
until the views of Congress were officially made known.
But, after a lively debate, the resolution was carried
by fifty-eight to twelve.   A Bill in conformity with
the resolution was thereupon presented to the House ;
and, notwithstanding the stress of the struggle over
the Rebellion Losses Bill, and the failure of Congress
to take action, was adopted on the third reading by
thirty-two Ayes to eight Noes.[1]   In moving the final
reading of the Bill, Mr. Merritt expressed his firm
conviction that a favourable arrangement would be
made with the United States Government in the near
future.   In the Legislative Council the measure did
not encounter any serious opposition.   As assented to
by the Governor-General, the Bill had a purely faculta-
tive character, since its operation was made dependent
upon the adoption of a similar measure on the part of
the United States.

Throughout the spring and summer of 1849, commercial conditions on the Lower St. Lawrence were
steadily growing worse.   The prospects of the colony
were as dark and gloomy as they well could be.   Abandoned by the motherland, disappointed by the United
States, and debarred from the markets of Europe, the
commercial public were driven by sheer desperation
into the dangerous course of disloyalty.   The local
government could render no assistance, for it was
itself on the verge of insolvency.   The condition of
affairs was very vividly described by an acute observer,
the Rev. Dr. Dixon, ex-president of the British Wes-
leyan Conference, who had recently made a tour of
the provinces and of the United States.   " Canada,"
he wrote, " now belongs to Great Britain by a figment,
a tradition of loyalty, a recollection of heroic deeds,
and not by any material interest or benefit.   Nay, in
the present depressed state of things, cast off by the

[1] March 6, 1849.

mother country, and left to their own resources, with the United States close by their side possessing vast political power and influence, a growing credit and monetary resources, a prodigious mercantile and commercial navy, an active, industrious, and virtuous people, a Government capable in all respects and equally disposed to foster, protect, and strengthen all its possessions—we say, with these things staring them in the face the policy of this country has made it the plain palpable interest of the Canadian to seek for annexation. This is as clear as any problem in Euclid. How long the traditions of loyalty will weigh against the interests now put in the balance against them, nobody need be at a loss to determine."

The uncompromising refusal of the English Government to reconsider the fiscal policy of the motherland, which was didactically pronounced [1] by the Colonial Secretary " to be best calculated to promote the permanent interests of the empire at large," at last convinced the Canadian people of the fruitlessness of further appeals to the British Parliament for the restoration of protective duties. In bitter disappointment at such ungenerous treatment from the mother country the commercial community anxiously turned their eyes to Washington in the hope of securing relief from that quarter. The Earl of Elgin continued to urge upon the English authorities the pressing necessity of securing a market for Canadian products in the United States; but so sorry was the condition of Canadian affairs, that His Excellency was forced to admit that the end of the imperial connection might be near at hand. The Governor-General, in fact, entertained grave doubts as to whether the empire which had been built up on the principle of a community of interest between the colonies and the homeland could long maintain its unity under the régime of free trade and colonial autonomy.[2]

---

[1] Letter of Earl Grey in reply to the petition of the Montreal Board of Trade, July 6, 1849.
[2] *Letters and Journals of Lord Elgin*, p. 113.

The position of the colony was made all the more difficult and dubious by the rapid growth in popular and parliamentary favour of a system of doctrines which aimed at a revolutionary change in the organization of the empire, and even appeared to threaten its total dismemberment. Since the close of the eighteenth century, English opinion in respect to the colonies had undergone several striking modifications. The loss of the American colonies, which was ascribed by the narrow-minded politicians of the time to an undue liberality of colonial policy, was followed by a long period of repression. Tory imperialistic ideas of the authority of the Governors, and the supremacy of the Colonial Office, were in the ascendency, and passed practically unchallenged. Democratic institutions were regarded as a source of discontent and a menace to the motherland. To the general public, the distant dependencies of the Crown were places of exile, the dumping-ground of convicts and other undesirables.

But in the second quarter of the nineteenth century a new, if somewhat artificial, interest was awakened in colonies and colonization. The rapid industrial development of England called for the opening of new markets. At the same time, the iniquitous operation of the Poor Laws, and the squalid poverty of the great manufacturing cities, were proving a serious burden on the tax-payers and a danger to the moral and social life of the State. Capitalists and philanthropists alike saw, or thought they saw, a happy means of escape from the ills that confronted them. The colonies, it was believed, would afford an expanding market for English manufactures, a profitable field for the investment of capital, and a promising home for thousands of emigrants. The Government caught the fever of the time. For the old policy of neglect, tempered by autocracy, was substituted a policy of benevolent, if often misguided, paternalism. Encouragement was granted to emigration, liberal appropriations were made to public works, and to the cost of the civil and military administration in the colonies ; and, most important of all, special fiscal advantages were extended to colonial products in the English markets.

On the political side, the powers of the governors were curtailed by the introduction of representative institutions and the promise was held out of a further extension of the principles of self-government, when the growth of population and the ripening experience of the colonists in local administration should warrant it. In short, the colonies were treated as the favoured children of the mother country. Though ofttimes vexed by the meddlesome interference of the Colonial Office in their domestic affairs, the colonies nevertheless took on a new lease of life. This development was undoubtedly partially artificial, and to that extent unhealthy, especially in fostering a spirit of undue dependence upon imperial favour. But, upon the whole, the paternal policy of the home authorities was helpful in assisting the weak dependencies over the hard pioneer stage of political existence.

But a new school of political economists arose, who boldly challenged the theories, and condemned the policies of the statesmen of the day. In opposition to the accepted doctrine of benevolent paternalism, they presented a new materialistic gospel of individual and national liberty. The tenets of free trade were only one phase, though a most important one, of the general political philosophy of the Manchester School. Their views on colonial policy were as clearly formulated, though not as fully developed, as their scientific opinions on economic questions. They abhorred the whole system of imperialism, as hostile to the interests of English democracy, and inimical to the spirit of colonial nationalism. They demanded the release of the colonies from the state of tutelage, and their elevation to the full rank of statehood, as equal and independent members of the family of nations.

In the House of Commons, the leaders of the Liberal

Party were constantly proclaiming that the government of the colonies should be surrendered to the
colonists themselves. They desired to throw off on
the colonies the financial burden and the political
responsibility of their own administration, and to
bestow upon them the same plenary powers of self-
government as were enjoyed in England, save in respect
to matters of exclusively imperial concern, such as
the regulation of foreign relations and questions of
war and peace. But the grant of national freedom
ought, in their opinion, to be accompanied by the
withdrawal of the special privileges the colonies
enjoyed in virtue of their colonial status; in particular,
the fiscal preference, the imperial contributions to the
civil and ecclesiastical establishments of the colonies,
and the maintenance by the mother country of the
military and naval forces in the various dependencies.

Some of the more advanced of the Radical thinkers
and politicians went even further in their political
speculations.[1] The retention of the colonies, in their
eyes, was incompatible with the maintenance of free
institutions at home, or the development of a democratic government in the distant dependencies. The
over-sea possessions represented to them the happy
hunting-ground of Tory imperialism. They were a
grand source of patronage and political corruption for
the English aristocracy. The colonies not only
imposed a heavy burden upon the British Treasury,
but were a constant source of discord in English
politics. In peace, they were a useless luxury; in
war, a menace to the security of the nation. The
frequent outbreaks of political discontent in the
colonies furnished, in their judgment, the most con-

---

[1] Professor Egerton has brought out clearly the essential difference
in the views of the early Liberal colonial reformers, as Lord Durham,
Butler, and Sir W. Molesworth, who were genuine imperialists, and
the narrow conceptions of colonial policy of Cobden, Bright, and
other Radical leaders, who were thorough-going Little Englanders.
Egerton, *British Colonial Policy*, pp. 366–7.

vincing proof of the incapacity of British officials at home and abroad to administer the affairs of distant possessions. The colonies, moreover, distracted the attention of the English public and Parliament from the consideration of more important social and political problems at home. They were a source of envy to foreign powers, and a frequent occasion of international difficulties. In short, they were an irksome, if not useless, encumbrance to the mother country. Under these circumstances, it was to the interest of both England and the colonies that the connection should be broken as soon as possible. It was evident, from the experience of the early American colonies, that the imperial tie could not be permanent. A distinct nationality was the manifest destiny of the self-governing dominions. Since independence was inevitable, it was better that the separation should take place peaceably, with the free consent and blessing of the mother country, rather than come as the result of bickerings, or, mayhap, of a bloody struggle, which might embitter their future relations for all time. As independent states, the colonies would take on a higher and nobler existence. Happily free from the dangers and complications of European politics, and rejoicing in the possession of civil and religious liberty, and a democratic form of social organization best suited to the development of their immense natural resources, the new-born states could aspire to play a prominent part in the affairs of the new world, and to wield a liberalizing influence upon the civilization of the old.

The doctrines of the Manchester School had just won a signal triumph in the field of economics in the adoption of the free-trade policy ; they now threatened to exert an equal influence upon the course of the political history of the colonies. Some of the Whig leaders, and many prominent members of Parliament, Tories as well as Radicals, accepted, in whole or in part, the colonial as well as the economic tenets of the Little Englanders.[1]   A large proportion of the most influential magazines and journals of the kingdom, including *The Edinburgh Review* and *The London Times*, openly espoused the new political philosophy.   The consecrated zeal of Cobden and the burning eloquence of Bright commanded the attention of the whole nation.   From a thousand platforms of the Free Trade League, the economic and political philosophy of the Manchester School was widely disseminated.

The new political doctrines soon crossed the seas and made their influence felt upon public opinion in the colonies.   It was, indeed, a stunning blow to the colonial loyalists to be frankly informed by the press and politicians of England, that loyalty was not necessarily a virtue, that their devotion to the Crown was no longer estimated at its full face value, and that it would probably be better for both England and the colonies if the latter should peacefully cut the painter. It was but natural that the colonial Tories should resent the appearance of a set of dogmas which placed a stigma on their time-honoured traditions ;   and this resentment was still further accentuated upon the adoption by the Whig Government of some of the detested principles of the Manchester School.   On the other hand, the new doctrines found much favour among the colonial Reformers.   The sympathy which they naturally felt for the English Radicals, from whom they derived their own political principles, was intensified in this case by the earnest desire to free the colonies from the meddlesome interference of Downing Street officials.   They were not ready as yet to sever the imperial bond, but they welcomed any doctrines which promised to extend the measure of colonial self-government.

In Canada, the moment was especially propitious

[1] Reid, *Life and Letters of the First Earl of Durham*, vol. ii. p. 137, Melbourne to Durham, July 22, 1837; Parker, *Sir Robert Peel*, vol. iii. pp. 388–90, Peel to Aberdeen, October 25, 1841.

for the reception of the new philosophy. The ground
had already been prepared by recent events for the
scattering of the seed. The Tories, sullen and embittered by the loss of power, were prone to adopt
the tenet of colonial separation, as a means of justifying
their vindictive spleen against the British Government.
The Reformers, on the other hand, were delighted at
the opportunity of putting into effect the constitutional
principles of self-government for which they had so
long struggled in opposition. The agricultural and
mercantile interests were almost forced by the law of
self-preservation into a movement to carry the political
doctrines of the Manchester School to their logical
conclusion. Surely, it was thought, a Government
which had sacrificed the vested interests of Canada,
could not complain if the colonists should, likewise,
adopt such measures as might seem best calculated
to restore their prosperity, without regard to imperial
considerations. Had they not been invited, in effect,
to relieve the motherland of her colonial obligations,
and to assume the responsibility of their own administration? In short, in the colonies, as well as
the homeland, the theories of Adam Smith and the
teachings of Cobden had prepared the way for a
peaceful revolution.

"All parties," *The Montreal Gazette* declared,[1] "are
convinced that the policy of England is to leave the
colonies to themselves in politics and commerce. The
withdrawal of colonial protection was followed by the
invitation to the colonies to abolish their system of
preferential duties. These steps indicate an intention
of directing the colonial education towards total
independence." *The Herald*, likewise, shared the
opinion that the British Government would gladly
give up the colonies. "The whole current of opinion,"
it maintained, "among England's most influential
statesmen, is evidently tending towards that point
where they will bid adieu to the colonies, with wishes

[1] April 13, 1849.

for their prosperity and hopes for continued friendship." Since England no longer retained a monopoly
of Canadian trade, there remained to her only " the
pride of sovereignty and the cost." The English
Government, it believed, would be especially pleased
to grant independence to Canada, since " British
supremacy had been mocked, and Great Britain disgraced," by recent political events in the colony.

The character of the agitation for annexation at
this time was admirably described by Lord Elgin in a
communication to the Colonial Secretary. " There
has been a vast deal of talk about annexation, as is
unfortunately the case when there is anything to
agitate the public mind. If half the talk on this
subject were sincere, I should consider an attempt to
keep up the connection with Great Britain as Utopian
in the extreme. For, no matter what the subject of
complaint, or what the party complaining ; whether
it be alleged that the French are oppressing the British,
or the British the French—that Upper Canada debt
presses on Lower Canada, or Lower Canada claims on
Upper ; whether merchants be bankrupt, stocks
depreciated, roads bad or seasons unfavourable,
annexation is invoked as the remedy for all evils
imaginary or real. A great deal of this talk is, however,
bravado, and a great deal the mere product of thought-
lessness. Undoubtedly it is in some quarters the utterance of every serious conviction ; and if England
will not make the sacrifices which are absolutely
necessary to put the colonists here in as good a position
commercially as the citizens of the States—in order
to which free navigation and reciprocal trade with
the States are indispensable ; if not only the organs
of the League, but those of the Government and the
Peel party, are always writing as if it were an admitted
fact that colonies, and more especially Canada, are a
burden to be endured only because they cannot be got
rid of, the end may be nearer at hand than we wot of."

CHAPTER II

THE SPIRIT OF DISCONTENT

IN the meanwhile, out of the troublous times, a
gradual reorganization of political parties was
taking place. It would, indeed, have been
strange if the existing political discontent and
economic distress had not given birth to a new party
with a new set of principles to remedy the ills of society.
The public were ready for a change, if not for a political
revolution. The Tory Party was wrecked. After
enjoying for so long the spoils of office and the special
favour of the Governors, it could not bear with
equanimity to be cast out into the cool shades of opposition. The proceedings of the Montreal mob had

thoroughly humiliated them. The social order had
changed ; democratic ideas were in the ascendency,
new constitutional principles were in vogue, the doctrines of divine right and special privilege in Church
and State were discredited. They had fought a losing
battle for a lost cause. The free spirit of the age was
against them.

Unfortunately, in this crisis, the leaders of the party
were unable to control the actions of their disunited
followers, or to formulate a new political programme
adapted to the necessities of the time. They stood
helplessly by, allowing matters to drift along a dangerous course. An extreme section of the party, embittered by their humiliating treatment at the hands
of the English Government, and freed from the re-
straining influence of their natural leaders, threw over-
board the time-honoured principle of loyalty, and
entered upon an active campaign in favour of annexation. The bulk of the party either groped around
blindly in the dark, or, like Micawber, idly waited for
something favourable to turn up. On the other hand,
a small body of progressive members sought to re-
habilitate the party by advocating the adoption of
some of the democratic principles of their political
opponents.

The condition of the Reformers, though seemingly
prosperous, was by no means reassuring. After a long
arduous struggle against heavy odds, they were at last
returned to power under favourable circumstances
which seemed to promise a long tenure of office. The
Governor was a statesman of well-known Liberal principles, the leaders of the party were strong and able
men, and the Assembly was overwhelmingly Reform
in its composition. But, from an early date, the party
had been divided in sentiment and policy into a Radical
and a Conservative wing. The long struggle in opposition for the principle of responsible government had
served to heal over the differences which the revolt of
1837–8 had caused among the leaders, and in the ranks

of the party. But on accession to office, the old cleavage threatened to open up again. The overwhelming strength of the party, together with the hopeless weakness of their opponents, weakened party discipline, accentuated personal rivalries and internal dissension, and aggravated the danger of a division of the party into two distinct and hostile camps. The Radical or Clear Grit wing preached the gospel of a triumphant democracy. They derived their political opinions to a large extent from the doctrines and experience of the neighbouring American states.

The Chartist agitation in the homeland, and the revolutionary propaganda in Europe, further contributed to spread the spirit of social discontent among the people, and to give them a roseate conception of the blessing of republican institutions. On the other hand, the Conservative element of the party were adverse to any important constitutional changes. They were satisfied with the grant of ministerial responsibility, and preferred, for the time being, to enjoy in peace the emoluments of office, rather than to go rushing forward into any further agitation. They were alarmed at the rapid growth of republican sympathies within the party, and fearful that these tendencies might develop into a distinct separationist movement. The leaders of the Government were placed in a most difficult and embarrassing position in their attempts to maintain the unity of the party, and, at the same time, to restrain the radicalism of a portion of their supporters. Unfortunately, their efforts were not attended with much success. The breach within the party grew wider and wider every day.

The policy of the English Government, as we have seen, had alienated the hearts of many of the colonists. The ruin of the colony was too high a price to pay for the reputed blessings of British citizenship. Not only was the vacillating policy of the mother country largely responsible for the prevailing commercial depression, but the British ministers had obdurately hardened their hearts against the petitions of the colonists for the restoration of the protective system. The commercial community of Canada were quick to learn the lesson of national self-interest. In their distress and resentment, they caught up the demand of the English Radicals for the emancipation of the colonies. A connection which was mutually burdensome and disadvantageous should not, and, it was contended, could not, be permanently maintained.

The Provincial Government also had to bear a share of the public criticism that falls to the lot of every Government which has the misfortune to be in power during a period of economic distress. The fact that the Ministry were in no way responsible for the existing depression was quite disregarded, whereas the failure of their efforts to induce the Governments at Westminster and Washington to grant concessions to Canadian trade was keenly felt in every home. Through no fault of their own, the Government were made to present to the public a spectacle of helpless incompetence. Many of the mercantile community did not fail to draw the conclusion that they must needs look to another source than their own Government for the relief of the country's ills.

The situation was still further aggravated by the intensity of partisan feeling and the bitterness of racial hatred which had developed out of the events of the last ten years. Since the days of Mackenzie and Papineau, the relations of the political parties had been particularly envenomed ; the struggle had been, not so much a conflict of men and of principles as a war between churches, races, and religions. The triumph of the Reformers in 1848, as we have seen, intensified the malignity of partisan and racial feeling. French domination was made the political issue of the day. A civil war was barely averted, and the danger was not yet past. A large part of the energies of the public was used up in these internecine struggles, which paralysed the economic vigour of the people, destroyed the social unity of the community, and endangered the future welfare and prosperity of the colony.

Within the province, there appeared to be no immediate escape from these direful conditions; the races were too nearly equal in number, and the issues too vitally concerned the social welfare and the religious convictions of the participants, to permit either party to lay down its weapons of war, and declare a permanent peace of God. Since there was no prospect of an extensive immigration from the British Isles, or the United States, it almost seemed as if the war of races, broken only by temporary truces, must needs go on for ever, unless the ascendency of the Anglo-Saxon race could be assured by a union with the United States. To many a loyal Briton, there appeared to be no other alternative to French domination than annexation to the neighbouring republic. To many others, who were comparatively indifferent to political and religious questions, annexation seemed the simplest remedy for the distracted state of the province. The commercial community longed, above everything else, for the cessation of the strife of parties and races and for the opportunity of pursuing their business interests under the more favourable conditions which prevailed across the border. The country was sick at heart and cried for peace.

Out of the economic distress, the social discontent, and the turmoil of race and party, arose the British American League, the primary product of an indeterminate spirit of political unrest and disaffection. "There is," declared *The Montreal Gazette*,[1] " a presentiment of approaching change. At no time has there been greater disaffection, or so strong a desire for something different. Men know what they feel without particularly analysing the causes or tracing them to their sources, although they may not be able to determine definitely the objects they desire or the means of attaining them."

[1] *The Gazette*, April 13, 1849.

The first branch of the League was formed at Brockville, with the avowed object of uniting the Anglo-Saxon population against the dominant influence of the French. Soon after a branch was established in Montreal,[1] which became the headquarters of the League's activities. The prime mover in the new organization was the Hon. George Moffatt, an able and prominent business man of the city, and an influential member of the Conservative Party. By reason of his well-known moderate views, and his extensive business connections, he exerted a wide commercial and political influence throughout Lower and Upper Canada. By gathering together all the disaffected elements in the country, he hoped to build up a strong organization upon the wreckage of the Tory Party.

An address, accordingly, was issued by the League to the public, pointing out in detail the evils, commercial, racial, and political, from which the country was suffering, and calling for a convention to take into consideration the commercial crisis, and the constitutional changes which the situation demanded. The address expressly disclaimed any desire to determine in advance the principles by which the convention should be guided, or the remedies which should be proposed for the manifold ills of the colony. All such matters were reserved for the determination of the convention itself. But upon the much-mooted question of the political future of the country in relation to Great Britain, the address spoke out in the most uncompromising language. " To maintain that connection inviolate has been, and still is, the ardent wish of every member of the League. We devoutly hope that no measure of injustice may ever be inflicted, no power may ever be abused, to the extent of provoking reflecting men to the contemplation of an alliance with a foreign power ; if there be, as some have said, a time when all colonies must, in the course of human events, throw off their dependence on the parent state,

[1] *The Gazette*, April 19, 1849.

and if, in our generation, that time should be destined to arise, we predict that, if true to ourselves, it will not come until no British hands remain able to hoist the flag of England on the rock of Quebec, and no British voices survive able to shout ' God save the Queen.' "

But the actions of the League by no means corresponded to its ultra-patriotic professions. The Montreal branch readily received into membership persons of the most varied beliefs in regard to the ills of the country and its political future. Annexationists, as the most active and energetic critics of the existing régime, were gladly welcomed into membership. In truth, the principles of the League were left vague and uncertain, in order the better to attract all the discordant opponents of the Ministry. The Annexationists on their part, either in the hope of converting the League to their own political purposes, or merely with a view to the more effective prosecution of their propaganda, joined the League in large numbers. Some of the officers of the League, and many of the members, were open and avowed supporters of continental union. Mr. Harrison Stephens, one of the vice-presidents of the local association, and moreover an American citizen, openly proclaimed his intention to do his best to bring about annexation.[1] Although not prepared to go so far as Mr. Stephens in advocating a breach of the British connection, many members sympathized with the movement to the extent of regarding the prospect of separation with complacency, as probably the simplest and best solution of the country's troubles ; while in the minds of others annexation was a sort of *arrière-pensée*, a last means of salvation in case all other means of relief should entirely fail.

The active propaganda of the Annexationists did not fail to produce a feeling of irritation among the loyalist members of the League. Strife soon broke out between the two factions. The immediate occasion of discord

[1] *The Montreal Pilot*, May 17, 1849.

was the fear of the Tory loyalists that their annexation
brethren might seek to procure the election of annexation delegates to the approaching convention, as a
first and necessary step to capturing the convention
itself, and committing the League to the policy of
annexation. The Hon. George Moffatt took alarm,
and, according to report, not only threatened to resign
the presidency of the local branch, but announced his
determination not to attend the approaching convention, unless all discussion of the subject of annexation
was excluded from its deliberations. The resolute
attitude of the President displeased many members of
the League, who did not find his policy sufficiently
progressive to suit their views. Some of the more
pronounced Annexationists accordingly deserted the
League, with a view to the formation of a distinct
Association to bring about a union with the United
States by peaceable means.[1]   A test of the relative
strength of the two factions took place soon after at
the election of delegates to the convention. This election, which was presided over by Mr. F. G. Johnston,
Q.C., a prominent member of the annexation group,
showed a decided majority for the candidates favourable to the British connection.[2]   Only one of the five
delegates chosen, Mr. Charles Backus, sympathized in
any way with the views of the separationists.

The condition of affairs in Quebec was somewhat
similar to that in Montreal. Thanks to the efforts of
Mr. Thomas Wilson, a branch of the League was formed
in Quebec, early in May. The League, he explained,[3]
was non-political in character, and had no connection
whatever with the recent riotous proceedings in Montreal. The primary object of the Association was to
devise some means of rescuing the country from its
political and commercial difficulties. While professing
the deepest loyalty to Great Britain, he declared that

[1] Montreal correspondent to *The Toronto Globe*, June 25, 1849.
[2] *The Montreal Pilot*, July 19, 1849.
[3] *The Quebec Gazette*, May 5, 1849.

if the day should ever come when the welfare and prosperity of the province were incompatible with the colonial status, he would no longer advocate a connection which was prejudicial to the best interests of the country. He expressly declined to pledge the convention in advance to the maintenance of the imperial union.

The equivocal attitude of Mr. Wilson and other prominent members of the League served to strengthen the opinion of many outsiders that the real object of that body was annexation. *The Quebec Gazette* endeavoured to remove the unjust prejudice which this suspicion had aroused amongst the English population, by assuring its readers that " such a design was entirely foreign to the purpose of the League." Notwithstanding this assurance, persons of well-known annexation views were not only received into membership, but were honoured with responsible positions in the local League. The question of the attitude of the League towards annexation was publicly raised at a subsequent meeting of the League, but no satisfactory response was forthcoming. The League in Quebec, as in Montreal, was committed to no general principles, but each member was left free to maintain his own private opinion.

Mr. Wilson, who was elected President of the local Association, advocated the adoption of a protective policy for Canadian labour and industries, and the maintenance of the British connection until it should be found that such connection was not likely to be advantageous to England, or profitable to the colony, while Mr. John Gordon, a prominent Tory politician, who was subsequently elected a member of the local Grand Council, emphatically declared that he was in favour of annexation, and considered that nothing else would " right the country." [1] Just prior to the meeting of the convention Mr. Wilson addressed an open letter to the members of the Association, in which, after pointing out the various courses which had been

[1] Quoted from *The Toronto Globe*, July 5, 1849.

suggested to meet the altered policy and extraordinary legislation of the Imperial and Colonial Governments —namely (1) the separation of Eastern and Western Canada with a readjustment of boundary, (2) a legislative union of the British American provinces with a change in the constitution of the Government, (3) Independence, (4) Annexation—he pronounced himself as strongly in favour of the second solution. Although Mr. Wilson was chosen as delegate to the Convention, the local Association was by no means committed to the views of its able President.

In the eastern townships, annexation sentiment was somewhat prevalent among the English population, but, as yet, the new political gospel had not found general acceptance. Of the various branches of the League throughout the district, only one, that at Melbourne, came out distinctly for annexation, provided it could be effected "peaceably and honourably." Many of the members of the League were undoubtedly in sympathy with the growing movement in favour of annexation, but they hesitated to commit their several Leagues or the approaching Convention to a definite policy. As a result of this non-committal attitude, the delegates to the Convention were left free to draw up a platform for the Association according to their own best judgment of the political situation and the needs of the country.

In Upper Canada, annexation feeling had not made much progress among the members of the League ; only here and there, at widely scattered points, was it at all in evidence. At Brockville, which was within the Montreal sphere of influence, several Annexationists were among those most active in organizing and directing the policy of the League. Even Mr. Gowan, the most loyal of Tory Orangemen, did not find it incompatible with his political principles to sit at the Council Board with fellow officers of well-known annexation views.[1] In the Hamilton district, an able and respect-

[1] *The Montreal Gazette*, April 13, 1849.

able member of the Tory Party, Mr. H. B. Willson, son of the Hon. John Wilson, formerly Speaker of the Upper Canada Assembly in the days of the Family Compact, took up the annexation cause with much energy and enthusiasm. He belonged to the interesting type of the democratic Tory ; in brief, he was a Tory by education, a Radical in feeling, and an Annexationist by interest.[1] He set himself to the difficult task of converting the Leagues of the west to more democratic principles, but he soon found that the undertaking far exceeded his power and ability, and that he could not hope to accomplish his object in the limited time at his disposal before the meeting of the Convention. Thanks, however, to his earnest advocacy of the principle of elective institutions, he was chosen by the Saltfleet Branch of the League as a delegate to the Convention. But the movement in favour of republican institutions did not spread much farther among the Leagues. *The Hamilton Spectator*, the chief Tory organ of the district, distinctly disavowed all connection of the League with the annexation movement ; and, with few exceptions, the members of the League in Upper Canada remained staunchly loyal to the British flag.

The Reform Party had been following the course of the League with anxious jealousy. The equivocal declarations of several of the leaders of the League, together with the open annexation proclivities of the Montreal Branch, furnished the Liberal press with plenty of material with which to throw suspicion upon the motives of the League. From one end of the country to the other, it was held up to scorn and ridicule as at heart a Tory annexation body. At a public meeting of Reformers at Peterborough, a resolution was adopted condemning the formation of the League, " the objects of which are to create strife and dissatisfaction in the country, and ultimately to sever the bonds between them and Great

[1] *The Toronto Globe*, August 4, 1849.

Britain." [1]   Just prior to the assembling of the Convention *The Toronto Globe* solemnly declared that the Tories of Upper Canada "were sold into the hands of desperadoes whose real object was annexation." [2]

As the time drew near for the assembling of the Convention, an increasing interest was manifested by the public as to its probable declaration of principles. The election of delegates in Upper Canada, where the League had the largest number of branches and the bulk of its membership, resulted in the return of an overwhelming majority of supporters of British connection.   On the other hand, the smaller group of representatives from Lower Canada were divided upon the question of separation.   However, the general result was so decisive, that even the Annexationists saw little prospect of winning the Convention over to their views. The Montreal correspondent of *The St. John's News*—a League paper—expressed the fear that there were too many Tories who "still clung to the exploded theory of Divine Right" to raise successfully the question of annexation in the Convention. [3]   The special correspondent of *The Globe* in the same city likewise wrote that, according to report, the question would not even be considered by the Convention, as the time was not yet ripe for its discussion, and "the people would not stand for it." [4]   Mr. Wilson of Hamilton, who was well acquainted with the state of public opinion in Upper Canada, similarly declared that the subject would not be broadly broached by its advocates at the Convention, but that the preliminaries, separation and independence, might be proposed, "as more likely to win general support." [5]   In truth, the election of delegates disposed of the question in advance, and the Annexationists saw the necessity of accepting the verdict against them.

[1] *The Toronto Globe*, June 23, 1849.
[2] *Ibid.*, July 26, 1849.
[3] Quoted in *The Toronto Globe*, July 26, 1849.
[4] *The Toronto Globe*, July 29, 1849
[5] *Ibid.*, July 28, 1849.

The Convention, which met at Kingston, July 26, was a most heterogeneous body, representing almost every phase of public opinion, save that of the French population. There were about one hundred and fifty delegates in attendance, from all parts of the country from Quebec to Sandwich. Although but comparatively few in numbers, the representatives from Lower Canada wielded a much greater influence than their voting strength warranted, partly owing to the superior ability of the delegates, and partly on account of their more advanced opinions on the questions of the day. Although the High Church Tories of Upper Canada formed the backbone of the Convention, yet among the delegates were to be found Annexationists, supporters of independence, advocates of a federal union of the British American colonies, provincial partitionists who demanded a repeal of the Act of Union, Orangemen with pronounced anti-French views, and even a few Radicals who clamoured for popular elective institutions.

In such a gathering, where the chief bond of union was opposition to the Reform Administration, it was practically impossible to suppress all reference to the question of annexation, however anxious the chairman, Mr. Moffatt, and the majority of delegates might be to shelve its discussion. The question kept cropping up at inopportune moments. A resolution of Mr. Wilson, of Quebec, in favour of the election of Legislative Councillors, greatly alarmed the ultra-Tory members, who saw in the resolution a dangerous step towards the adoption of republican institutions. An amendment was accordingly moved by Mr. Ermatinger, setting forth in fervid language the loyalty of the Convention to the Crown and to the principles of the British Constitution. In the ensuing discussion, several of the delegates from Lower Canada bitterly arraigned the Imperial Government for its political and commercial policy. Although not venturing openly to avow themselves Annexationists, they were eager for a change in the form of the local constitution, and for the adoption of such strong political measures as would teach the English Government to respect colonial opinion. A few Upper Canadians supported them in this attitude, but the vast majority, restrained by their Tory traditions, were desirous only of building up a working political organization of moderate views upon the basis of the old Conservative Party. The amendment was carried by 89 to 19.

Upon a resolution of Mr. Gowan for the organization of a National Association of the Leagues, the question was more directly raised by Mr. Backus of Montreal, who, in a fighting speech, declared : " If we are to be told by every succeeding Government in England that we are nothing in their eyes, that we are at perfect liberty to go whenever it is our interest to do so, let us raise ourselves at once to the standard of a nation." (Cheers and disapprobation.) It was unreasonable to suppose that nothing was to be said here but what would agree with their wonted feelings of loyalty ; they must be prepared to forget that they were colonists, and take a step for themselves. This frank declaration got the speaker into difficulties, and he was forced to defend himself against the charge of being an annexationist. Annexation, he explained, ought to be adopted only as a final resort, in case all other measures should fail to bring relief. A subsequent resolution by Mr. Gowan expressing unfaltering attachment to the British connection, and praying for the recall of the Earl of Elgin, called forth several warm speeches in condemnation of annexation. Mr. Parsons of Beauharnois declared that it was necessary that the Convention should show the falsity of the representations of their opponents, who had led the whole American public to look forward to a declaration in favour of independence on the part of the Convention. Annexation, in his judgment, would be the greatest calamity which could befall a British subject ; but, nevertheless, he would prefer annexation to a change in the Constitution. Still another speaker [1] attacked the annexation movement on the ground that Canadians would thereby degrade themselves to the level of slaveholders. Both the United States and France should be made to realize that they would never see the severance of Canada from the British Empire. An effort was made by Mr. Wilson of Quebec and his colleague from Saltfleet to side-track the resolution, but without success. It was adopted unanimously.

The question again came up, this time, fortunately for a more general and dispassionate discussion, on a resolution in favour of a union of the British American colonies, the *chef-d'œuvre* of the Convention, upon which its fame chiefly rests. In an able speech in support of the resolution, Mr. Duggan maintained that such a union would not only establish the supremacy of the Anglo-Saxon race in Canada, but that it would make of the colonies a great nation, would strengthen the motherland instead of burdening her as at present, and would set up an equipoise to the preponderant power of the United States in America. If, he declared, he had to choose between French domination and annexation, he would prefer the latter, a view which found considerable favour in the Convention.

The ultra-Tories of Upper Canada, as was to be expected, were vigorous in their denunciation of separation. Annexation, in their opinion,[2] would not take place unless the loyalists were driven to desperation by the unfriendly action of the English Government. Mr. J. W. Gamble, leader of the progressive wing of the Convention, devoted considerable attention to the topic. He confessed that, at heart, he was in favour of the independence of Canada, provided the consent of Great Britain could be obtained. He was

[1] Mr. Ruttan of Cobourg.
[2] See speeches by R. MacDonald (St. Catharine's) and Strachan (Goderich), son of Bishop Strachan.

convinced that a relationship with Great Britain of the nature of a personal union, similar to that of the Ionian Islands, would be best suited to the condition of Canada, but for the sake of harmony he would yield his opinions in favour of the project of a federal union of the provinces. Notwithstanding the material advantages which annexation would bestow in doubling the value of property, the vast majority of the inhabitants of the province could not easily lay aside their inherited British feelings. Annexation, in his opinion, could only be looked upon as a last resort.

In conclusion, he indulged in some interesting prophecies as to the future relations of Canada and the United States. Before many years had elapsed, there would be a terrible convulsion in the neighbouring republic, which would rend that nation in twain. Some of the northern states would then desire to form a union with Canada. The topography of the continent, and the natural sequence of events " marked this out as our ultimate fate." An equally interesting opinion as to the future of the colony was expressed by Mr. Wilson of Quebec, who supported the proposed union of the provinces as the best means of overcoming the difficulties which would arise from Canadian independence. The time, he believed, was near at hand when Great Britain would cast off the colonies. She had already deprived them of all the commercial advantages of their connection with the empire, and was now retaining her political advantages at their expense.

The scheme of a federal union, it must be admitted, won favour among the delegates, not so much from its own inherent merits as a truly national policy, as from the evils it promised to avoid. To the loyalists, it held out the prospect of rendering a resort to separation unnecessary ; and to the English population, it brought the hope of freeing the country from the danger of French domination. Of these two motives of policy, the former probably predominated in the minds of a majority of the Convention, though the latter found the more positive expression among the Orange members. Thanks to the combination of these two forces, the resolution was agreed to unanimously.

As a final summing up of the labours of the Convention, the League adopted an address in which, after strongly condemning the commercial policy of the motherland, and censuring the local Government and Legislature for their conduct in respect to the Rebellion Losses Bill, they set forth the political programme of the newly organized party. In respect to the economic condition of the province, the Convention adopted the materialistic view of the Montreal Board of Trade, that the loyalty of the province was a commercial product to be purchased or rewarded by fiscal considerations. They accused the British Government of responsibility for the " extensive bankruptcy and general distress of the colony." Local political conditions were likewise portrayed in sombre colours. The sins of the Government were heaped up measure on measure ; the Government had kindled racial animosity, legalized rebellion, increased the debt of the province by the payment of traitors, juggled with the system of representation, interfered with the elective franchise, and abused the power of appointing legislative councillors As a cure for the ills of the country, three principal remedies were proposed—Protection, Retrenchment, and a Union of the British American provinces.

The proceedings of the Convention clearly showed how weak was the annexation sentiment among the members of the League. Notwithstanding their general dissatisfaction with the conduct of the British Government, on both political and commercial grounds, the great bulk of the Tory Party in Upper Canada could not be brought to join hands with, or even countenance the seditious outbreaks of, their friends in Montreal. The Reform press, in attaching an undue importance to the disloyal utterances of the Montreal branch of the League, had, in truth, grossly misrepresented the real state of public opinion among the Tories. The bulk of the party were loyal at heart, notwithstanding occasional murmurings of disaffection. The anxiety of the loyalists was relieved at the outcome of the Convention, for at one time they feared that it might be rashly committed to annexation. " We dreaded," said the Montreal Transcript, " lest a handful of disappointed politicians should drag their party, and it might be the country, into the arms of a republican confederation. This intent, we had been told, lurked in the minds of many of the Leagues. Had this folly been committed, our opponents would have won a great triumph. Had the question been even seriously discussed, the result would have been most injurious to the country. But, thanks to the good sense of the League, the question was shelved. Not even the sense of injustice could extort such a thought from an assembly of British colonists."

The deliberations of the Convention were a great disappointment to the Reform Party. They had hoped that the heterogeneous elements in the League would break up in discord, without being able to frame a political programme, or else that the Convention would be led to declare for independence or annexation. But the Convention had not only strongly asserted its loyalty to the Crown, but had succeeded in formulating an attractive and statesmanlike policy that promised to appeal with much force to the disheartened mass of the electorate. The League could no longer be fairly or honestly accused of annexation aims, however much many of its members might be suspected of sympathy with that policy.

The proceedings of the Convention were followed with very great interest by that portion of the American press which was watching the trend of Canadian events. It was expected by many Americans, according to

The New York Herald, " that the League would declare
for annexation, but after reading the debates we are
convinced that it is contemplated by only a few of the
people." When the Convention made its declaration
of loyalty, " we knew that the annexation game was
over." *The Herald* was happily able to comfort its
readers with the assurance that, under the circumstances, it was probably best " if a union were not
consummated at present." The delight of a section of
the Tory press over the disappointment of their
American cousins could scarcely be concealed. The
Americans, declared *The Kingston Chronicle and News*,
" have been taught that the Conservatives value too
highly their liberty to throw off their allegiance."
The Canadian people, it concluded, could and would
settle their own difficulties without the assistance of
the United States.

The social and political influences which operated
most strongly in diverting the current of public opinion
among the English-speaking inhabitants of Upper and
Lower Canada, away from England towards the
United States, had but comparatively slight effect
upon their French fellow citizens. The annexation
movement among the French population was distinctive in origin and character. The growing disaffection of the English residents of Montreal had, as
we have seen, no historical connection with the events
of '37-8 ; it arose out of an unhappy combination of
political and commercial circumstances which strained
the loyalty of the English Tories to the breaking-point.
On the other hand, the concurrent expression of annexation sentiment among a section of the French population traced its origin almost directly back to the
rebellion in Lower Canada.

Papineau, the leader of the revolt, was a republican
who derived his political principles from the doctrines
of the French Revolution and the experience of the
American states. He never properly understood the
genius of the English Constitution. The principle of

responsible government was a mystery to him. The
only true expression of the will of the people was, in
his opinion, to be found in the popular election of
the chief administrative officials, as in the American
states. His experience in exile served only to
strengthen his convictions as to the true basis of popular
government. On his return to Canada he again
plunged into the bitter political struggle then going
on. Although elected to Parliament as a supporter of
Lafontaine, his natural ambition and his Radical
opinions soon rendered it impossible for him to co-
operate with that statesman. He accordingly dis-
sociated himself from the Liberal leader and the
constitutional wing of the party, in order to carry on
an independent democratic propaganda. Although
isolated in Parliament, he soon succeeded in attracting
to his standard a band of clever young men of Radical
opinions, who received the name of Le Parti Rouge.
In Parliament, the exigencies of politics led him to
join forces, for the moment, with. his erstwhile foe,
Sir Allan MacNab, in an effort to defeat the Reform
Government, whose cautious policy blocked, and, he
believed, would continue to block, all efforts to usher
in a democratic régime.

The new party, which was quickly organized under
his leadership, soon after issued a political programme
of an extremely radical and anti-clerical character.
They advanced the principle of the popular election
of all administrative officials from the Governor-
General downwards ; they bitterly attacked the interference of the clergy in social and political questions ;
they strongly condemned the existing colonial régime as
inimical to political freedom and the natural progress
of the province ; and last, but not least, they loudly
called for a constitutional union with the United
States. Several newspapers were established in Montreal and Quebec to support these principles. But the
Radical views of the party, and especially their unfriendly attitude towards the Church, aroused the

vigorous opposition of the clergy, who in self-defence rallied to the support of the Government. The Church and the Ministry alike were greatly strengthened by this tacit alliance against the common foe. There were, declared *The Montreal Witness*, two French parties in Quebec, " the priests' party and the party of progress."

The Rouge Party, though greatly inferior in numbers and influence to the Ministerialists, and, moreover, discredited by their connection with the revolt of 1837, made up for their inherent feebleness by the enthusiasm of their propaganda. At first, the organs of the party directed their efforts chiefly to the advocacy of the principles of republicanism and independence. But the course of events soon forced them to come out plainly for annexation. Far from accepting the doctrine, that union with the United States would destroy French nationality, they boldly avowed that annexation would best preserve and maintain their language, laws, religion, and political institutions. In an early article, *L'Avenir*, the principal organ of Papineau, declared : " The United States, far from extinguishing in our hearts the sacred fire of nationality, would fan it into a blaze. For they knew well that in confiding the safety of the St. Lawrence to the French of Canada, it would be as well guarded as was New Orleans by the French of Louisiana." [1]

And again, in a later editorial, fittingly written on the Fourth of July, *L'Avenir* took up the challenge of *Le Journal de Quebec*, to demonstrate how the French could preserve their nationality in case of annexation. Under the American federal system, it carefully explained, each state was allowed to preserve its own social good life and political constitution. In case of a political union, " we shall enjoy the protection of one of the first empires of the world, be assured of our own nationality, and shall not have to suffer, as to-day,

[1] Quoted in *The Toronto Globe*, April 4, 1849.

the rage of our embittered enemies. We shall not be subject to the mercy of the first English Governor who shall have the caprice to tyrannize over us, and to make heavy the burdens that we already bear. Further, we repeat it, masters of the election of our own officials, we shall have a legislature and an executive truly French-Canadian in personnel; our laws will be in reality official laws, and our language an official language; we shall be no more forced, as to-day, to submit our laws to the stroke of the pen of an English Queen, or to sacrifice our language to the necessity of being understood by our public officials. Furthermore, our general interests will be represented in the House of Representatives and the Senate of the United States by a sufficient number of members to make them known and respected. We shall have freedom of commerce with the entire world and the United States; we shall enjoy liberty of education and the largest and most complete political rights; we shall possess direct control over the policy and expenses of our Government, over our growing population, over the conservation intact of our rich and extensive territory, and over the improvement of our agricultural industry, by means of a strong and universal system of education."

Le Moniteur Canadien, the reputed organ of Mr. Viger, in a careful analysis of the political situation, declared, in effect, that there were three parties in Quebec: first, the Ministerial; second, the Tory; and third, the Democratic. The first was made up of the larger part of the French-Canadians, a few Irishmen and a small number of English Liberals. The organs of the party were discreetly reserved on the questions of democracy and annexation, although professing a loyalty to British institutions equal to that of the staunchest Tories. But, it alleged, should the Reformers be driven into opposition, they would almost unanimously declare for independence or annexation. The Tory Party, likewise, in order to dominate over the French, would gladly join in any attempt to break the British connection. If the commerce of Canada developed as that of the United States, and the English Government restored to them their former political ascendency, they would soon stop calling for separation ; but if, on the other hand, they were kept out of office, they would continue to frighten the imperial authorities by threats of secession, and seek to popularize themselves with the electorate by crying for annexation. Canada, it prophesied, would be annexed to the United States in five years. Upper Canada would be formed into one state, Lower Canada into another, and New Brunswick into a third. The independence of the country would be obtained by means of petitions addressed to the parent country, signed by men of all parties, and, amongst others, by 60,000 French-Canadians. Papineau would be chosen as the first representative of the State to the United States Senate.[1] *Le Courier des Etats-Unis*, which closely followed the course of Canadian affairs, summed up the situation in the statement, that, despite the opposition of the clergy, and the intolerant attitude of the Tory Annexationists, which outraged the sensibilities of the French population, and made co-operative action extremely difficult, the French-Canadians would rally *en masse* to the cause of annexation, when they became truly acquainted with the operation of republican institutions.[2]

At first, the attitude of some of the French ministerial papers was doubtful. For the most part, they kept discreetly silent, awaiting their cue from the Government. A strong attempt was made by the Annexationists to win over *La Minerve*, the principal organ of Lafontaine, to their cause. For a moment the paper wavered in its allegiance. On one occasion it went so far as to express an opinion somewhat favourable to annexation ; but, at the same time,

---

[1] Quoted from *The Colonist*, July 27, 1849.
[2] Quoted from *L'Avenir*, June 14, 1849,

guarded itself with many limitations, as became a
ministerial organ doubtful of its position, but inclined
to strike out a new policy if the future should appear
propitious. "Annexation," it declared, "does not
frighten us ; the colonial status is only transitory."
But, it added : "We can, we ought even, to wish for
annexation ; but the time is not yet come, we must
wait." Although somewhat disappointed at the
hesitancy of *La Minerve's* utterance, the annexation
press were quick to interpret it as an evidence of a
favourable movement within the ministerial ranks
which would soon lead the whole party into the annexation camp. But the leading article of *La Minerve*
was evidently written without sufficient knowledge
of the real attitude of the Government upon the
question. A few days later, the hopes of the Annexationists were blasted. *La Minerve* came out with an
open disavowal of the interpretation which the opposition journals had placed upon its recent article. It
emphatically denied the imputation that the Government was in any way responsible for its editorial
policy on this or any other question. As though to
atone for its temporary defection, it roundly declared
that, not only had it not become an advocate of
annexation, but that it did not even place it on the
order of the day for discussion. "We are quite ready
to admit that all those who desire order and security,
uphold, and must uphold, as one basic principle, both
the Reform Ministry and the connection with Great
Britain, and that frankly and without reserve." Now
that England had granted to the Canadians a Liberal
Constitution, they should show their appreciation of
her action by their loyalty to the Crown.

The ministerial papers quickly followed the load of
La Minerve. They threw aside their non-committal
attitude, which had caused them to be suspected of
annexation proclivities, and came out boldly against
the new movement. *Le Journal de Quebec*, the chief
organ of the Government in the ancient capital, was

especially outspoken in its criticism of the French Annexationists ; while *L'Ami de la Religion et de la Patrie* appealed to the faithful to remember their duty of allegiance to the Crown. The old theory of Divine Right was again called into requisition to prove the heinousness of resistance to constituted authorities. By converting the question into a strict party issue, by representing it as a scheme of their ancient enemies, the Montreal Tories, to recover their ascendency, and by appealing to the religious zeal of the faithful to withstand the insidious doctrines of the enemies of the Church, the organs of the Government succeeded in checking, to a large extent, the rapid spread of annexation views among the mass of the French population.

Since early spring, the condition of affairs had been steadily growing worse. The continuance of the commercial depression, and the growing social and political unrest were rapidly preparing men's minds for a radical change in the constitution of the province. The Montreal correspondent of *The New York Herald* vividly described the state of public feeling in Montreal just prior to the decision of the English Government on the Rebellion Losses Bill. " Let this Bill receive the royal assent, and the second ministerial measure of increasing the representation be passed, and the struggle will have commenced. Canada will go peaceably, if possible, forcibly if necessary. The year 1850 will see the Stars and Stripes float over the battlement of the Gibraltar of the New World, Quebec. The inattentive observer of affairs may doubt the probability of such an event, but let him carefully look into the causes which are bringing about this event, and he will at once see those shadows which portend the coming events. The colonies have lost all protection in the home markets ; they can therefore no longer compete with the American exporter. The United States Congress have refused to pass the Reciprocity Bill ; Canadians cannot, therefore, reap any advantage from the Republic. And, lastly, the hatred of race against race has risen to such a pitch, that nothing but the succumbing of one will ever allay it."

Some of the Tory papers were already open to conviction as to the merits of annexation. On June 11, *The Montreal Gazette* came out with a feeler in favour of separation, in which, after depicting the bitter feelings which pervaded all English hearts, since the home Government had cast such unmerited scorn upon their loyalty, it concluded by raising the question, whether it was not a moral law of nations for colonies to be weaned, sooner or later, from the parent state. Similar, and even stronger, language was frequently heard in private conversations. The end of the month saw *The Herald* break ground cautiously in favour of annexation. It presented the policy of separation as essentially an English question. It was the duty of the motherland to grant independence to Canada, rather than the business of the latter to ask or demand the same. Some change was obviously necessary, since the country could not go on as it was. Canada, it concluded, should not do anything prematurely or designedly to bring about separation; she should rather throw off on England the entire responsibility of determining the future of the province, of leaving to the latter no alternative but independence or annexation.[1]

The same day there appeared the prospectus of a paper intended " to advocate the peaceful separation of Canada from the imperial connection." Although the paper failed to materialize, the prospectus served the valuable purpose of a campaign document, of clearly setting forth the complex conditions which were forcing upon the public the question of a possible change of allegiance. The prospectus was, in fact, a manifesto rather than a business proposition. Mr. Sydney Bellingham, whose name was attached to the prospectus as *pro tempore* secretary of the organization

[1] *The Montreal Herald.* June 29, 1849,

committee, was one of the most active Annexationists in the city. The previous summer he had presided at an unsuccessful annexation meeting at which his fellow countryman, Mr. O'Connor, was the chief speaker,[1] and subsequently, according to report, had departed on a mission to New York, to solicit subscriptions towards the scheme of annexation.[2] He was a man of rather uncertain reputation. By *The Montreal Gazette* he was described as a " gentleman well known as a man of energy and talent " ; on the other hand, his portrait was painted in the most unfavourable colours by the Governor-General,[3] and by *The Hamilton Spectator*, which referred to him as " the toady of Lord Sydenham," and " the bosom friend of the New York repealers." [4]

The prospectus of Bellingham's paper was cordially greeted by both *The Courier* and *The Gazette*, the latter declaring that it would not be long before there would be but few journals in opposition to that policy. " We do not object to see our new companion succeed, and when the time comes we may not be found backward in seconding its efforts." An even more striking evidence of the rapid change of public opinion in the city was seen in the open display of many American flags on the Fourth of July. Such a display, as was pointed out by a keen observer, could scarcely have occurred a year or so previously.[5]

Just at this critical moment appeared the speech of Lord John Russell in the House of Commons, in which he stated that he would permit the Rebellion Losses Bill to go into operation. This last blow shattered the loyalty of the Montreal Tories. For some

---

[1] See letter of Lord Elgin, July 18, 1848, *Letters and Journals of Lord Elgin*, p. 57.

[2] *The Montreal Transcript*. Quoted in *The Toronto Globe*, July 12, 1849.

[3] Canadian Arch.

[4] Letter of Sir Francis Hincks to the London *Daily News*, August 10, 1849.

[5] Special correspondent, *St. John's News*, July 5, 1849.

months past, they had been wavering in their political
faith. Now, partly from choice, partly from chagrin,
the principal papers of the party, with one exception,
came out more or less openly for separation.   The
outburst was, to a large extent, " an ejaculation uttered
in a moment of passion, rather than a deliberate conviction." [1] But several of these same journals were
by no means certain of their own attitude ; their utterances were weak and vacillating, the fitful expressions
of editors who were anxiously following the varying
course of public opinion, rather than seeking to direct
the current of events by strong and clearly pronounced
views. Nor were they agreed among themselves as
to the future of Canada, or the mode in which she
would work out her political destiny. *The Herald*
alone was ready to commit itself to the policy of
annexation. *The Courier* came out in favour of independence under an English guarantee of protection.
It showed its sympathy with annexation, however, by
throwing open its columns to a series of articles upon
that subject.[2] For a time *The Gazette* wavered in its
course ; it adopted the attitude of a friendly critic of
annexation, which, it claimed, would not be as beneficial to the province as the supporters of that policy
maintained, since the effect would be to deprive the
colony of its revenues, and to burden it with a portion
of the United States debt. Before the end of the
month, however, *The Gazette* had made up its mind
in favour of independence.

Notwithstanding their superficial differences of
opinion, all three papers were at last united in demanding a separation from Great Britain. Their tone
towards the motherland was harsh and censorious.
They bitterly attacked her as the source of all the
colony's misfortunes. Far from discussing the question of annexation in a calm and reasonable spirit,
they used it rather as a medium for venting their

[1] *The Toronto Examiner*, July 11, 1849.
[2] *The Montreal Courier*, July 5, 1849.

dissatisfaction with the existing conditions of government. Without actually hoisting the Stars and Stripes, they showed quite clearly in what direction their sympathies were turning, and what would be the inevitable end in case matters did not mend according to their several wishes. The unseemly and seditious conduct of the Tory press of the capital almost justified the bitter arraignment of *The Toronto Globe*: " Mercantile embarrassment, added to political discomfiture, appears to have upset them completely. They seem to have gone fairly demented; they rave against French domination, free trade, responsible government, in fact, against anything and everything on which they can vent their ill-temper." [1] Of the four Tory journals of the city, only *The Transcript* remained loyal to the British connection.

Side by side with *The Transcript* in hostility to any scheme of independence or annexation stood *The Pilot*, the sole English organ of the Reform Party in Montreal. It denounced the annexation cry, at the outset, as a Tory scheme, gotten up by " the most bigoted and selfish part of the people." [2] It questioned the motives and sincerity of the Tory Annexationists, since the result of such an agitation, if long protracted, would necessarily be the utter ruin of the Tory Party, and the destruction of their special privileges. But, as the movement took on a more serious character, *The Pilot* saw the necessity of treating the question in a more reasonable spirit. Nothing, it declared, but dire necessity could justify the severance of the imperial tie. It warned the Annexationists of the danger which such a policy might inflict, not only on Canada, but on the nations at large. Mr. Roebuck, an influential member of the English Parliament, had recently pointed out that the annexation of the British American colonies might prove dangerous to the liberties of the world, by making the United States too powerful and

---

[1] *The Toronto Globe*, June 20, 1849.
[2] *The Montreal Pilot*, April 28, 1849.

tyrannical in her relations with other powers.   Over
against the abolition of ecclesiastical privileges, the
greatest boon which annexation promised to confer,
The Pilot set the introduction of the curse of slavery
into Canada.   "We ask the annexationist if he is
prepared to sacrifice justice and benevolence on the
altar of Mammon, if he is prepared to enter into
partnership with the owners of human flesh and bones,
the oppressors of human souls, if he is willing that
his country should become part and parcel of a system
which denies the right of citizenship to men whose skin
is of a darker hue than that of their neighbours, and
takes from them the key to knowledge, lest they should
learn to assert the dignity of their nature, and claim
to be treated as brothers."

The remaining English paper, *The Montreal Witness*,
an independent journal of high moral tone, was from
the first sympathetic towards the annexation cause.
After a period of hesitancy, it at last came out frankly
for annexation.   In a long editorial of August 13, it
discussed the question in its own original manner,
with special regard to the effect of a political union
on the religious, temperance, and financial interests of
the province.   Annexation, it concluded, was "the
natural and probable gaol [an amusing misprint]
towards which we are tending."

The French-Canadian papers divided upon the question according to strict party lines.   *L'Avenir* and *Le
Moniteur*, the two Rouge organs, were as ardent advocates of annexation as Papineau himself.   On the other
hand, *La Minerve*, the mouthpiece of the Ministry,
after a brief period of irresolution, threw the whole of
its powerful influence against the movement.   The
religious press, which was seriously alarmed at the
prospect of the introduction of American liberal ideas
in Church and State, was even more strongly opposed
to annexation.

By the middle of July, political discontent was so
far advanced in Montreal, that five of the leading papers

of the city were won over to the policy of separation ; only three, including the two ministerial organs, still clung to the British connection. The two extreme parties of the city, the ultra-Tory loyalists on the one hand, and the ultra-French Radicals on the other, had raised their voices in loud protest against the maintenance of the imperial tie. The moderate section of the Conservative Party and the great bulk of the Reformers still remained loyal. Public opinion, however, was flowing strongly in the direction of annexation. In view of these unfavourable conditions, the prophecy of Isaac Buchanan that Lord Elgin would be the last Governor-General of Canada seemed destined to be soon fulfilled.

During the remainder of the summer months, public interest in the question of annexation rapidly increased among all sections of the population. At the same time, a gradual modification in the character of the movement was taking place, the evidence of which may be clearly traced in the changing tone of public discussions of the question. In its origin, as we have shown, the annexation issue was the product of an unusual combination of economic, social, religious, and political conditions. On account of the bitterness of partisan feeling, the political element was predominant in the earlier stages of the agitation. The strident note of a bitterly disappointed party rose highest in the cry for annexation. It is easy to follow the ascending scale of Tory indignation : at first they murmured, then they threatened the English Government ; and finally a small section of the party denounced the British connection. But the outburst which greeted the acceptance by the Whig Government of the Rebellion Losses Bill soon spent itself, though the bitterness of spirit and the sense of injustice still remained. The hopes of the Annexationists rose high when the exasperation of the Tories against Lord Elgin and the English Ministry first broke forth ; but, with the subsidence of party feeling, these hopes were seen to be premature and unfounded. Something more than political discontent was necessary to produce a revolution.

Moreover, the calling of the League Convention had a steadying effect upon the moderate section of the Tory Party. The organization of the League and the adoption of a political programme turned their energies in another direction, and helped to restore discipline in the disorganized ranks of the party. The party was no longer a mob ; it was again provided with accredited leaders and an attractive set of political principles. The scheme of a colonial federation not only held out some promise of relieving the social and economic difficulties of the province, but was also much more acceptable to all true Britishers than annexation. " A union of the provinces," *The Gazette* declared, " would give the colonists practical independence, so much desired, and remove the idea of annexation now existing among many influential persons." In a similar spirit, a few days later, it asserted : " We feel with the League that it is the duty of British subjects to exhaust all means left to them of remaining under the government of the Queen in spite of all disagreeable and all adverse circumstances." Still the idea of annexation always remained as an *arrière-pensée* in the mind of *The Gazette*, as in the minds of the leading public men of the city, for it went on to declare that, in case the Maritime provinces saw fit to join with Canada in an intercolonial legislative union, well and good, " but, if they have made up their minds to go one step further, we have no objections to follow them."

But, in truth, neither the unpopularity of the Colonial and Imperial Governments nor the proceedings of the Convention was the determining factor in the life of the movement. The source of discontent went much deeper than mere partisan feeling. The pronouncement of the Convention had undoubtedly quieted, to a large extent, the cry for annexation which arose from the excess of party spirit. But an ally, more powerful even than the League, was fighting on the side of the Annexationists. In Montreal, business was at the lowest ebb ; both local and foreign trade were palsied ; property was unsaleable ; capital was un-productive ; labourers tramped the streets in search of work ; homes were deserted, and families were fleeing from the stricken city.[1] The seriousness of the commercial situation overshadowed all other matters. The angry cry of the partisan gave way to the anxious sigh of the merchant and the despairing groan of the workman. The political aspect of annexa-tion was forced into the background ; from this time forward, commercial considerations were all-powerful.

"When annexation was first spoken of," said *The Bytown Packet*, "it was merely held out as a threat. But, latterly, it has assumed a different aspect. Many are now annexationists whose views are not directed by party violence, and whose position and character entitle them to respect."[2] The mercantile community was seeking a way of escape out of the slough of despair. Some change was imperatively demanded, and that right speedily. For the moment, it appeared as if the interests and the allegiance of the mercantile com-munity were in deadly conflict. The business interests of the city were suffering from the British connection, and out of that suffering there arose, in the minds of many honourable and public-spirited men, the certain conviction that prosperity could not be secured as long as that connection was maintained. "Herein," declared a keen-sighted American observer, "is the mainspring of annexation. All other grievances can be smoothed and obviated, but this reaches every man and is felt every hour."[3] In annexation alone appeared the hope of financial salvation.

[1] Lucas, *Historical Geography of the British Colonies*, part 2, p. 195.
[2] *Bytown Packet*, November 10, 1849.
[3] *The Rochester American*, quoted in *The Colonist*, September 7, 1849.

As time went on with but hazy prospects of a union of the provinces, the tone of the Montreal Tory press became increasingly favourable to annexation. Early in September, *The Gazette* declared that loyalty in Canada was shaken among the loyal, and totally lost in the hearts of many. "Canada has turned the corner, and will not return upon her trail. The second Parliament that will be elected from this date will address the Queen to be absolved from their allegiance, or else something extraordinary will happen to prevent it." [1] Nevertheless, it still hesitated to pronounce outright in favour of annexation, on account of the many obstacles in the way. It severely criticized the policy of those papers, more especially the French, which advocated immediate annexation without the intermediate step of independence. It threw upon them the difficult task of proving that such a step would be beneficial and possible of accomplishment. In the judgment of *The Gazette*, annexation could not take place without the consent of Great Britain and the co-operation of the Maritime provinces, whose sentiments were apparently unfavourable to such a policy at the present time. [2]

The utterances of *The Herald* and *The Courier* were even more friendly in tone. In announcing the projected publication of an annexation paper in Toronto, the latter declared that the views of Mr. H. B. Wilson "were only about six months in advance of the whole of the British population of the Canadas." The former, for some time past, had been carrying on an active propaganda in favour of annexation. Even the most partisan of the Reform papers were obliged to admit that the campaign of *The Herald* was conducted in good faith, though the gravest doubts were cast upon the sincerity of the cry for annexation on the part of the other Tory journals. It was suspected, and openly alleged, that the utterances of several of the latter were intended for English consumption,

[1] September 3, 1849.　　　　[2] September 8, 1849.

with a view to intimidating the home Government into compliance with Tory demands, rather than for the education of the Canadian public in the doctrine of annexation. But, whatever the political motives, whether partisanship, racial antipathy, or commercial discontent, the press of Montreal was surely preparing the way for annexation in the most effective way by preaching the gospel of social and economic discontent with the colonial status.

But, in other portions of the province, the efforts of the Annexationists did not meet with the same degree of success. In the ancient capital, the advocates of separation obtained a respectable, if not enthusiastic, hearing almost at the very outset of the movement. Early in the year, it was reported that annexation rumours in the city were " as plentiful as blackberries in season." [1] At first the chief Tory paper, *The Quebec Gazette*, was inclined to discountenance the threats of separation, voiced by some of its contemporaries, as likely to prejudice the Tory Party, and prove injurious to the credit of the country.[2] But when the Whig Government supported the Baldwin-Lafontaine Ministry, its loyalty was strained almost to the limit of endurance. Although not yet prepared to support annexation, it could not help but sympathize with its Montreal friends, and even justify their seditious utterances.[3] " Responsible government," it declared,[4] " was the prelude, free trade laws the first act, the modification of the Navigation Laws the second, the royal sanction to the Indemnity Bill will be the third, and we doubt not that we shall soon have to chronicle the *dénouement*."

Strong declarations in favour of separation were common throughout the city, and sometimes gave rise to excited feelings. On one occasion it was found necessary to call in the police to stop a fight which broke out in the city council over the statement of a

[1] *The Quebec Gazette,* January 22, 1849.
[2] *Ibid.*, March 30, 1849.
[3] *Ibid.*, June 13, 1849.
[4] *Ibid.*, July 5, 1849.

member that they would all be Americans in three months.[1] But the majority of the papers were not carried away by the excitement of the moment. *The Quebec Chronicle*, an influential Tory journal, determinedly set itself against the movement. Although it admitted that annexation might be financially advantageous to the country, it nevertheless expressed the hope that the British connection would not be sacrificed for mere material ends. *The Mercury*, the third Tory organ of the city, solemnly warned its political friends against having anything to do with annexation. " We still more distinctly maintain that the desperation cry of annexation to the neighbouring states is unreasonable, impudent, and highly prejudicial to the Conservative cause, and that no declaration from the British Canadians could be more pleasing to the Lafontainists, than that of an intention to hoist the Stars and Stripes."

Among the French population of Quebec, the gospel of annexation was able to make but little progress, partly owing to the racial isolation and conservatism of the people, but more particularly on account of the silent opposition of the clergy and the unfavourable attitude of the ministerial leaders and press. The charges of disloyalty, levelled against the French-Canadians by some of the Tory papers of Upper Canada, were, according to *The Quebec Gazette*, most unjust. The French-Canadians, it contended, appreciated the value of the British connection as much as their English fellow citizens ; and, moreover, did " not feel the less need of it, because they were threatened with a war of extermination by some of the latter."[2] The French ministerial organs did not hesitate to affirm that the French-Canadians would turn out to a man to put down the Tories, should the latter attempt to annex them to the United States. With the launching of *Le Canadien Indépendant*, a Papineau

---

[1] *The Quebec Gazette,* June 12, 1849.
[2] *Ibid.,* April 4, 1849.

paper, the views of the Quebec Annexationists at last found expression. Mr. Aubin, the editor-in-chief, was a warm supporter of the annexation cause, and both by pen and counsel contributed largely to the spread of annexation sentiment among his countrymen. But, notwithstanding the advent of the new organ, the progress of the movement among the French habitants continued to be much less marked than among the English population.

In the eastern townships, the question of annexation possessed a special significance for the English population. Both political and commercial considerations combined to render their position most precarious. They could not help but contrast their social isolation and the deep commercial depression on their side of the line with the ethnic solidarity and the financial prosperity of the New England states. Their interests, both racial and material, appeared to lie with their fellow Anglo-Saxons across the border, rather than with their foreign fellow countrymen at home. The substance of the matter was stated very clearly by Dr. Colby, one of the leading Tories of the district, in a public address early in the year. Although he considered it premature as yet to discuss the subject of annexation, since the consent of both Great Britain and the United States would be requisite to make such a measure operative, he admitted, nevertheless, that in the end annexation " would be desirable," as a means of emancipating the English minority of the district from French domination. But, notwithstanding this confession, he was not prepared to support the movement, since " such a union would, on some accounts, be premature, and also unjust on the score of humanity "—premature, since the district would not willingly submit to the higher taxation of Vermont, and unjust, as subjecting the province to the legal obligation of returning runaway slaves.[1]

In the early stages of the discussion, the views of

[1] *The Montreal Gazette*, June 8, 1849.

Dr. Colby expressed, with fair accuracy, the opinion of the majority of the English-speaking public. The tirades of Colonel Gugy and other extremists, by arousing a very lively fear of French domination, had estranged the hearts of the people from the motherland, and prepared their minds for a favourable consideration of proposals of annexation. But with the deepening financial depression, the attention of the people in the eastern townships, as in other parts of the province, was directed more and more to the commercial aspect of annexation. The question of how to secure an entrance for the local produce into the American market became the most vital issue of the day.

In Upper Canada, the progress of the annexation movement was much less encouraging than in other parts of the province. On the one hand, the English population of the west did not stand in the same constant dread of French domination as their eastern brethren, who were in daily contact with the problem of racial relationship; and, on the other, they had not experienced the same measure of financial suffering as the merchants and agriculturists of the lower St. Lawrence. Among the Tories and some of the Clear Grits, though for entirely different reasons, there was, however, a strong feeling of dissatisfaction with the existing régime, and a growing desire for a change in the political constitution of the province. But this desire did not commonly assume the form of a demand for separation.

From a very early date, the Tories of Toronto had justly enjoyed a reputation for loyalty, but the attitude of the English Government upon the Rebellion Losses Bill put that reputation to the severest test. They could not help but sympathize with their political friends in Lower Canada. For the moment their devotion to the Crown weakened, and some of them were prone to follow the example of their Montreal brethren in demanding a release from the British connection. The loyalty of *The Colonist*, which voiced the sentiments of the moderate Tories, was rudely shaken ; at times, it adopted a tone not unfavourable to the cause of annexation. In the midst of the commercial unrest consequent upon the change in England's fiscal policy, it came out with the frank declaration that separation was inevitable. " Our opinion, declared repeatedly within the last three years, has been that commercial wants and intercourse would bring it (annexation) to pass in a very short period, independently of collateral circumstances of a purely political nature. Setting aside, therefore, all private and sectional considerations, a glance at the features of our present colonial position will establish clearly what is the early and inevitable destiny of the whole British North American provinces." [1]

Out of this editorial, there subsequently arose a lively controversy between *The Patriot* and *The Colonist*, in which each endeavoured to clear its reputation by accusing the other of having favoured the movement. A hasty visit of the Hon. G. Moffatt to Toronto served to remove the erroneous impression that the League at Montreal was committed to the principle of annexation, and revived, to some extent, the doubtful loyalty of *The Colonist*. It denied the accusation that it had attempted to force annexation dogmas on the public ; it had merely " argued the subject in full, confining its remarks rather to the current of events and the facts of history, than to the expression of particular inclinations." [2] A few days later, in a critical review of the political situation in the United States, Great Britain, and at home, in relation to the future of the colony, it expressed the view that the fate of Canada would depend upon future circumstances outside the determination of the province itself. All the elements of political, social, and commercial change were in full operation. Much would depend upon the character of the agitation in

[1] *The Colonist*, July 3, 1849.   [2] *Ibid.*, July 13, 1849.

the province, but even more upon external influence ;
the success of the annexation movement would depend
" on the extent to which it may be encouraged by the
conduct of the Colonial Office ; by the pressure of the
anti-colonial mob of the manufacturing district of
England ; and by the amount of the commercial and
political sympathy infused from the United States." [1]

But, after the League Convention, when evidence
rapidly accumulated from all parts of the country that,
for the present at least, the Conservatives of Upper
Canada would have nothing to do with annexation,
The Colonist recovered its wonted loyalty so far as to
declare that it " was opposed to any agitation in favour
of separation from Great Britain," especially in view
of the possible submission in the near future of a satisfactory form of government for the North American
provinces.[2] It contended that the only Annexationists were to be found among the Reformers, and,
as that party was now in power, they would not, for
the best of reasons, take any part in the agitation for
separation. The greatest security against an early
attempt to bring about annexation was to keep the
Reformers in office ; for, should they be forced from
the Treasury Bench, the country might look for a
revival of the seditious propaganda of 1837-8.

The loyalty of *The Patriot*, the organ of the High
Church Tories, was not made of such flimsy material.
True, its hatred of the Government led it at times to
indulge in language that sounded almost seditious ; [3]
still it never altered in its attachment to the Crown
and British institutions. Although opening its
columns at first to the Annexationists, it nevertheless
declared itself " altogether opposed to the discussion
of a subject so inimical to all true British feeling.
The views of *The Patriot* were endorsed by the great
bulk of the Tories of Upper Canada, a fact which was

---

[1] *The Colonist*, July 27, 1849.
[2] *Ibid.*, September 11, 1849.
[3] *The Toronto Patriot*, July 5, 1849;

admitted by the Reformers themselves. At the very moment when *The Globe* was bitterly denouncing the partisan and mercenary action of the Montreal Tories in supporting annexation, it freely acknowledged that " a large and respectable portion of the Canadian Conservatives are thoroughly attached to Great Britain, and will not knowingly be led into an annexation agitation." [1]

To *The Toronto Globe* is due the chief credit for preventing the spread of annexation opinion in Canada West, especially among the Reformers. From its very first number, *The Globe* had secured, and later successfully maintained, a political ascendency over the Liberal Party. It wielded an influence and an authority greater than that of any other paper in the province. To almost all of the Scotch Reformers, the editorial utterances of George Brown were both the law and the gospel. From the very outset of the annexation movement, the attitude of *The Globe* was clear and decisive. The whole of its tremendous influence was thrown on the side of the British connection, and never for a moment throughout the whole contest did it swerve from its allegiance. The cry of annexation, it claimed, was a plot of the Conservative Party to frighten Lord Elgin into a change of ministry. Against those papers which affected to look on annexation as a mere matter of time, it poured forth its righteous indignation. " Show us the Liberal journals," it demanded, " which use such language, which would chain our free Canada to a republic whose desperate efforts to extend the region of slavery were continued up to the very last moment of the last sitting of Congress. We are told that capital would flow in from the States by annexation. But, if it did, and brought with it the deep degradation of a connection with slavery, better it were sunk in the deepest waters of Lake Superior." [2] The connection with Great Britain, it maintained, should and would be

---

[1] *The Globe*, June 20, 1849.　　[2] *Ibid.*, April 14, 1849.

perpetuated in the face of the most adverse circumstances. It gloried in the loyalty of the people of
Upper Canada, and their jealousy for the preservation
of provincial freedom, which had disappointed and
discomfited the plottings of the Montreal Tories.[1] It
especially appealed to its fellow Reformers to demonstrate their faith in the liberal institutions they had so
recently acquired, by a loyal support of the efforts of
the Ministry to put the principles of political responsibility into practice in the present dangerous crisis.

The attitude of *The Examiner*, the leading organ of
the Radical section of the Reform Party, was somewhat doubtful, and variable at times. It maintained a
critical and almost hostile attitude towards the Baldwin
Government, whose conservative policy it constantly
contrasted with the more liberal principles of the
Governments of the American states. Its eyes were
turned from England, and were longingly cast across
the boundary line. Although not prepared to support
the cause of annexation, and even at times scorning that
policy in no uncertain language, it assisted in spreading
the belief that, sooner or later, the bond between
England and the North American colonies would be
broken. In short, it accepted and inculcated the
principles of the Manchester School. It was opposed
to an immediate separation, but looked forward
without misgivings to its ultimate attainment by a
peaceful process of evolution. The subject of annexation, in its opinion, should be approached in a
spirit of earnest inquiry. It was a topic of the social
circle, "a thing of which men speak as of a family
arrangement." To many, it had become the all-
important question. Men thought soberly upon it,
weighing the advantages and disadvantages of such
a step. Within a brief time, a revolution had taken
place in the sentiment of the Tory Party, and the
spread of the agitation threatened to work still further
political disorganization.[2]

[1] *The Globe*, May 12, 1849.   [2] *The Examiner*, March 14, 1849.

The Examiner, however, refused to be rushed into annexation. At the moment when the cry of the Montreal Conservatives rang loudest for annexation, it calmly pointed out that Canada must first become a nation before she could contract an alliance with the United States. The people must be converted to the principles of independence before they rashly talked of annexation.[1] For its part, *The Examiner* preferred to await the course of events, and to watch the varying currents of public opinion, rather than to commit itself to any definite policy upon the question.

The growth of annexation sentiment in Canada West, though slow as compared with its progress in Lower Canada, was, nevertheless, steady. Early in September, the Annexationists believed that public opinion had become sufficiently favourable to warrant the establishment of an annexation paper. The progress of the movement had been greatly crippled by lack of an organ through which to carry on the propaganda. Almost the whole of the press of Upper Canada was opposed to separation, and even those papers which were sympathetic refused to commit themselves to a whole-hearted support of the cause. An independent organ was required to carry on an educational campaign throughout the western half of the province. A prospectus was accordingly issued by Mr. H. B. Willson, setting forth at length the purpose of the paper, and the political and economic conditions which had brought it into being. Although inexperienced in newspaper work, Mr. Willson assumed the editorship of the new publication.

The Canadian Independent was, according to the prospectus, " chiefly designed to promote by peaceable means separation from the mother country." Mr. Wilson emphatically disclaimed " all connection with either of the great political parties." The paper would confine itself to the advocacy of independence, " which must hereafter take precedence in importance over all

[1] *The Examiner*, July 11, 1849.

other questions." The necessity of an organ in Upper Canada was evident. In Lower Canada, with two or three exceptions, the entire press, both French and English, had declared for the cause of independence. In this section of the province, however, the virulence of party feeling, and the complete subserviency of the whole press to party purposes, had been such as to deter from espousing the cause even the conductors of those journals whose opinions were known to be favourable. The reasons for advocating independence were " of both a political and commercial nature, and the measure would be advocated on the broad grounds of political and commercial necessity.

"From the sentiments distinctly enunciated on various occasions during the last few years by English statesmen and writers of eminence, no reasonable doubt can be entertained that, whenever a majority of the people of these colonies shall, through their representatives in Parliament, ask to be freed from the imperial connection, their request will be conceded. Indeed, those who have attentively noted the sentiments propounded by the leading politicians in Britain of the present day must have noticed a growing desire to be released from the government of their colonies, as soon as it can be done with honour and safety ; whilst others, whose influence has already effected one of the greatest changes in the commercial policy of the empire which the world has witnessed, do not hesitate to express an opinion that the colonies should be abandoned without delay. It is believed that a great majority of the people of Canada, influenced by the opinion that the province would be permanently and materially benefited by the attainment of this end, are already favourably inclined. In Lower Canada, which contains considerably more than one-half of the entire population of the province, and where the press has taken the initiative, the feeling amounts almost to unanimity ; and in Upper Canada a very large proportion, if not an actual majority, of the

people may be regarded as entertaining similar sentiments.''

The causes which had led to the desire for mutual
separation were known to all. The recent measures
of the Imperial Government had not only placed the
colonies on the same footing as strangers, but actually
restricted them from participating on favourable terms
in the trade of any country in the world. Over these
limitations upon its commercial freedom the province
had no control.

" As the British provinces are so situated geographi-
cally in relation to the United States as to render them
commercially dependent upon each other to a very
large degree, the attainment of Canadian independence
can only be regarded as a necessary preliminary to
admission into the American Union. The advocacy
of the one necessarily involves that of the other. The
subject is, therefore, one of equal interest to our
neighbours on the other side of the line.''

In order to devote his energies exclusively to *The
Independent*, Mr. Wilson soon after withdrew from
the League.[1] It had not been his original intention
to advocate immediate annexation. He had intended,
on the contrary, to limit the policy of the paper to
the advocacy of independence, leaving the question of
annexation open for future determination, when independence had been attained. But the pressure of the
Montreal Annexationists forced him out of this equivocal
position. In a trenchant editorial of September 5, *The
Herald* declared that the Annexationists of Lower
Canada would prefer to see the province remain as it
was, than to have independence without annexation.
Although doubtful of the expediency of such precipitate action, in view of the traditional loyalty of the
people in Upper Canada, Mr. Wilson yielded to the
wishes of his Montreal friends to join in the annexation
campaign they were about to start.

The advent of *The Canadian Independent* was awaited

[1] *The Globe*, September 22, 1849.

with considerable interest throughout the province. In the Montreal district, its appearance was welcomed as an evidence of the changing sentiments of the people of Upper Canada, but in the western district its advent was greeted with mixed feelings of chagrin, curiosity, and good-natured tolerance. As a mark of their disapprobation of its policy, *The Patriot* and *The Globe* refused to publish the prospectus in their columns, notwithstanding the fact that they were offered most favourable advertizing rates.[1] *The Colonist* was not so squeamish, and gave due prominence to the new publication. It refused to be a party to the attempt to gag the new paper, the object of which was limited to peaceful agitation. "At any rate," it asserted, "peaceful separation would not be productive of a tithe of the disaffection" which had been occasioned by the action of the Government in rewarding rebels. It charged the Ministry with responsibility for the distracted condition of the province, out of which the agitation for annexation had arisen, and accused *The Globe* of hypocrisy in endeavouring to discount the strength of the movement.[2] So far as *The Independent* was concerned, the Tory Party repudiated all responsibility for its policy; the views of the editor of that paper were purely personal, and found no favour in the League.[3] The loyalty of the people of both Upper and Lower Canada, it asserted in conclusion, was too firmly established to be easily moved by the annexation views of one man. The friendly tone of *The Colonist* was doubtless due, in part, to a desire to placate the growing body of Annexationists, with a view to enlisting their support in overturning the Reform Government.[4] Such an alliance, it thought, might prove politically useful, even though the views of the annexationists were most objectionable.

[1] *The Globe*, September 4, 1849.
[2] *The Colonist*, September 11, 1849.
[3] *Ibid.*, September 7, 1849.
[4] *The Examiner*, September 5, 1849.

The Examiner did not believe that the utterances of the Montreal press were a true reflection of public opinion in the province. The annexation cry of the Tories of Upper and Lower Canada was, it maintained, essentially political in intent, and was designed to frighten the English Government rather than to effect a change of allegiance. But, notwithstanding this hypocrisy of the Tory Annexationists, there were scattered throughout the province many mute republicans and genuine Annexationists who believed with Papineau that the British connection was incompatible with the development of free democratic institutions, and who felt, with *The Quebec Gazette*, that colonial dependence unduly restricted the expanding energies of a free-born people. Whatever the strength of these unorganized elements (for the Annexationists had not yet attained sufficient cohesion to be called a political party) the issue they presented was one which must be seriously considered by the country at large.[1]

The discussion of the question was carried into the columns of the ecclesiastical press. *The Church*, the recognized organ of the Bishop of Toronto, maintained the historic loyalty of the Anglican clergy by rallying its adherents to the British cause. " The very idea of annexation to the United States," it declared, " was indignantly scouted by the immense majority of Western Canada, and we have reason to believe it meets with as little encouragement in the lower portion of the province." [2]

In the rural section of the west, interest in the subject of annexation was by no means equal to that in the chief cities. The question, as we have seen, was primarily commercial in character ; it affected the merchants of the city much more than the independent farmers of the western district. The issue was quickly taken up by the metropolitan press as a matter of real vital interest to their urban readers,

[1] *The Examiner*, September 5, 1849.
[2] *The Church*, September 27, 1849.

but considerable time elapsed before the local town
and village papers deigned to treat the question in
any other than a very desultory manner. They were
inclined to look upon the hue and cry of the Montreal
Tories as a passing whim, or a sudden outburst of
irresponsible opinion.

But, here and there throughout the western district,
the question was given due consideration. In the city
of Hamilton the views of the separationists found little
sympathy. The columns of *The Spectator* were thrown
open to a free and frank discussion of the subject, in
which Mr. H. B. Willson took a leading part.[1] But
in its editorial page, *The Spectator* took care to vindicate
its unimpeachable loyalty by attacking the views of
its annexation correspondents in an unsparing manner.
Although bitterly opposed to Lord Elgin, on both
personal and political grounds, it disavowed the attempts of some of its Tory contemporaries to convert
that hostility into an attack on the British connection.
It distinctly disclaimed the views of Mr. Willson as to
the cause, extent, and cure of the manifold evils which
affected the country.[2] It was especially zealous in
repudiating the attacks of the Reform press upon the
motives and the loyalty of the League. The Ministry
itself was responsible, because of its maladministration,
for the spread of annexation dogmas. Notwithstanding
the intensity of its political feeling, *The Spectator* still
preferred the mismanagement of the Reformers to the
democratic heresies of the United States.

The Hamilton Journal and Express, and the *Guelph
and Galt Advertiser* were equally hostile to annexation.
At the very outset of the agitation, the former declared, " as a true representative of the Reformers of
Canada West, and in their name," that the United
States would " not annex Canada just yet " ;[3] the
latter proudly affirmed that the loyalty of the Reform

[1] *The Spectator*, March 28, April 4, etc., 1849.
[2] *Ibid.*, March 28, 1849.
[3] Quoted from *The Spectator*, April 25, 1849.

Party was not in question. It was true, it admitted, that a few of the French-Canadian papers professing Liberal principles had unfortunately supported annexation, but " as a body the Liberal press of Canada has spoken out plainly and firmly for the continuance of British connection and responsible government, believing, as they do, that under responsible government we shall have all the advantages of limited monarchical government, with as much liberty and equality and civil justice, and smallness of national expenditures, as if we were a republic. And we do say that, as a body, the Tory press of Canada has come out as boldly for annexation as the Liberal press has denounced it." It acknowledged, however, that all the Tory papers had not gone over to the enemy, since " a few, such as *The Guelph Herald*, are still strong in their professions of loyalty to the British flag."

In the Midland district, *The Kingston British Whig* expressed the opinion that the Conservative Party was dead in every part of the country save Montreal. The province, it declared, would " not be ready for annexation for fifty years yet." [1]

The question was altogether too important to escape the attention of the politicians, especially when it afforded such a splendid opportunity to the Reformers to make party capital at the expense of their opponents. During the summer, several of the Reform members of Parliament took occasion to refer to the matter in their public addresses. At a large Reform meeting at Brantford, the Hon. Malcolm Cameron scouted the idea of annexation,[2] harped upon the loyalty of the party, and denounced the action of the Conservative press in lending their sanction to the movement. In like manner, Mr. Morrison, in an address to his constituents of the county of York, attacked the

---

[1] Quoted from *The Globe*, September 15, 1849.
[2] *The Amherstburg Chronicle* accused Mr. Cameron of having formerly supported annexation as necessary to the prosperity of the country.

separationist proclivities of the League, and declared
that the latter would soon find that Upper Canada
repudiated the idea of annexation.[1]

As autumn came on, Lord Elgin undertook a trip
through the western provinces in order to familiarize
himself with the condition of the people, and check, if
possible, the growing separationist sentiment. Notwithstanding the semi-political character of his progress (for the Reformers turned out *en masse* to honour
him with all the distinction of a party leader), he was
greeted with loyal addresses from the various municipal
bodies, and was accorded a friendly reception by the
people at large. The Conservatives, for the most part,
joined with the Reformers in testifying their loyalty
to the Crown by a respectful, if not a hearty, reception
to the royal representative. Even in Toronto, in spite
of the intensity of party feeling, the corporation adopted
an address emphasizing the loyalty of the city.[2]   Only
here and there, as in Brockville and London, were
there spasmodic evidences of disaffection on the part
of a small number of extreme Tories. The tour of
the Governor-General had a beneficial effect in rallying
the Reform Party to a heartier support of the Ministry,
and in recalling the people at large to a sense of their
duty and allegiance to their gracious sovereign. It
served to dispel the suspicion, that at heart a considerable minority, if not a majority, of the people
of Upper Canada favoured a peaceful separation from
England. Many were undoubtedly dissatisfied, but
few had been attacked by the virus of disloyalty. So
strongly, indeed, was the spirit of loyalty shown throughout the tour, that the Annexationists found it advisable
to avoid all hostile demonstrations, and to manifest
a respectful deference towards the Governor-General.

[1] Letter of Hon. F. Hincks to *The London News*, August 10, 1849.
[2] *The Globe*, September 17, 1849.

CHAPTER III

THE MANIFESTO AND THE COUNTER MANIFESTOS

Disaffection in Montreal—Alliance of the ultra-Tories and Rouges
—The commercial interests demand a change—Preparation
of the Manifesto—An Address to the People of Canada—
Signatures to the Manifesto—Minority of French-Canadians—
Battle of the Montreal press—The *Herald, Courier,* and *Witness*
declare for annexation—The *Gazette* favours independence—
The *Transcript* and *Pilot* support British connection—The
French-Canadian papers divide on party lines—Organization
of Annexation Association—Declaration of Papineau—Annexation demonstration—Speeches and resolutions—Officers of the
Association—Policy of the Association—Loyalty of the Reform
Government—Letter of Baldwin—Protest of French Liberal
members against annexation—Criticism of their action—Letter
of Francis Hincks—Effect upon the Reform Party—Address
of Montreal loyalists—Character of signatures—Dismissal of
annexation officials—Criticism of action of Ministry by Tory
press—Conduct of the Conservative leaders—Loyalty of the
Orangemen—Opinion of the Governor-General—Criticism of
Movement—Opinion of correspondent of *London Times.*

BUT we must return to the fountain-head of the annexation movement, the city of Montreal. Here, as we have seen, at the beginning of September the Annexationists were seeking to marshal their forces for a vigorous forward campaign. Disaffection was rife on every side. The people were distracted by radical jealousies and economic losses. The Ministry was powerless to grant relief, and the programme of the League had proved abortive. The spirit of unrest was abroad. The sharp but petulant cry for separation gave way to the general conviction that relief could be found only in annexation. The anti-colonial policy of the Whigs, according to *The Kingston Chronicle and News,* had strained the loyalty of the Montreal merchants to the breaking-point. " When poverty enters at the door, love is said to fly out of the window, and it is very much the same with loyalty. The dollar is found by experience to be as potent on this as on the other side of the line 45. The Montreal Annexationists doubtless desire to retain their loyalty, but they flatly declare they can no longer afford the luxury. Cobdenism has rendered it too costly for them ; and Elginism has led many of them to doubt whether the article is not dear at any price."

But up to this moment, the forces of discontent had remained unorganized. They were merely a rabble, or, at best, a loose group of hostile factions. The Tories were the traditional enemies of the French-Canadian democrats. The two opposing factions were separated from one another by race, language, religion, social usages, and political principles and ideals. Where, then, was to be found the mutual bond of sympathy, or common interest, to unite the Tory annexationist with his French-Canadian compeer ? Apparently, they had nothing in common except their hostility to the Government. But, in politics, necessity often makes strange bed-fellows. We have already seen how Papineau, the Radical, had joined forces with MacNab, the reactionary, to overthrow the Reform Government. Much as these two leaders disliked one another, they hated Lord Elgin and his ministers even more. This unnatural parliamentary alliance prepared the way for future political co-operation. The popular clamour for annexation in Montreal brought about a temporary *rapprochement* of the Tories and the Rouges in that city. Here was an issue on which they could get together. They were alike convinced of the general advantage of annexation, though they widely differed as to the specific benefits they severally expected to derive from a union with the United States. The goal was the same, but the objects in view were fundamentally different.

Since neither the French nor the Tory Annexationists were strong enough of themselves to direct the course of events, political prudence demanded that they drop their ancient enmity, and unite to promote their common cause. To that end, a change of tactics was required on the part of the Tory Party of the capital. The violent language of the Tory press had long wounded the susceptibilities of the French population, and had driven them into the ranks of the Reform Party, through fear of an anti-clerical crusade. Unfortunately for the cause of annexation, the French democrats had very grave doubts as to the motives of the new-born Tory desire for annexation. "If," said *Le Courier des Etats-Unis,* "the French-Canadians believed in the sincerity of the Tories, the party [referring to the Annexationists] would be all-powerful here." It was folly, according to *Le Courier,* for the Conservatives to dream of freeing themselves from the British yoke without the co-operation of at least a portion of the French population.

But mere political blandishments would never have sufficed to draw the two parties together. The reciprocal attraction of their common misery was required to bring about the necessary co-operation. In their common suffering, they forgot for the moment their social, political, and religious differences. To both there was held out the glowing prospect of escape from insolvency. The appeal was made with particular success to the wealthier members of the mercantile community. For many years, they had been accustomed to look upon the British connection as a commercial relationship out of which financial profit was to be derived. Loyalty under the preferential tariff was a part of their stock-in-trade. But upon the withdrawal of the imperial preference, their loyalty became a drug on the market. All considerations of party policy or political allegiance were lost sight of in the demand for a restoration of their accustomed profits. On this fundamental basis of the common material interests of the two nationalities, the Annexationists determined to found a new political party.

The moment was favourable for the commencement of a vigorous propaganda. The press, for the most part, was friendly. The public was ripe for a change, and the interests of the merchants demanded it. The relations of the French and English inhabitants of the city had become more cordial. By the beginning of October, the plans of the Annexationists were well under way. The French and English Annexationists agreed to sink their differences, and to unite in the common cause. A small but influential group of representative merchants set to work to draw up a declaration of political principles.

The press took the lead in preparing the minds of the public for the coming announcement. *The Herald* came out with a frank declaration in favour of immediate annexation. " We have reason to wish for an incorporation with the states of the American Union ; like reason prompts us to desire that this incorporation should take place as speedily as possible. A state of political transition is a state of personal and social misery. Here is no tranquillity, no improvement. It is of the utmost importance for the inhabitants of Canada, as the world believes that they are about to pass through a revolution, that they should do it at once." [1] It drew an unfavourable contrast between the policy of the League for a federal union of the provinces and the scheme of annexation. The choice in reality must needs be made between annexation and independence, since a federal union of the colonies necessarily involved independence. The latter would be much more costly, especially in the matter of defence, whereas the former would save the expense of maintaining a distinct administration and, what was even more important, would afford relief to the economic distress of the province by opening

[1] *The Herald*, October 3, 1849.

up the American market, and affording means for transportation of Canadian products.

The same day *The Courier* made a similar avowal of annexation principles. " When," it declared, " men find things irretrievably bad, they must needs think of desperate remedies. Annexation is that remedy ; it will be foolish now for us to wait to see what England will do for us. England can do nothing." [1] A couple of days later, it declared, in more offensive language, that while Canada remained a dependency of a distant empire, she would never be rich enough to make the internal improvements which were necessary to open up trade, nor would English capital be attracted to a colony which was certain to separate in the near future. The principles of free trade, it contended, were incompatible with the maintenance of a colonial empire. *The Pilot* and *Transcript* might " stick like lice to a dead corpse," but they could not revive the loyalty of the Canadian people.[2]

The Montreal Witness endeavoured to give a religious sanction to the annexation movement. " It is precisely because we think the indications of Divine Providence are pointing directly, constantly, and, we might add, urgently in the direction of annexation, that we have felt constrained to discuss the subject at some length, ere it becomes involved in the whirl of party strife." The most striking indication of providential direction was to be seen in the conversion of the Tory Party, which for many years had manifested " a passionate and chivalrous attachment to the British Crown," into an Annexation Party, " thus dissolving the only bond that was sufficiently strong to retain the Canadas for Britain against their own interest."

The city was on the tip-toe of expectation in consequence of a rumour that the Annexationists were about to issue a public manifesto.[3] The preparation of such a document was taken in hand " by a committee of

---

[1] *The Courier*, October 3, 1849.   [2] *Ibid.*, October 5, 1849.
[3] *The Gazette,* October 5, 1849.

gentlemen of wealth, education, and influence," with a view to ascertaining to what extent public opinion was prepared to support them in their efforts. According to their own profession, they had " no desire to assume the leadership, or draw others into ill-advised measures "; but if the manifesto were favourably received, they were prepared to go ahead with the organization of a general association. The immediate object of the committee was limited, however, to setting before the public the advantages of annexation. They did not wish at the moment to discuss the future policy of the Annexationists, or the means by which the object in view might be attained.

The preparation of the manifesto was, according to *The Gazette*, a delicate undertaking, since much of the success or failure of the propaganda depended on the first impressions of the public. The committee were solemnly advised to attend carefully to the form of the declaration, to see to it that the statement was " well conceived and well matured," and not to be deficient in weight and strength, as it was reported. The secrecy with which the committee set about the preparation of the manifesto awakened considerable criticism from those who were not within the inner circle of the movement. The motives of the committee were undoubtedly good, declared *The Gazette*, but " we cannot help feeling that the issuing of such a document is beginning where we ought to end." Before such a publication was issued, there should be a full opportunity of ascertaining the opinion of the masses. The question of procedure was, after all, one of good political tactics. " An organization," in the opinion of *The Gazette*, " should take place first, and then a declaration of opinion. We have to consider what Upper Canada and the other provinces will do." [1] The people of Lower Canada, however unanimous, ought not to think of dictating to the majority of their fellow citizens in North America. An association, if

---

[1] *The Gazette*, October 5, 1849.

properly organized, would always be in a position to make a declaration of principles, when the feeling of the public appeared favourable to such a statement.

But, notwithstanding this criticism of the tactics of the annexation leaders, *The Gazette* did not hesitate to affirm that the prevailing opinion in Canada was decidedly hostile to the British connection. " In Lower Canada, both the English and French are ripe for a change. In Upper Canada, we believe that there is still a majority of the population pretending to be desirous of continued connection with England, but the inhabitants of the towns along the lake are fast changing their opinions, and in a short time the old feeling— the loyal feeling—will be confined to the old country settlers in the back townships." Even the feelings of the latter would change when they realized the difference in the price of wheat on the two sides of the boundary line. This striking revolution in public sentiment was due, in the opinion of *The Gazette*, to the annihilation of every tie of interest between England and her colonies ; and, as Canada withdrew from social and commercial intercourse with the motherland, she as surely cemented her relations with the United States.[1] *The Courier*, likewise, declared : " The desire for annexation has taken fast hold on all classes of the community, and every minor issue is about to be absorbed in this all-important question. The difficulty now is to find a man who is opposed to annexation," whereas, six months ago, the man who would have ventured to stand up openly in favour of such a measure would have been a *rara avis*. Such was the revolution in sentiment, which, in the opinion of *The Courier*, had been brought about by the incapacity and maladministration of the Government.[2]

At last the expected manifesto, the most important document in the history of the annexation, made its appearance.

[1] *The Gazette*, October 8, 1849.   [2] *The Courier*, October 6, 1849.

An Address to the People of Canada

The number and magnitude of the evils which afflict our country, and the universal and increasing depression of its material interests, call upon all persons animated by a sincere desire for its welfare to combine for the purpose of inquiry and preparation, with the view to the adoption of such remedies as a mature and dispassionate investigation may suggest.

Belonging to all parties, origins, and creeds, but yet agreed upon the advantages of co-operation for the performance of a common duty to ourselves and our country growing out of a common necessity, we have consented, in view of a brighter and happier future, to merge in oblivion all past differences of whatever character, or attributable to whatever source.

In appealing to our fellow colonists to unite with us in this, our most needful duty, we solemnly conjure them, as they desire a successful issue and the welfare of their country, to enter upon the task at this moment- ous crisis in the same fraternal spirit.

The reversal of the ancient policy of Great Britain, whereby she withdraws from the colonies their wonted protection in her market, has produced the most disastrous effects upon Canada. In surveying the actual condition of the country, what but ruin or rapid decay meets the eye ? Our Provincial Govern- ment and civic corporations embarrassed, our banking and other securities greatly depreciated, our mercantile and agricultural interests alike unprosperous, real estate scarcely saleable upon any terms, our un- rivalled rivers, lakes, and canals almost unused ; whilst commerce abandons our shores, the circulating capital amassed under a more favourable system is dissipated, with none from any quarter to replace it. Thus, without available capital, unable to effect a loan with foreign states, or with the mother country, although offering security greatly superior to that which readily obtains money, both for the United States and Great Britain, when other than the colonials are the applicants—crippled, therefore, in the full career of private and public enterprise, this possession of the British Crown, our country, stands before the world in humiliating contrast with its immediate neighbours, exhibiting every symptom of a nation fast sinking to decay.

With superabundant water power and cheap labour especially in Lower Canada, we have yet no domestic manufactures, nor can the most sanguine, unless under altered circumstances, anticipate the home growth or advent from foreign parts of either capital or enterprise to embark in this great source of national wealth. Our institutions, unhappily, have not that impress of permanence which can alone impart security and inspire confidence ; and the Canadian market is too limited to tempt the foreign capitalist.

Whilst the adjoining states are covered with a network of thriving railways, Canada possesses but three lines, which, together, scarcely exceed fifty miles in length, and the stock in two of which is held at a depreciation of from 50 to 80 per cent.—a fatal symptom of the torpor overspreading the land.

Our present system of Provincial Government is cumbrous and too expensive, so as to be ill-suited to the circumstances of the country, and the necessary reference it demands to a distant Government, imperfectly acquainted with Canadian affairs, and somewhat indifferent to our interests, is anomalous and irksome. Yet in event of a rupture between two of the most powerful nations of the world, Canada would become the battlefield and the sufferer, however little her interests might be involved in the cause of the quarrel or the issue of the contest.

The bitter animosities of political parties and factions in Canada, often leading to violence, and in one case to civil war, seem not to have abated with time ; nor is there at the present moment any prospect of diminution or accommodation. The aspect of parties becomes daily more threatening towards each other, and under our existing institutions and relations little hope is discernible of a peaceful and prosperous administration of our affairs, but difficulties will to all appearance accumulate until government becomes impracticable. In this view of our position, any course that may promise to efface existing party distractions, and place entirely new issues before the people, must be fraught with undeniable advantages.

Among the statesmen of the mother country—among the sagacious observers of the neighbouring Republic—in Canada—and in all British North America—amongst all classes, there is a strong pervading conviction that a political revolution in this country is at hand. Such forebodings cannot really be dispelled, and they have moreover a tendency to realize the events to which they point. In the meantime serious injury results to Canada from the effect of this anticipation upon the more desirable classes of settlers, who naturally prefer a country under fixed and permanent forms of government to one in a state of transition.

Having thus adverted to some of the causes of our present evils we would consider how far the remedies ordinarily proposed possess sound and rational inducements to justify their adoption.

1. " The revival of protection in the markets of the United Kingdom."

This, if attainable in a sufficient degree, and guaranteed for a long term of years, would ameliorate the condition of some of our chief interests, but the policy of the empire forbids the anticipation. Besides, it would be but a partial remedy. The millions of the mother country demand cheap food ; and a second change from protection to free trade would complete that ruin which the first has done much to achieve.

2. " The protection of home manufactures."

Although this might encourage the growth of a

manufacturing interest in Canada, yet without access to the United States market there would not be a sufficient expansion of that interest, from the want of consumers, to work any result that could be admitted as a remedy for the numerous evils of which we complain.

3. "A federal union of the British American Provinces."

The advantages claimed for that arrangement are free trade between the different provinces, and a diminished governmental expenditure. The attainment of the latter object would be problematical, and the benefits anticipated from the former might be secured by legislation under our existing system. The market of the sister provinces would not benefit our trade in timber, for they have a surplus of that article in their own forests ; and their demand for agricultural products would be too limited to absorb our means of supply. Nor could Canada expect any encouragement to her manufacturing industry from those quarters. A federal union, therefore, would be no remedy.

4. "The independence of the British North American colonies as a Federal Republic."

The consolidation of its new institutions from elements hitherto so discordant—the formation of treaties with foreign powers—the acquirement of a name and character among the nations, would, we fear, prove an over-match for the strength of the new republic. And having regard to the powerful confederacy of states conterminous with itself, the needful military expenses would be too costly to render independence a boon, whilst it would not, any more than a federal union, remove those obstacles which retard our material prosperity.

5. "Reciprocal free trade with the United States, as respects the products of the farm, the forest, and the mine."

If obtained, this would yield but an instalment of the advantages which might be otherwise secured.

The free interchange of such products would not introduce manufactures to our country. It would not give us the North American continent for our market. It would neither so amend our institutions as to confer stability, nor ensure confidence in their permanence; nor would it allay the violence of parties, or in the slightest degree remedy many of our prominent evils.

6. Of all the remedies that have been suggested for the acknowledged and insufferable ills with which our country is afflicted, there remains but one to be considered. It propounds a sweeping and important change in our political and social condition, involving considerations which demand our most serious examination. THIS REMEDY CONSISTS OF A FRIENDLY AND PEACEFUL SEPARATION FROM BRITISH CONNECTION, AND A UNION UPON EQUITABLE TERMS WITH THE GREAT NORTH AMERICAN CONFEDERACY OF SOVEREIGN STATES.

We would premise that towards Great Britain we entertain none other than sentiments of kindness and respect. Without her consent, we consider separation as neither practicable nor desirable. But the colonial policy of the parent state, the avowals of her leading statesmen, the public sentiments of the empire, present unmistakable and significant indications of the appreciation of colonial connection. That it is the resolve of England to invest us with the attributes, and compel us to assume the burdens, of independence is no longer problematical. The threatened withdrawal of her troops from other colonies—the continuance of her military protection to ourselves on condition that we shall defray the attendant expenditure, betokens intentions towards our country against which it is weakness in us not to provide. An overruling conviction, then, of its necessity, and a high sense of the duty we owe our country, a duty we can neither disregard nor postpone, impel us to entertain the idea of separation; and whatever negociations may eventuate with Great Britain, a grateful liberality on the part of Canada should mark every proceeding.

The proposed union would render Canada a field for American capital, into which it would enter as freely for the prosecution of public works and private enterprises as into any of the present states. It would equalize the value of real estate upon both sides of the boundary, thereby probably doubling at once the entire present value of property in Canada, whilst by giving stability to our institutions, and introducing prosperity, it would raise our public, corporate, and private credit. It would increase our credit both with the United States and foreign countries, and would not necessarily diminish to any great extent our intercourse with Great Britain, into which our products would for the most part enter on the same terms as at present. It would render our rivers and canals the highway for the immigration to, and exports from, the West, to the incalculable benefit of our country. It would also introduce manufactures into Canada as rapidly as they have been introduced into the Northern States ; and to Lower Canada especially, where water power and labour are abundant and cheap, it would attract manufacturing capital, enhance the value of property and agricultural produce, and give remunerative employment to what is at present a comparatively non-producing population. Nor would the United States merely furnish the capital for our manufactures. They would also supply for them the most extensive market in the world, without the intervention of a Customs House officer. Railways would forthwith be constructed by American capital as feeders for all the great lines now approaching our frontiers, and railway enterprise in general would doubtless be as active and prosperous among us as among our neighbours. The value of our agricultural produce would be raised at once to a par with that of the United States, whilst agricultural implements and many of the necessaries of life, such as tea, coffee, and sugar, would be greatly reduced in price.

The value of our timber would also be greatly

enhanced by free access to the American market, where
it bears a high price, but is subject to an onerous duty.
At the same time there is every reason to believe that
our shipbuilders, as well at Quebec as on the Great
Lakes, would find an unlimited market in all the ports
of the American continent.   It cannot be doubted that
the shipping trade of the United States must greatly
increase.   It is equally manifest that, with them, the
principal material in the construction of ships is
rapidly diminishing, while we possess vast territories,
covered with timber of excellent quality, which would
be equally available as it is now, since under the free-
trade system our vessels would sell as well in England
after annexation as before.

The simple and economical State Government, in
which direct responsibility to the people is a distin-
guishing feature, would be substituted for a system at
once cumbrous and expensive.

In place of war and alarms of war with a neighbour,
there would be peace and amity between this country
and the United States.   Disagreement between the
United States and her chief, if not only, rival among
nations would not make the soil of Canada the san-
guinary arena for their disputes as under our existing
relations must necessarily be the case.   That such is
the unenviable condition of our state of dependence
upon Great Britain is known to the whole world ; and
how far it may conduce to keep prudent capitalists
from making investments in the country, or wealthy
settlers from selecting a foredoomed battlefield for
the home of themselves and children, it needs no
reasoning on our part to elucidate.

But other advantages than those having a bearing
on our material interests may be foretold.   It would
change the ground of political contest between races
and parties, allay and obliterate those irritations and
conflicts of rancour and recrimination which have
hitherto disfigured our social fabric.   Already in anticipation has its harmonious influence been felt—the

harbinger, may it be hoped, of a lasting oblivion of dissensions among all classes, creeds, and parties in this country. Changing a subordinate for an independent condition, we would take our station among the nations of the earth. We have now no voice in the affairs of the empire, nor do we share in its honours or emoluments. England is our parent state, with whom we have no equality, but towards whom we stand in the simple relation of obedience. But as citizens of the United States, the public service of the nation would be open to us—a field for high and honourable distinction, on which we and our posterity might enter on terms of perfect equality.

Nor would the amicable separation from Great Britain be fraught with advantages to us alone. The relief to the parent state from the large expenditure now incurred in the military occupation of the country —the removal of the many causes of collision with the United States, which result from the contiguity of mutual territories so extensive—the benefit of the larger market, which the increasing prosperity of Canada would create, are considerations which, in the minds of many of her ablest statesmen, render our incorporation with the United States a desirable consummation.

To the United States, also, the annexation of Canada presents many important inducements. The withdrawal from their borders of so powerful a nation, by whom in time of war the immense and growing commerce of the lakes would be jeopardized—the ability to dispense with the costly but ineffectual revenue establishment over a frontier of many hundred miles— the large accession to their income from our customs— the unrestricted use of the St. Lawrence, the natural highway from the Western States to the ocean, are objects for the attainment of which the most substantial equivalents would undoubtedly be conceded.

Fellow Colonists,—we have thus laid before you views and convictions on a momentous question, involving a change which, though contemplated by many of us with varied feelings and emotions, we all believe to be inevitable ; one which it is our duty to provide for, and lawfully to promote.

We address you without prejudice or partiality—in the spirit of sincerity and truth—in the interest solely of our common country, and our single aim is its safety and welfare. If to your judgment and reason our object and aim be at this time deemed laudable and right, we ask an oblivion of past dissensions ; and from all, without distinction of origin, party, or creed, that earnest and cordial co-operation in such lawful, prudent, and judicious means as may best conduct us to our common destiny.

A committee of six prudent Annexationists undertook the task of securing signatures to the document. Their efforts met with immediate success, for in five hours 325 names were obtained, almost without solicitation.[1] After that, when the first wave of enthusiasm had somewhat subsided, and the calmer second thought of the public began to prevail, progress was much slower, yet withal encouraging. Within ten days somewhat over 1,000 signatures were secured without much labour on the part of the canvassers.[2] But the personnel of the signers was even more significant than the number of signatures. On the list were to be found many of the leaders in the political and financial life of the city, including John Redpath, John and David Torrance, Robert Jones, a prominent Conservative politician and member of the Legislative Council, Jacob Dewitt and Benjamin Holmes, Liberal members of the Legislative Assembly, John and William Molson, D. L. Macpherson, subsequently Lieutenant-Governor of Ontario, L. H. Holton, later a member of the Mackenzie administration, J. Rose, afterwards Sir John Rose, Minister of Finance in the Cabinet of Sir John

---

[1] *La Minerve*, October 11, 1849.
[2] *The Toronto Examiner*, October 24, 1849

Macdonald, T. Workman, and J. J. C. Abbott,[1] a future premier of Canada. A stronger and more influential body of men could scarcely have been recruited. The banking and the larger industrial and commercial interests were especially well represented.

Although the great majority of the signers were Conservatives in their political affiliations, the names of a few prominent Reformers were included in the list. " Taking the newspapers as our guide-book," said *The Montreal Transcript*, " we are forced to the conclusion that, in this city, the friends of annexation are to be found in the ultra-Conservative party and the most democratic and republican of the French. One by one," it reluctantly admitted, " the Conservative journals have come over to that doctrine, and many influential Conservatives, who not long ago would have rejected the address with scorn, are now its shameless and unflinching advocates. And it cannot be doubted

---

[1] In a speech in the Senate, March 15, 1889, Sir John Abbott said : " The annexation manifesto was the outgrowth of an outburst of petulance in a small portion of the population of the Province of Quebec, which is amongst the most loyal of the provinces of Canada. Most of the people who signed the annexation manifesto were more loyal than the English people themselves. There were a few people of American origin who seized a moment of passion into which the people fell, to get some hundreds of people in Montreal to sign this paper. I venture to say that, with the exception of those American gentlemen, there was not a man who signed that manifesto who had any more serious idea of seeking annexation with the United States than a petulant child who strikes his nurse has of deliberately murdering her. They were exasperated by the fact that when 10,000 men, who had suffered distress and disaster in the unfortunate rising before those days, petitioned the Governor for the time being to retain for the consideration of Her Majesty a Bill which they believed to be passed for paying the men whom they blamed for the trouble, the Governor-General, with an ostentatious disregard, as they believed, for their feelings and in contempt of their services and their loyalty, came down out of the usual time in order to sanction the Bill. The people were excited and did many things they ought not to have done ; they behaved in a very rough manner to His Excellency, which they ought not to have done, and within two or three days, while still under the influence of this excitement, a number of them signed this paper. But there was no evidence of any agitation by these people for annexation. Before the year was over, it was like the shower of last season. . . ." Pope, *Life of Sir John Macdonald*, vol. i. p. 70.

but that a great part of their supporters go with them in this strange and sad revulsion of opinion." To a similar effect was the declaration of *The Kingston Herald*. " It is worthy of remark that the proposition has not been introduced by the old tried and faithful adherents of reform and equal rights, but on the contrary by men who have ever been the stern and uncompromising enemies of both. The bigot, the exclusive High Churchman, the man of rectories and ecclesiastical domination, the excusers of book-burning and vandal ruffianism, who have been in the habit of calling themselves *par excellence* ' Britons ' and ' Loyal Anglo-Saxons,' have been and are the promoters of the treasonable proposition." The names of the officers of the Montreal branch of the League were particularly in evidence ; almost one-half of the Executive Council, including two of the Vice-Presidents, signed the manifesto, and the example of the officials was followed by a large number of the private members of the League. " The warp," declared *The Pilot*, " is high rampant Toryism " ; the weft, a few scattered British, Irish, French, and American Liberals, whose presence there is somewhat of a mystery. " By far the largest portion of the names appended to the annexation address " were, according to *The Pilot*, members of the League.[1] The conduct of these gentlemen was, indeed, the more remarkable, since but a few months before the League had issued an address of a diametrically opposite character. Many other members of the League, according to *Le Courier des Etats-Unis*, felt themselves debarred from signing the manifesto by reason of the Kingston declaration, although they were secretly in sympathy with the movement ; and it was fondly believed by the Annexationists that many such would gladly support the address as soon as they could recover their freedom of action.

The position of the free-trade Liberals, such as

[1] *The Pilot*, October 18, 1849.

Holmes, MacDougal, Holton, and Glass, was equally inconsistent, since less than a year before they had protested against the petition of the Montreal Board of Trade as disloyal. But, despite the fact that England had repealed the obnoxious Navigation Laws, and that the effect of the remedial legislation for which they had pleaded could not, as yet, be fully felt, their boasted loyalty had evaporated, and they were found clamouring for such a protective tariff under the United States flag.[1] But, in the face of economic distress, consistency was not a virtue of which the adherents of either party could boast.

Of the names appended to the address, barely one-thirtieth were those of French-Canadians. Of the signers only one, the Hon. S. De Bleury, a former member of the Legislative Council, was a person of any political distinction.[2] With the exception of a few young men connected with *L'Avenir* and *Le Moniteur*, there was, declared *The Gazette*, "hardly a name on the list of signatures connected with politics that one knows."[3] The signers were almost all either young Radical-republican followers of Papineau (of whom the ablest representative was A. A. Dorion, subsequently leader of the French-Canadian Liberals) or small retail merchants who, by reason of the hard times, had adopted the fiscal views of their English fellow traders. Both in numbers and personnel the French signers were manifestly inferior to the formidable array of English Annexationists. The French republicans were, indeed, a feeble minority, without economic strength or political prestige ; the English Annexationists, on the contrary, were representative of the best elements in the city's life.

The appearance of the address was the signal for an outburst of public criticism. From one end of the province to the other, it became the chief topic of

---

[1] *The Montreal Transcript*, quoted from *The Globe*, October 8, 1849.
[2] *Le Canadien*, October 12, 1849.
[3] *The Gazette*, October 18, 1849.

conversation. In Montreal, in particular, excitement was at fever heat. For the moment, it appeared as if the movement would sweep the city and the surrounding district. It was the absorbing subject of discussion in the counting-house, at the market-place, and even in the home. The press exploited the matter for all it was worth. Public opinion was greatly divided, but amongst the English population the majority appeared for a time to favour the Annexationists. With the publication of the manifesto, *The Herald* came out unequivocally in favour of annexation. Mr. Kinnear, the editor, was one of the first to sign the address, notwithstanding the fact that, shortly before, he had contributed an eulogistic article to an American magazine upon the prosperity of Canada. Thanks to his earnest championship of the movement, *The Herald* came to be looked upon as the mouthpiece of the annexation party. *The Herald* did not fail to point out with pride that the cause of annexation had won a splendid victory at the outset, in the calm, masterful tone of the address, and the truly cosmopolitan personnel of the signers. "The names which are attached to the document prove how false are the accusations that there is not in this country a sentiment in favour of annexation."

Such a sentiment, it contended, was not confined to a few disgrunted adherents of a disappointed party in quest of office, but was equally in evidence among members of both political parties, and among citizens of the highest social rank, and representative business men who were not identified with any party organization. The heartiness and alacrity with which the address was adopted afforded the most convincing proof "of the unanimity of almost the entire population." In subsequent editorials, *The Herald* strongly supported the scheme of annexation in preference to a federal union of the provinces. With the defeat of the Baldwin Ministry, it believed, all the factions in Lower Canada would be fused into one independent party, and thus put an end to racial issues. It denounced the fiscal policy of the motherland as sufficiently provocative in itself to justify the colonies in throwing off their allegiance. Since England had withdrawn the preferential policy, it behoved the people of Canada to demonstrate their spirit of independence by " emerging from the state of pupilage." The conduct of the English Government, it continued, had absolved them from their allegiance to the Crown. Moreover, the interests of the homeland had " from various circumstances become distinct from ours ; they have not been slow in telling us so, and even in regretting the necessity which forced an anti-colonial policy upon them. The very suggestion of separation and independence was not, it is notorious, first broached on our side of the Atlantic, but by British statesmen and British journalists."

But after the first enthusiasm was over, *The Herald* began to modify the positiveness of its original declarations. Annexation was no longer represented as the all in all, but rather spoken of as a *dernier ressort.* " If," it asserted, " the interests of the people at large are likely to be best promoted by annexation, our loyalty has ceased to be so strong as to make us postpone them to sentiment ; but if, on the other hand, they are best subserved by the maintenance of the British connection, then we will perforce put up with British affronts." The question of separation was thus freed from sentimental considerations and reduced to the basis of comparative material advantage.

The Courier was not a whit less enthusiastic about the appearance of the manifesto. It published a declaration of political independence, setting forth the reasons which had determined its policy. In a few brief words it summed up the case for annexation in the most effective statement of facts and fancies to be found in the whole literature on the subject. " We are annexationists as much from necessity as from choice, because it affords a simple escape from the complicated political, religious, and social obstacles which beset our path, because it would give us a written constitution, preserve us from a war of races, enlarge our fields of commerce, foster manufacturing interests, augment the value of real estate, and elevate our labouring classes from their present degraded and depressed condition." From these motives, and for these reasons, "and in order to get rid of a vicious administration, we should proclaim our independence, and invite our beloved Mother to sanction, and other nations to recognize, the same." In a moment of petty chagrin and disappointment, it assailed its fellow Conservatives of Upper Canada for their hostile attitude towards annexation and more popular democratic institutions. Towards the close of October, *The Courier* suspended publication, only to reappear, however, a few days later, as an organ of the Annexationists.

The erratic attitude of *The Gazette* furnishes a most interesting commentary on the course of the annexation movement. Prior to the issue of the manifesto, *The Gazette*, as we have seen, had been suspicious of the "hole-in-the-corner methods" of the annexation leaders. It was, however, duly impressed by the eminence and respectability of the signers of the manifesto, towards whom it showed an unusual degree of courtesy and consideration, but it still kept up its adverse criticism of the political methods of the Annexationists. "A great portion," it admitted, "of the men of wealth and standing among the inhabitants of British origin in Montreal have arrived deliberately at the conclusion that the colonial connection ought to be dissolved." But the sudden and private manner in which the address was prepared, and the unsatisfactory form of its composition, were not in its favour. Although a great mistake in judgment had been made in failing to consult the outside public about the preparation of the document, *The Gazette* admitted that the sincerity of the leaders of the movement, and the respectability of the signers, could not be questioned in any way even by the most captious critic. If the address had been prepared by a popularly selected delegation, it would have been received with much greater confidence by the general public. It should not have been the product of a Cabal, but the result of a great public movement.

The Gazette professed itself " unable to go as fast as the signers of the manifesto." But as there was little prospect of the continuance of the British connection, unless a great change should come over English public opinion, " it did not feel opposed to the ultimate decision of fate, when the time should come." As British subjects, however, they should exhaust all means of alleviating the prevailing distress before finally determining upon separation. "Nor do our private views differ materially from those who have signed the manifesto. It is only from our anxiety to proceed with due caution, and a proper regard to the effect that the action of Montreal ought to have upon the country at large, which leads us to point out the preferable mode of attaining the common ultimate end. There should be no hesitation or division of opinion among the opponents of the existing régime about thoroughly informing the English Government and people of the real state of public feeling in Canada. But to attempt to hasten the prospect of separation would, in its opinion, only defeat the object in view." [1]

The equivocal attitude of *The Gazette* lent some credence to the accusation that its editor had been offended because the paper had not been permitted to play the leading part in the movement. This charge *The Gazette* indignantly denied. All those who favoured annexation, but disapproved of the style or material of the address, had, it contended, a right to complain of the injury done to the cause by the publication of an unsatisfactory document. The manifesto was neither well written nor properly arranged. The premises were totally inadequate to carry the conclu-

[1] *The Gazette*, October 11, 1849.

sion, and many of the statements were unsupported by any official evidence. Under these circumstances, *The Gazette* announced that it would not take a prominent part in the agitation, but would limit itself to supporting the Annexationists where they did right, and to endeavouring to check them where they went wrong.[1]

It especially warned the Annexationists against attempting any hasty action, since there were several most important matters on which the public would require assurances before they finally determined to sever the imperial tie. Canadians were entitled to know first of all the terms of separation from the motherland, and the relation of England to the United States after the incorporation of Canada in the Union. The slightest consideration of England's past favours towards the colony must lead to the conclusion that Canadians ought to establish the incompatibility of English and Canadian interests to the satisfaction of the English people before they ventured to approach the British Government with a request for release from the colonial tie. Furthermore, the country ought also to be assured that, in case of annexation, there would be a settlement of the most dangerous domestic question, the racial issue, and that there would be neither a war of races nor the domination of one race over another.[2]

The matter of the terms of annexation raised, in the mind of *The Gazette*, very serious and critical questions.[3] They ought not to take a leap in the dark, nor trust to the generosity of their neighbours.[4] Among the questions which demanded serious consideration were the following: Should Canada be admitted into

---

[1] *The Gazette*, October 12, 1849.
[2] *Ibid.*, October 13, 1849.
[3] *Ibid.*
[4] In a subsequent editorial *The Gazette* stated: " We must have an opportunity to understand what we are called to participate in, before we can with prudence or honour throw ourselves unreservedly into the annexation fad " (October 20, 1849).

the Union as a single state, or divided up into several distinct states? What should be done with the Maritime Provinces, with the imperial property and guarantees, and with the public debts? Would the United States assume the provincial debt of Canada, or would the latter be burdened with a full share of the American indebtedness? What arrangements would be made in respect to the seignorial tenure, the clergy reserves, and provincial boundaries? These and many other questions demanded satisfactory answers before the country could properly consider the general question of annexation. In forcing the issue on too rapidly, without due preliminary consideration, the leaders of the annexation party would assuredly meet with a repulse, and find it necessary to retrace their steps, if they desired to carry the country with them.[1] Indeed, the hasty promulgation of the manifesto was likely to retard rather than to advance the cause of annexation; for although the injustice of the Rebellion Losses Bill had released the loyalists from their allegiance to the Crown, the old feeling of affection for the homeland was as yet too strong to permit of the dissolution of the imperial tie in an indecent and improper manner.[2]

But notwithstanding this criticism, *The Gazette* concluded: "The feeling is without a doubt spreading that the final result of all our moves in Canada, unless checked by Great Britain, will be into the arms of the United States. We believe so ourselves." After all its dubious wobblings, *The Gazette* at last came out freely for Canadian independence, in preference to annexation, "because we are convinced that it is worth a trial, and that it is attainable, while we believe that Great Britain will never consent to a bare, unqualified demand to hand us over to the United States."[3]

The Witness was so much pleased with the manifesto, that it began a series of articles in favour of annexation;

---

[1] *The Gazette*, October 15, 1849.   [2] *Ibid.*, October 17, 1849.
[3] *Ibid.*, October 23, 1849.

but the sharp protest of the Hon. M. Cameron, together
with the criticism of some of its readers, led it to stop
the publication of the articles in question. It declared,
by way of explanation, that there were certain other
reforms, such as the abolition of the clergy reserves
and ecclesiastical tithes, which ought to precede annexation, and that it would consequently devote its
attention, for the present, to the discussion of these
more pressing matters.

The Transcript, as was to be expected, came out
flat-footed against the address. In an exceptionally
keen analysis of the social, economic, and political
conditions which had produced the manifesto, it declared : " We doubt if an act so questionable in itself
was ever before sent forth in so questionable a manner.
Notwithstanding the unanimous refusal of the Kingston
Convention to sanction annexation, a handful of
Montrealers " decide on their own mere motion on
this most delicate and difficult question." Of the
signers, it continued, there are some " who really
believe that annexation to the States would be a remedy
for the evils from which we suffer, and who desire it,
therefore, on patriotic grounds as being best for the
interests of the country. Many of these parties fly
to annexation as a relief from the turmoils of our own
Government. They see no other cure for the dissensions which divide us." But however much " we may
admire the unselfish motives and the high-minded feelings " by which they are influenced, we cannot but
realize that annexation, far from relieving these evils,
would rather increase them. " Next to this class, we
find a considerable number of merchants and traders
who have suffered severely from the depression of the
times, and who have no hope in the revival of our
system. They lay everything to the withdrawal of
protection, and will not wait to see what a little time
will do. Among them are some quondam free traders
who are in an amazing hurry to falsify their own
theories. Doubtless they feel uneasy at the economic

outlook ; but with the many evidences of a revival of trade about them and knowing full well as business men the liability of all countries to periods of commercial depression, they act impatiently in seeking to drive the country into immediate annexation. But there is still another class of annexationists, the most zealous, though not the most numerous, whose feelings are certainly far less disinterested than those of either of the previous classes. These are the holders of real estate in the city. We have not a great deal of sympathy with these gentlemen in their desire for higher rents. As a mere Montreal real property movement, we look upon annexation as anything but a patriotic agitation.''

On one point only, *The Transcript* continued, were the Annexationists agreed, namely, to get rid of the British connection. To that end, they showed the greatest eagerness in " accentuating the evils of the country, and in assigning to the whole province a condition of wretchedness which is mainly existent in Montreal. To all such clamours, we need only reply that prosperity will return in time without the abandonment of British allegiance." Besides, it was most unfair for the Annexationists to present only the dark side of the picture, and to hold the colonial régime responsible for the depression which was partly due, at least, to their own unlucky speculations.

The reference of the manifesto to the dangerous position of Canada in case of war between England and the United States would bring a blush of shame to the cheek of thousands of honest-hearted Britons throughout the country. It was criminal to think that England would engage in an unjust war ; but, should war occur, she would make every sacrifice for the defence of Canada. There must needs be a great change in the sentiments of Canadians of English stock, before they would allow their allegiance to be affected by such a miserable pretext.

The belief that a " political revolution " was at hand

in Canada was, according to *The Transcript*, much more prevalent in the minds of Yankees and English Radicals who favoured such a revolution, than amongst the Canadian people. Although the virus of annexation was widely scattered throughout the province, it was not likely to produce serious effects. Already the public press of Quebec had condemned the manifesto as false in its premises and misleading in its conclusion —false, inasmuch as it misrepresented the economic situation of Canada and the attitude of the English public ; and misleading, in that it professed to make the consent of England a condition precedent to separation, when, if the premises were true, annexation would be desirable even if England should object thereto. The country at large would doubtless ratify this judgment, notwithstanding the alluring promises of material prosperity and social rest held out by the Annexationists.

However much the question might be openly canvassed in Montreal, it had not yet been seriously considered by the country at large. To have any chance of success, annexation must cease to be a local or a party question and become the great provincial issue. " At the present time we have no evidence of this national movement, nor do we think that it is at all likely that it will take place. Men will require much more evidence than they now possess, before they will agree to abandon their present allegiance. All we see at present is a small party in this city, a party respectable, we acknowledge, in the character of its members, but certainly not in a position to dictate either to the province at large or to this community. The party has only had a few weeks' existence as a party, and presents nothing in its composition which can invite confidence." [1]

The Transcript was especially earnest in warning its fellow Conservatives against any alliance with the French republicans. The Conservative Party was not

[1] Quoted from *The Globe*, October 16, 1849.

" cut out " for republican institutions. "Every natural thought, every natural act, every impulse of the party gives, and has given, the lie to such a union. They may cheat themselves into the belief that annexation is practicable and desirable, or be led away by a sense of injury, but they can never be reconciled to republicanism." It would involve a recasting of their social usages and habits, a total surrender " of the soul and body to the imperious tyranny of a democratic republic " ; it would mean more than a change of Government, " it would bring about a social revolution."

Besides, there could be little real sympathy between them and their French allies. The aim of Papineau was French domination, an idea fundamentally opposed to that of his Anglo-Saxon supporters, who " probably imagine that by making a bargain with the neighbouring Union their influence will be all in all, and that the influence of their French allies will count for nothing." One or the other party was being deceived, and that party was certainly not the French. " So far from their influence prevailing, the influence of Mr. Papineau and his friends is much more likely to turn the scale than that of the British ultra-Conservative Party." Under such circumstances, Conservatives should be especially careful how they involved themselves in a dangerous movement. British citizenship, *The Transcript* concluded, was no valueless thing to be exchanged for a mess of pottage. If the Annexationists pursued their present blind policy, the people of the colony would go down in history as guilty of the basest ingratitude towards the parent state, in using their newly acquired constitutional freedom " to sell themselves to the Yankees."

The New Era, a recently established Tory paper, followed the lead of *The Transcript* in opposing annexation, and supporting the principles of the League, protection and a union of the provinces.

The Pilot was equally vigorous in its condemnation of the manifesto. So far did it carry its opposition, that it refused to open its columns to the publication of the address. A protest by a small group of prominent Liberal Annexationists,[1] against what they considered the unfair attitude of the paper, served only to call forth the crushing reply that, even if the address had been handed to *The Pilot* at the same time as to the other journals (which, however, was not the case), it would not have been inserted. *The Pilot* " would not lend its columns to the dismemberment of the empire." The Annexationists could get the Tory organs to do their publishing for them; for the ministerial press would refuse to do so. The Liberals of Montreal would not throw away the substance of good government they now enjoyed for the shadowy benefits of annexation. That was the spirit in which they rejected the pressure placed upon them to sign an address which they had never read. The Annexationists, it believed, had adopted a mistaken policy in issuing a manifesto instead of establishing a paper to advocate their principles.[2]

With the majority of people, annexation was, as yet, " more a matter of feeling than of reflection." The disaffected " and the disappointed wish for a change, and that is the change which appears easiest and most feasible." Although annexation was an open question in both parties, it was especially disconcerting to the great mass of loyal Reformers to find a few Liberal politicians uniting with the Tories in promoting the cause of annexation. *The Pilot* loudly called upon all Reformers to avoid such an entangling alliance and to range themselves loyally under the party flag.

In a series of able editorials it attacked seriatim the arguments of the address. Canada, it declared, was now suffering " from mushroom organizations." The majority of the signers were members of the League which had recently proposed a different means of saving

[1] Messrs. Boyer, McKay, Holton, Workman, De Witt, Hart, Glass, Bruneau, Holmes, and Knapp.
[2] *The Pilot*, October 11, 1849.

society. " Such extraordinary tergiversation in their past conduct bodes ill for their future consistency, as such extreme haste in adopting a new system betokens little study and labour in the concoction of it." They had simply accepted it without due consideration as the best means at hand for promoting the prosperity of Montreal. But before distracting the country by such an agitation, the Annexationists should offer the most convincing proof—first, that the Canadian public desired annexation; second, that the majority of the inhabitants of the other British North American colonies supported it; third, that England was prepared to grant it; and finally, that the United States was ready to incorporate Canada in the Union. But on all these points there was a signal lack of satisfactory evidence. Only in Montreal was annexation regarded as a really vital issue. All the Reform and most of the Conservative papers, especially in Upper Canada, had pronounced against it. Neither was any evidence offered on the second proposition, to prove that public opinion in the Maritime Provinces was less unfavourable to annexation than in Canada. In regard to the third proposition, it was entirely unwarranted to assume that either the British Government, or the nation at large, desired to compel, or even to induce, the colonies to dissolve their allegiance, merely because Lord John Russell and other English statesmen favoured the policy of throwing off on the colonies the whole burden and responsibility of their own administration. The fourth and last proposition, which required to be established, was equally doubtful. For, even though Great Britain should agree to peaceful separation, annexation " could be effected only after long and difficult negotiations, even if it were possible to be effected at all with the Union as it is now composed."

The Pilot did not hesitate to attack the blue-ruin cry which the Annexationists had unscrupulously made the chief issue of the day. It endeavoured to prove by a liberal use of statistics that the existing depression was mainly confined to the Montreal district, and that business conditions throughout the province were already improving, as was evidenced by an increase in the public revenue and the canal tolls.[1] The action of the Montreal Conservatives in raising the annexation cry at the very moment when the Government was about to enter upon negociations for reciprocity with the United States was, according to *The Pilot*, exceedingly unpatriotic. A continuance of the present agitation would inevitably weaken the hands of the British Government in dealing with a foreign power, and might even endanger the success of the negociations. *The Pilot* explicitly denied the contention of the Annexationists that the expenses of the Government of Canada were higher than those of the neighbouring states, and that the danger of international complications would be less if they were American citizens instead of British subjects.[2]

On the other hand, it concluded, Canadians would lose by annexation the healthy and liberal spirit of public criticism, which was characteristic of English public life as contrasted with that of the United States, a loss which could not well be estimated in terms of mammon. Throughout the whole controversy the tone of *The Pilot*, unlike that of several of its contemporaries, was admirable. Although arraigning the conduct of the Tory Party in no uncertain terms, it did not permit its partisanship to run away with its judgment. It recognized the seriousness of the issue which was presented, and endeavoured to discuss the question in the calm and reasonable spirit which its importance demanded.

The skill of the political cartoonist was likewise placed at the service of the British connection. *Punch in Canada*, the one distinctive comic paper of the province, used the gentle art of raillery with telling effectiveness against the Annexationists. It pictured the sorry state in which Papineau and his young Radical

[1] *The Pilot*, October 16, 1849.   [2] *Ibid.*, October 25, 1849.

compatriots would find themselves in case of a political union with the United States. Even more effective were the cartoons at the expense of the English Annexationists at Montreal. Mr. Benjamin Holmes was made a special object of attack. He and his friends were represented as small boys who were caught in the act of trying to pawn their mother's pocket-handkerchief to Uncle Sam. It did not even hesitate to attack the convivial propensities of the member for Montreal. The commercial side of the annexation movement was hit off admirably by " a business flourometer " :

> " Flour, 33s. per barrel—loyalty up.
> Flour, 26s. per barrel—cloudy.
> Flour, 22s. per barrel—down to annexation."

It must be admitted that in the battle of the press the pro-British papers had considerably the better of the argument over their opponents. The latter were by no means sure of their own position, and were divided in their counsels between annexation and independence. They were prone to appeal to racial prejudices and partisan antipathies ; they engaged in general denunciation of both the local and English Governments without seriously attempting to analyse the situation of affairs, or to ascertain to what extent the free-trade policy of England was really responsible for existing conditions in the colony. The pro-British papers, on the other hand, were much less partisan and intolerant in their views ; with few exceptions, they endeavoured to argue the question out on its merits, trusting that the calm judgment of the public would sustain their reasoning.

The French press again divided on strict party lines. *L'Avenir* hailed the manifesto as the most important doctrine since the Ninety-Two Resolutions. It expressed the greatest satisfaction at finding the names of many leading French Canadians in the list of signatures : " C'est un appel fait à toutes les classes, et à toutes les parties, d'oublier les anciennes causes de division, pour se reunir dans le bout d'obtenir ce dont le pays a le plus puissant besoin, la prospérité avec l'annexion." By remaining outside the movement, the French-Canadians would sacrifice the future of their race and of the colony, and subject themselves for all time to the tyranny of the Colonial Office, from which they had suffered so long. The movement, according to *L'Avenir*, was spontaneous in its origin, and had met with a ready response from the French merchants. The bearers of the address, it boasted, had found only three persons who really objected to annexation, although several had desired time for consideration before attaching their signatures. *L'Avenir* thought that a better way of verifying public sentiment might perhaps have been found ; but, since the manifesto was issued, all sympathizers should lend their hearty support to the movement.[1]

La Minerve, on the contrary, looked upon the address as a sad page in the history of Canada. It accused the Conservative Party of taking up the question of annexation for the purpose of defeating the Government, rather than from any real desire for a political union with the United States.[2] The attitude of several of the other French papers was likewise critical. *L'Ami de la Religion* declared that it was not at all surprised at the appearance of the manifesto, since events had been pointing towards annexation for some time. It did not regard the address as an occasion for either gratification or chagrin and shame. Looked at from the standpoint of French nationality, annexation was undesirable, but any opposition to annexation on this ground was greatly weakened by the bitter controversies of the French press and parties, which threatened to destroy all sense of racial solidarity.

It was admitted, on the other hand, even by those who were opposed to separation, that annexation was inevitable in the not far distant future. *L'Echo des Campagnes* approached the subject from a very in-

---

[1] *L'Avenir*, October 13, 1849.
[2] *La Minerve*, October 18, 1849.

teresting but practical standpoint. There were, it declared, three classes of annexationists : first, partisans calmes ; second, outrés ; and third, partisans tièdes. In the third class were to be found the former Tories, who had been in despair since the day of their defeat. They had at first raised the cry for annexation in the hope of overthrowing the Government by causing a division in the Liberal ranks. They had played with fire, and got burned in consequence. To-day the demand for annexation was serious, but they could not well draw back ; they were led on unwillingly, and even in spite of themselves. Very little sympathy could be felt for those persons of wealth and ambition who had joined the movement with a view to exploiting it to their own advantage.[1]

Although on general principles annexation would be advantageous, nevertheless, the benefits of union would, it contended, be more than offset by the restrictions which annexation would place upon the powers of the local legislature to deal freely with the greatest of local problems, the seignorial system of tenure. The judicial interpretation of Article 1, Section 10 of the United States Constitution, in respect " to the impairment of the obligation of contracts," would effectually prevent the local government from abolishing the burdens of the feudal system.[2] The validity of this argument was denied by *L'Avenir*, but without greatly weakening its effect upon the intelligent part of the French-Canadian public.[3]

The sober demeanour of the great majority of the French Ministerialists showed the splendid discipline of the clergy and the party leaders. The rank and file of the party refused to commit themselves in any way to the annexation movement, until there had been an official expression of opinion from their spiritual and political guides. The Papineau party, it was

[1] *L'Echo des Campagnes*, October 18, 1849.
[2] *Ibid.*, November 2, 1849.
[3] *L'Avenir*, November 15, 1849.

admitted, had gained considerable strength by its union with the Annexationists, but it was still too weak to grapple alone with the Government. The real state of French opinion would, in the judgment of *The Montreal Gazette*, never be known until the Lafontaine Ministry was driven out of office.[1]

The favourable reception of the manifesto encouraged the annexation leaders to proceed to the formation of a permanent organization somewhat after the type of the English Anti-Corn Law League. The organization of such an association was, in the opinion of *L'Avenir*, all that was required to make the Annexationists " the strongest and most numerous political party in the country." The association, it was proposed, should enter upon an aggressive educational campaign, and flood the country with tracts and speakers. A call was accordingly sent out by about one hundred of the signers of the address, summoning a meeting to organize an association. The committee of arrangements requested several prominent politicians and merchants, including Papineau, Holmes, De Witt, De Bleury, Workman, and others to address the meeting, and otherwise assist in the work of organization.

Papineau, however, much to his regret, was unable to be present ; but in a letter to the Committee he expressed the strongest sympathy with the judicious efforts which were being made to obtain for all Canadians the right to govern themselves, instead of being governed by a distant authority. Under the colonial régime, he declared, the interests, desires, and necessities of Canada were being sacrificed. Distance alone, not to mention the essential differences in the social conditions and economic interests of the two countries, made good government from Westminster impossible.

As far back as 1823, in consultation with English political leaders, he had advocated the independence of Canada, and they had all admitted that it would be to the mutual advantage of both countries to part

---

[1] *The Gazette*, October 18, 1849.

company. Voluntary separation, he urged, was much preferable to a warlike dissolution of the imperial tie, such as had been effected by the United States. British statesmen did not maintain that the connection should be perpetual, but only that it should be prolonged, for fear that if Canada were incorporated in the American Republic, the other North American colonies would soon follow suit. Such a splendid addition of wealthy states to the American Union would, it was feared, make the United States a dangerous economic competitor in the markets of the world. The government of the colony had, he declared, become most corrupt and expensive. The grant of responsible government could not rescue the country from depression, since England would not change her fiscal policy to please the colonies. Had he been in Montreal at the date of the issuance of the manifesto, he would have been one of the first to support its judicious, patriotic, and reasonable declaration of principles.

On account of ill health, the Hon. S. De Bleury also found it impossible to be present at the meeting. In a letter to the committee expressing his regrets, he deplored the evils from which the country was suffering. The condition of affairs was, he declared, even worse than at the time of the Ninety-Two Articles. The only hope of relief was to be found in peaceful separation, to be followed by annexation to the United States. But Annexationists must first show to England by public demonstrations and petitions that the majority of the people of Canada desired a change of allegiance. "Courage, then, citizens of Quebec; to the work, and at once."

Although the purpose of the meeting was merely to effect a permanent organization, the gathering took on the character of a public demonstration in force. According to the annexation papers, the hall was incapable of holding the crowd who sought admission. The audience was largely composed of prominent business men of the city. Apparently only a few French-

Canadians were present, and such of them as participated in the proceedings belonged to the " Young
Canada " party. John Redpath was chosen chairman,
and Messrs. John Glass and G. P. E. Dorion acted as
joint secretaries. In his opening remarks, Mr. Redpath
declared that the commercial distress of the colony
was due to the action of Great Britain in withdrawing
protection from colonial products. Canada, he admitted, could not properly question the right of England
to change her fiscal policy, even though such change,
as in the present instance, inflicted the severest suffering
upon the colonies. But, under these circumstances,
Canada must needs look to her own interests. It was
incumbent upon them to take measures to stop the
drain of thousands of skilled artisans to the United
States.

He enlarged at length upon the prosperity of the
States as contrasted with the poverty of Canada :
prices were 20 per cent. and property 50 per cent.
higher across the line than in this province. To save
the country from impending ruin, annexation was
absolutely necessary. The League was, in his opinion,
" going in a roundabout way to attain what they, as
Annexationists, sought to secure by direct means "
(cheers). Annexation was the only subject which had
aroused real interest at the Kingston Convention. He
was advocating annexation, not for any party purpose,
but solely for the advantage of the country. Partisanship had been the curse of the province, and he hoped
that the Canadian people would now bury all past
dissensions and unite on the policy of annexation.

In moving the first resolution in favour of the formation of an annexation association, Mr. H. Taylor
declared that he respected the motives of those who
were strongly opposing the present movement, for he,
too, honoured the Queen as much as any of them.
Some of their opponents, however, were actuated by
personal interests and considerations. He felt that he
owed his first loyalty to the country in which he lived.

Union and organization were necessary to attain the object they had in view. In seconding the resolution, J. De Witt, M.P., instituted a comparison between the economic conditions of Canada and of the United States, most unfavourable to the former. The agricultural, railroad, and steamship interests, in fact, every interest in the country was suffering severely. The people of Canada should rise up, and make their country truly great. They should act like men, and not like children and dependents. Above all, they must place their country above party.

The second resolution, which was proposed by B. Holmes, M.P., read : " That our state of colonial dependence can only be prolonged at the sacrifice of our most valuable interests ; and that this meeting, considering the social, commercial, and political difficulties of Canada, and feeling the weight of the evils which oppress our society, believe that the only attainable measure capable of improving permanently our condition consists in a peaceable separation from Great Britain, and the annexation of Canada to the United States of America."

In moving the resolution, the local member denied that the Annexationists were unfriendly to the motherland. The address, he stated, had limited itself to a simple statement of the facts of the case. The Annexationists had an equal right with the pro-Britishers to express an opinion on the existing situation. The manifesto of the latter had been signed by hundreds " who are unknown in the city, and by a large number of officials, and by others who are advocates of restriction and protection, and by a few free traders." Every one admitted that separation would come in time, and why not now, when thousands were crossing the line on account of the free-trade policy of England. So far from criticizing the action of England in this regard, he would rather cut off his right hand than see the English people starve owing to the Corn Laws. The repeal of the Navigation Acts, though tardily granted, would be of some advantage, but it could not alter the Canadian climate. Reciprocity was unfortunately not now obtainable, though it might have been a few years ago, before Canada had uttered threats of secession. The United States desired the whole of Canada, in order to round out their empire, and " they know that by withholding reciprocity they can force us into annexation." The Canadian farmers could not successfully compete with their American neighbours. They could afford " to admire England, but not to starve for her." The economic interests of England were incompatible with those of Canada. England would not return to a protective policy, nor would she encourage, but rather discourage, the growth of colonial manufactures. One of the important effects of annexation would be to bring American capital into the country, which would raise the rate of wages, and enable the manufacturers of Montreal to compete on an equal footing with the Lowell manufacturers. In order to attain their end, Annexationists must go to the polls, and elect a majority of members to the local legislature. England, he was convinced, would not refuse to accede to the demand of the Canadian Parliament for separation.

A similar view was expressed by Mr. Molson in seconding the resolution. He desired to make annexation the test question at the coming elections. For his part, he would not support any candidate for Parliament, Whig or Tory, who was not an annexationist. He summed up his political principles in the statement that " this country and himself were first," and he would stick to that. Mr. Robert McKay declared that, although the Annexationists were now charged with treason, time would prove that they were right. As their opponents were endeavouring to deny them the right of expressing their feelings, they should start an active campaign for the extirpation of the ignorance, bigotry, and intolerance of their critics.

The third resolution, which ran to the effect that,

" burying all past dissensions," they should bind themselves to co-operate by all lawful means to promote
the object of the association, and that to this end
they should invite the Canadian people to form similar
associations in the same fraternal spirit, was moved by
Mr. John Rose, Q.C., one of the most influential lawyers
of the city. He urged that they should not allow
their zeal to be chilled by the strength of the opposition.
The demand for separation had arisen in England, not
in Canada. In proof of this statement, he cited the
opinions of many English statesmen to the effect that
Canada was not wanted. Lord Vincent had predicted
that Canada would be a " running sore " to the motherland ; Mr. Sherwin, one of the permanent Under-
Secretaries, had recently stated before a Committee
of Parliament that he would not regard a colonial
revolt as treason. Lord Ashburton had also told them
plainly that they were free to join the States, if they
so desired. When English statesmen said these things,
why should Canadian Annexationists be charged with
treason ? For his part, he regretted the necessity of
a separation from the mother country, but they could
still keep alive their old affection for her. It was a
sublime, and not a base, ideal for England to adopt
the policy of training up the colonies to take their
places among the nations. He was convinced that
he could best prove his loyalty by endeavouring to
promote the interests of his adopted land, in accordance with the desires of the English Government and
nation.

The Hon. Robert Jones stated that he had signed
the address only after long consideration, and that he
was prepared to assume full responsibility for his
action. Both the aims and methods of the Annexationists were legitimate and proper. The principle of
responsible government, in his judgment, could not be
worked successfully in this country ; in fact, the people
had been worse off since its introduction. The progressive opinion of the day laid it down as a political

maxim, that the republican form of government could alone promote the prosperity of the human race.

In an able legal argument, Mr. F. G. Johnston, Q.C., maintained that the members of the association were acting within the limits of their constitutional rights as British citizens. As the object of the association was peaceful, there could be no question of treason or disloyalty. The movement was not designed, as some of their opponents maliciously represented, to secure annexation at all hazards and by any means whatever. The movement was not specious or artificial ; it arose out of the dire necessity of the time. Protection was now out of the question in England, and reciprocity with the United States was impossible, since the latter country could dictate to Canada what terms it desired, and those terms would undoubtedly be annexation. Several of the French-Canadian speakers urged their compatriots to join with their English fellow citizens in the movement for annexation. Canada, Mr. Latté declared, could never become great as a colony ; she must first become independent before she could hope for national prosperity.

The audience was enthusiastic in its support of the speakers, and all the resolutions were carried unanimously. A committee was appointed, consisting of Messrs. McKay, Dorion, Torrance, Mulholland, and Ostell, to nominate a ticket of officers, to be submitted, and voted upon, at a future meeting of the association. A constitution, setting forth the object of the association, and providing for the administration of its affairs, was drawn up by the committee in charge, and duly adopted. The association mapped out an ambitious programme. It proposed to offer a prize of from $300 to $500 for the best monograph on annexation, to be distributed at the lowest possible price, to send public lecturers over the province, to organize branch associations in local centres, to lend financial assistance to annexation papers, to participate in elections by securing the return to Parliament of members who were favourable to independence or annexation, and to hold a provincial congress, when sufficient branches should have been organized throughout the colony to assure a representative gathering. The association expressly repudiated any idea of resorting to party violence to promote its objects.

At the adjourned meeting of the association for the election of officers, only about sixty persons were present.[1] The nominating committee brought in its recommendations, and the following officers were duly elected : President, John Redpath ; Vice-Presidents, John D. Torrance, J. De Witt, L. H. Holton, W. Workman, D. E. Papineau, P. Drumgoole, and F. B. Anderson ; Councillors, H. Stephens, W. Molson, D. Kinnear, J. Rose, J. Papin, J. Bell, R. Laflamme, and J. Ostell ; Treasurer, D. Torrance ; Secretaries, R. McKay and A. A. Dorion.

In pursuance of the policy of carrying on an active agitation, the secretaries subsequently sent circulars to all parts of the provinces, announcing the formation of the Montreal association, soliciting the assistance and co-operation of friends and sympathizers, urging the formation of branch associations, and enclosing copies of the manifesto.[2] An office was established in St. Jacques Street, to serve as a permanent bureau of the association. Mr. Perry, of *The Herald*, was installed as assistant secretary, at a salary of £150 a year, with instructions to keep in touch with the movement in all parts of the country. A very interesting pamphlet was prepared by the association for general circulation. It set forth in detail the comparative advantages and disadvantages of the Canadian and American forms of government. Special attention was devoted to a statement of the cost of the executive, judicial, legislative, and military departments of the State of New York, as compared with the cost of administering the same departments in Canada.[3] Need-

[1] November 15, 1849.   [2] Weir, *Sixty Years in Canada.*
[3] *L'Avenir,* November 30, 1849.

less to say, the comparison in almost every item was made to appear most unfavourable to Canada.

The bold manner in which the Annexationists carried on their treasonable propaganda demanded the serious attention of the Canadian Government. As long as the agitation was confined to the Tory Party, the Ministry did not deem it advisable to interfere ; but when the movement began to spread among a section of the Reformers of Upper Canada, it was felt that the time had come for a definite declaration of policy on the part of the Government. Upon the Hon. Robert Baldwin devolved the unpleasant duty of dealing with the dangerous situation which had arisen in the ranks of the party. It was a fortunate thing for the empire that there stood at the head of the Provincial Government at this moment a man of the character of Robert Baldwin. By reason of his ability, soundness of judgment, unquestioned probity, and long and valiant service in the struggle for constitutional freedom, he had gained a striking ascendency in the councils of his party and at the same time had won the respect of many of his opponents. His strong feelings of attachment to the British connection had been proved by his conduct during the revolt of 1837. Even a keen sense of political injustice, and a strong feeling of resentment against the partisan and arbitrary action of the Tory Governor, had not been able to drive him into the seditious plots of the more extreme Reformers. He had been throughout his career loyally attached to the British Crown, and a great admirer of British institutions.

The approaching bye-election for the Third Riding of York afforded Baldwin an excellent opportunity of voicing his opinion on the question of annexation. In this case there was the greater reason for a decisive expression of party policy, since Mr. Peter Perry, the prospective Reform candidate, was known to be more or less sympathetic towards the views of the Annexationists. During a visit to Montreal a short time before, he had, according to report, openly avowed himself an annexationist. In the candidature of Mr. Perry, the annexation issue was unmistakably presented to the party and to the electorate. Mr. Baldwin did not hesitate to throw down the gage of battle to the suspected Annexationists within the party. On the very eve of the publication of the Montreal manifesto,[1] he addressed an historic letter to Mr. Perry in which he declared, in no uncertain language, that the maintenance of the British connection was a fundamental principle of the Reform Party. His letter read as follows:

" MY DEAR SIR,

" The expediency of applying to the mother country to give these colonies a separate national existence, or to permit them to annex themselves to the neighbouring Republic, has become a subject, not only openly discussed in some of the leading journals of the province, but appears to be entertained, to some extent at least, in quarters where we would naturally have looked for the existence of very different sentiments. It becomes necessary, therefore, that no misapprehension should exist on the part of any one, friend or opponent, as to my opinions, either on the question itself, or on the effect which a difference respecting it must necessarily produce on the political relations between me and those of my friends (if any there be) who take a different view of the subject. And I take the liberty of addressing this letter to you, as well from the political connection which has so long subsisted between us, as from the circumstance of an election about to take place for the Riding in which you reside. At that election, whether you may become a candidate or not, . . . it is due to my friends that no room should be left to suppose me undetermined upon, or indifferent to, this question. It is but right that they should be made aware that I have not changed

----

[1] October 4, 1849.

my opinion in relation to it, but that I retain unaltered my attachment to the connection with the motherland, that I believe now, as I did when last I addressed my constituents from the hustings, that the continuance of that connection may be made productive of material good to both the colony and the parent state.

" It is equally due to my friends that they should, in like manner, be made aware that upon this question there remains, in my opinion, no room for compromise. It is one of altogether too vital a character for that. All should know, therefore, that I can look upon those only who are for the continuance of that connection as political friends—those who are against it as political opponents.

" The mother country has now for years been leaving to us powers of self-government, more ample than ever we have asked, and it does appear a most impious return to select such a time for asking for a separation. . . . I can, at all events, be no party to such proceeding, and must not suffer it to be supposed that I have a moment's doubt respecting it. Let the declaration which I have above made lead to what it may, as respects the relative political position of either myself or others, I feel that I am in the path of duty in making it. I abide the consequences."

Scarcely had the manifesto made its appearance, before other members of the Government took steps to assist the Attorney-General in checking the spreading contagion of unrest. The Hon. Malcolm Cameron sent a letter to *The Montreal Witness* protesting against its attitude on the question of annexation, and characterizing the movement as the conspiracy of a set of disappointed men to dismember the empire.[1] Thanks to his initiative, a formal protest was drawn up, a few days later, and signed by all the ministers of the Crown then in Montreal, and by all the French Liberal

---

[1] *The Globe*, October 13, 1849.

members of the city and vicinity. The protest ran as follows :

" We, the undersigned members of the Provincial Legislature, residing in the city of Montreal and its vicinity, have read with astonishment and regret a certain address to the people of Canada, recently published by divers persons, with the avowed intention of exciting, in the midst of our population, a movement in favour of the separation of this province from Great Britain, and of its annexation to the United States of America. Sincerely attached to the institutions which the mother country has acknowledged, and convinced that those institutions suffice, through a system of wise and judicious legislation, to secure prompt and efficient remedies for all the evils which the province can complain of, we consider ourselves urgently bound to protest publicly and solemnly against the opinions enunciated in that document.

" We deem it our duty at the same time, and without awaiting the concurrence of the other members of the Legislature—upon the approval of whom, with few exceptions, we may, however, confidently rely—to appeal to the wisdom, the love of order, and the honour of the inhabitants of this country, and to call upon them to oppose, by every means in their power, an agitation tending to subvert a constitution which, after having been long and earnestly sought for, was received with feelings of deep gratitude towards the metropolitan Government ; an agitation, moreover, which can result in nothing beyond the continuation of the scenes from which this city has already so severely suffered, the disturbance of social order, and a renewal of the troubles and disasters which we have had to deplore in time past."

To the protest were appended the names of twenty members of the Legislative Council and Assembly,[1]

[1] Messrs. Leslie, Bourett, Morin, Viger, Cameron, Price, Drummond, Dumas, Cartier, Davignon, Lacoste, Nelson, Jobin, Massue, Methot, Chabot, Lemieux, Cauchon, etc.

including the following members of the Government :
Messrs. Leslie, Price, Taché, Caron, Cameron, and
Drummond. Of the signers, all but Price and Cameron
hailed from Lower Canada, and almost all were of
French extraction. The document was, in fact, a
joint declaration of the Government and the French
Liberal members, in repudiation of the annexation
movement. Shortly after, two other French members
signed a similar protest, as officers of militia.[1]

In times of bitter racial and political feeling, when
the loyalty of the French-Canadians is sometimes
called in question, this fact should not be forgotten,
that the first protest against the annexation manifesto
was made by the French Reformers, not by the English-
speaking Conservatives. This circumstance is rendered
all the more interesting by the fact that several of the
signers, such as Morin, Cartier, and Nelson, had taken
part in the revolt of 1837. After the grant of responsible government, these men rallied to the support of
the English connection, and by their prompt action
checked the spread of annexation sentiment among
their compatriots.

The decisive action of the French Reform members
aroused the severest criticism of the Papineau organs,
which accused them of supporting the British connection from purely mercenary motives. *Le Canadien
Indépendent* recited at length the salaries of the Executive Officers of the Crown, and the special remuneration
of certain other members of the Legislature who had
signed the counter manifesto. Chabot, it declared,
was the advocate of the Jesuits, and as such the
humble servant of the Crown. *L'Avenir* denounced
the perfidy of the former patriotic leaders of 1837,
Messrs. Morin, Leslie, and Nelson, who for the sake
of personal preferment had sacrificed their political
principles, and had gone over to the enemy. Cartier
was accused of having changed front, since, for some
years past, he had been an avowed advocate of annexa-

[1] Messrs. Duchesnay and Laurin.

tion, and had only recently pronounced himself as still in favour of it.[1] However this may be, there can be little doubt but that at the time of signing the protest Cartier was a loyal supporter of the British connection. He had recovered his faith in the future of the colony, and he entertained a lively hope of its economic development when its resources should have been opened up by an improved system of communication.[2]

The intense interest of the Government in the political situation in Upper Canada was clearly shown in a letter of the Hon. Francis Hincks to Mr. C. Crosby, a leading Reformer of Markham. The question of annexation was, in the judgment of the hon. minister, primarily a commercial question. Setting aside those subjects with which the local Parliament could satisfactorily deal, the single cause of discontent sprang, he declared, from the restriction on trade across the American border. Public opinion was agreed that " the inconsiderate cry for annexation would be at once stifled by the establishment of reciprocal free trade with the United States."

There was, however, he continued, a general opinion that the American Government would not make fiscal concessions to Canada. One thing was certain, the annexation movement was not calculated to assist the local government in its efforts to obtain reciprocity. If the Annexationists would drop their ill-advised agitation, he held out the hope that the Imperial Government, which at last was fully alive to the seriousness of the Canadian situation, would be able to secure from the United States the free admission of Canadian products into the American market.

The Montreal manifesto, he declared, was based upon a misconception of the state of English public opinion. " The generous sentiments expressed by the British statesmen to the effect that they had no desire to retain the colonies against the wish of their inhabi-

---

[1] *L'Avenir*, October 18, 1849.
[2] De Celles, *Life of Cartier*, p. 45.

tants, have been construed into indifference as to the
permanency of the connection, an indifference which
is most assuredly not felt by any numerous party.
Not only are the leading statesmen of the political
parties . . . most favourable to the subsisting connection, but the warmest advocates of Colonial Reform,
such as Hume, Molesworth, and Roebuck, would view
annexation with deep regret." It would be especially
mortifying to the Liberals in England, as well as in
the colonies, if the recent concession of self-government
should lead to the severance of the imperial tie, instead
of the strengthening of the connection as had been
anticipated. He appealed to the Reformers to rally
to the support of the Government in the struggle which
was apparently about to take place between the
loyalists and the Annexationists in the Third Riding.
Every member of the Ministry, he concluded, entertained the views of Baldwin, as set forth in the letter
to Perry, and would carry them out if backed up by
the party. But if their former supporters should fail
them, the Government had a primary duty to their
sovereign and country " to sustain any administration
favourable to the British connection which could command a larger share of public opinion than themselves."[1]

The Government was using every effort, both of a
personal and partisan character, to stop the spread of
annexation views within the Reform Party. Baldwin
officially read all the Annexationists out of the party.
Cameron and his associates denounced the movement
in unsparing terms, and Hincks declared in effect that
the Ministry placed their allegiance to the Crown before
their party, and were prepared, if necessary, to support
a loyal Tory Government, rather than to retain office
by the grace of annexationist Reformers. The ministers were undoubtedly alarmed at the growing strength
of the Clear Grit Party, and at the tolerant, if not
sympathetic, attitude towards annexation of some of
the papers, and many of the supporters of that faction

[1] October 22, 1849.

of the party. But they did not lose courage, nor hesitate for a moment as to the proper policy to pursue under the circumstances. They boldly attempted to stifle the spirit of sedition at the outset. To this end they cleverly represented the annexation movement in the light of an act of treason to the party and to the Crown, and adroitly appealed to the fealty of their supporters, to the constitutional principles of the party, and to the old chivalric affection of the colonists for the motherland, in the hope of stemming the rising tide of republicanism which was threatening to carry away so many of their former supporters. The appeal was to a large extent successful. The timely intervention of the Ministry rallied the bulk of the party around the British standard, and enabled the Government to direct its full strength against the Annexationists in another quarter.

Meantime, the loyalists of Montreal had taken steps to counteract the impression that the city had wholly gone over to the Annexationists. Thanks to the energetic initiative of Mr. John Young, a prominent Reformer President of the Free Trade League, and business partner of Benjamin Holmes, a counter declaration of loyalty was prepared and circulated throughout the city. Prominent members of the League [1] joined hands with leading Reformers to make the protest a success. The address ran as follows :

" We, the undersigned inhabitants of the city of Montreal, owing and acknowledging allegiance to Her Majesty the Queen, having read a certain address to the people of Canada, in which separation from the British connection and a union with the United States of America are recommended as presenting the only practicable remedy for the evils which affect this province, do hereby solemnly and deliberately record our dissent from the precipitate and ill-advised conclusions

[1] Messrs. Mack, Montgomerie, Smith, Isaacson, officers of the League, signed the protest.

which the authors and signers of that address have arrived at.

" We believe that there is nothing in the depressed condition of Canada which may not be promptly and effectually remedied by the adoption of a well-considered system of legislation, without having to resort to a measure revolting to our feelings, revolutionary in character, and tending to the dismemberment of the British Empire. These views we are anxious to maintain by all constitutional means. Anxiously alive to the importance of promoting the material interests of this our native and adopted country, and of preserving unanimity and good-will amongst all classes of our fellow citizens, we cannot but express an earnest hope that means may be devised without delay to restore prosperity to this province, cement the ties which have so long existed with the mother country, and allay all agitation which may otherwise prove formidable."

To this protest over a thousand names were subscribed, notwithstanding the fact that no regular canvass of the city was attempted. The counter declaration represented, according to *The Transcript*, but a feeble reflex of Montreal feeling upon the question, since in matters of this kind it was exceedingly difficult to put aside their personal opinions. In this case, a large number of gentlemen had refused to sign the declaration, because they were of the opinion that no protest was necessary, and that the good common sense of the public, without outside efforts, would put down the agitation of the Annexationists. A still larger number of citizens objected on political grounds, " from a fear lest the movement might weaken the Conservative Party, and strengthen that of their opponents." On the other hand, the annexation press threw out the insinuation, which was subsequently repeated by Mr. Holmes in the Assembly, that every stipendiary and office-holder in the city was compelled to sign the protest on penalty of dismissal ; and it was further alleged that there were many false names upon the roll.

The truth of the first of these accusations was challenged by *The Pilot*, which declared in rebuttal that much less pressure was exercised in securing signatures in the case of the counter, than in that of the original manifesto. However this may be, it must be admitted that the names of Government officials occupied an important place on the list, and that, in point of social and commercial standing in the community, the adherents of the counter declaration made a much less pretentious appearance than the formidable array of the original manifesto. The larger commercial interests of the city were undoubtedly in favour of annexation. Amongst the mass of the English population opinion was very evenly divided. On the other hand, the overwhelming majority of the French inhabitants were unresponsive and unsympathetic ; their passive attitude constituted the strongest barrier against the spread of annexation tenets.

Encouraged by the many evidences of loyalty throughout the province, the Ministry proceeded to carry the war into the camp of the enemy. The Government had already been challenged by a section of the Tory press to dismiss from the public service any or all of its supporters who had signed the annexation manifesto.[1] Although the task was an exceedingly unpleasant one, and likely to react disadvantageously upon the Government, the Ministry did not hesitate to do its duty. No other course, in fact, was open to it. The question presented to the Government was not one of party expediency, but of public honour and of true allegiance. No matter how liberal the principles of the Government might be, it could not permit its officials to forswear their allegiance at will, without proclaiming thereby its own powerlessness and dissolution. The Government, from its very character as the ruling organ of the State, was not only entitled

[1] *The Montreal Gazette*, October 31, 1849.

to demand obedience from its citizens, but was compelled to assert and maintain its authority, even by arbitrary means, against its recalcitrant servants.

A circular letter was accordingly addressed by Colonel Leslie, the Provincial Secretary, to the magistrates, Queen's Counsels, militia officers, and other servants of the Crown, whose signatures were appended to the manifesto, " with a view of ascertaining whether their names had been attached to it with their consent," and, if so, demanding an explanation of their conduct.[1] To this communication an interesting variety of responses was forthcoming. Some of the recipients disavowed their signatures ; a few of the Annexationists courteously acknowledged their offence, and in some cases attempted to justify their action ; but several, on the other hand, refused to afford the desired information, and even denied the right of the Government to question them in regard to the matter.[2]

With striking inconsistency, *The Gazette*, which had taunted the Ministry with weakness in dealing with the Annexationists, now faced about, and denounced the Government for its inquisitorial proceedings. The Queen, it declared, would lose through this persecution the services of many brave and loyal men whose places would be vacated in order to make way for traitors. The Bar, it ventured to assert, would resist this dangerous attack upon its independence. The recipients of the circular were advised to consult together, " to meet so unprincipled and despotic an invasion of public liberty and the right of free discussion."

The Ministry was in no way deceived or intimidated by the bluffs and threats of the opposition, but calmly proceeded to deal with the offenders. At a meeting

[1] Despatch of Lord Elgin to Earl Grey, December 3, 1849.
[2] Prominent among the recalcitrants was Mr. Johnston, Q.C., who denied at first the power of the Executive to interrogate him, since he held no office of profit under the Crown, and was not a servant of the State. Later, he sought to justify his refusal to reply on the ground of his high regard for the privileges of the Bar.

of the Executive Council, on December 1, it was resolved that those officials who had admitted being parties to the annexation address, and those who had failed to give a direct answer to the Government's inquiry, should be dismissed from the service, and that the guilty Queen's Counsels should be deprived of their gowns. The attitude of the Government was clearly set forth in a minute of the Executive Council, a copy of which was addressed by the Provincial Secretary to the dismissed officials.[1]

" There can be no doubt in the opinion of the Committee of Council that His Excellency must feel bound by a sense of duty, as well to his sovereign and the empire at large, as to the people of Canada themselves, not only to maintain the connection of the province with the parent state by the fullest exercise of all the prerogatives conferred upon him by Her Majesty, but to discourage by all the means constitutional within its control every attempt calculated to impair it. In the performance of this duty there can be no desire to question any one upon mere abstract speculations regarding different forms of government. It is for parties to satisfy themselves to what extent they may proceed with such speculations, without the risk of compromising themselves by a breach of the laws of the land. When, however, an individual arrives at the deliberate conclusion, that what he deems the evils under which his country labours require not merely a reformation of the Constitution, but its entire overthrow, and when such person entertains this opinion not as a mere speculative theory, possibly to be realized in some remote and undefined future, but actually takes measures directly intended to bring about such revolutionary change, it appears to your committee perfectly obvious that, apart from all considerations or inquiry as to consequences of a still more serious character, such party should not be permitted to remain in the anomalous and invidious

[1] December 5, 1849.

position of holding a commission during the pleasure of a sovereign power which he desires to subvert."

The Government was no respecter of persons : Reformers and Tories, magistrates, officers and civilians, men of high and low degree alike, felt its displeasure.[1] Conspicuous in the list of the dismissed Justices of the Peace were Jacob De Witt, Benjamin Holmes, and the Hon. Robert Jones ; John Molson was dropped from the Wardens of Trinity House, and Messrs. Johnston and Rose lost their status as Queen's Counsellors. The victims were found in all parts of the province, but the Montreal district and the Eastern Townships especially suffered from the expurgatory process.

The decisive action of the Ministry aroused the vindictive ire of the Annexationists and their friends. The dismissed officials very cleverly endeavoured to gain the sympathy of the public by posing as the victims of an arbitrary Government, and by standing forth as the champions of liberty of speech. In reply to his notification of dismissal, Mr. Holmes endeavoured to assume the patriotic rôle of a John Hampden. He claimed that he had acted for the advantage of the province in promoting the manifesto, the representations of which he believed to be true, and the object of which was not looked upon as seditious by the English Government. In conclusion, he expressed the deepest regret " to find that a full and free discussion of political questions, even though they might involve the ultimate severance of this colony from the parent state, was denied, and to be suppressed and punished by the Provincial Executive, while in England, even in the Imperial Parliament, the self-same questions were freely mooted."

In an elaborate argument, Mr. Rose also endeavoured

---

[1] *The Kingston Whig* alleged that, while the Government was dismissing annexationist magistrates in Lower Canada, it was appointing Annexationists to the Government service in the Kingston district. *The Examiner* also charged that Mr. Wilson, of *The Independent*, was permitted to retain his commission in the militia.

to clear himself and his friends from the charge of treason. The objects of the association, he contended, were perfectly peaceful and constitutional. The Annexationists did not aim at a revolution, nor did they intend to resort to illegal practices to attain their ends; they merely asserted the constitutional right of every British subject to seek to bring about by public discussion a change in the political organization of the country, by and with the consent of the English Government and people. The annexation journals, as was to be expected, raised a hue and cry against the " tyrannical conduct " of the Ministry, the result of which, they prophesied, would yet prove disastrous to the British connection. The action of the Government, declared *L'Echo des Campagnes*, would not suppress the annexation movement, but only serve to give a more personal character to the struggle, and separate more widely the partisans and the opponents of English supremacy in the province.

The Tory and Clear Grit journals were divided upon the question. Some of the Tory papers, such as *The Quebec Mercury* and *The Toronto Colonist*, condemned the dismissal of worthy officials who had proved their loyalty to the Crown during the revolt of 1837. A few of the Clear Grit organs joined in the clamour against the policy of the Government. The dismissals, according to *The Examiner*, were a violation of constitutional principles, and a bad piece of political tactics; such a policy would not make converts of the Annexationists, nor convince the public of the impropriety of a political union with their neighbours; neither the loyalty nor the honesty of the servants of the Crown would be promoted by a policy of coercion.[1] The chief result of this mistaken policy would be, *The Mirror* added, to arouse a general sense of injustice, and to harden the hearts of the Annexationists.

On the other hand, the leading Reform papers heartily approved of the conduct of the Ministry,

[1] *The Examiner*, November 14, 1849.

though a few of the more timid journals questioned the wisdom of the policy of the Government, on grounds of political expediency. *The Pilot* severely arraigned the contention of Mr. Rose that annexation could be peaceably obtained with the free consent of England. However peaceful, it concluded, the professions of the Annexationists might be, they could only attain their object by force—in other words, by treason. Even among the Clear Grit sections of the party but little sympathy was felt for the ex-officials. The feelings of the Upper Canada Reformers were voiced at a public meeting at Pickering of the Radical wing of the party, at which a resolution was adopted expressing approval of the dismissal of avowed republican office-holders.[1]

This lack of sympathy was doubtless due in part to the fact that the great majority of the dismissed officials were Tories in politics. At the same time it is but fair to add that neither the Ministry in making the dismissals, nor their adherents in supporting the same, were primarily influenced by vindictive motives, or by mere partisan considerations. It was not a case of the application of the spoils system under the most favourable circumstances. Even *The Globe*, which could scarcely be accused of undue consideration for Tory officials, expressed the hope that many of the offenders would recant their errors, and be restored to their former posts on showing works meet for repentance.

The vigorous action of the Ministry had a salutary influence upon both the civil and military services. The great body of the servants of the Crown were undoubtedly warmly attached to the British connection. A few were admittedly wavering in their allegiance; but, however sentimentally inclined they might be towards annexation, the majority of them were not prepared to play the part of martyrs. The Government made it more profitable for them to be

[1] *The Examiner*, April 10, 1850.

loyal, than to profess sentiments of disloyalty, and they were not beyond the reach of worldly wisdom. Henceforth, the Executive had very little occasion to exercise its disciplinary authority over its officials on account of their seditious conduct.

The tactics of the leaders of the Conservative Party were strikingly different from those of the Ministry. Although the great majority of the most influential members of the party, as MacNab, Macdonald,[1] Sherwood, Allan, Moffatt, Gugy, and Badgley, were personally opposed to annexation, but few of them ventured to take any active part in opposing the movement. For the time being, they surrendered their position as political leaders, and became passive spectators of the struggle between the Government and the Annexationists. They did not even endeavour to suppress, like the Liberal Ministers, the annexation propaganda within the party ranks. Their party was thoroughly disorganized ; in the Montreal district some of the most prominent members had gone over to the Annexationists, and many others in different parts of the province were wavering in their political allegiance. Under these circumstances, the Conservative leaders thought it best to await developments, and to adopt the safe, if not highly honourable, rôle of political opportunists, in the hope of reaping some advantage from the internecine struggle of their opponents.

The course of political events had strained the loyalty of the Orangemen. They had been in the forefront of the battle against the Rebellion Losses Bill. No section of the Tory Party had been so

---

[1] (Sir) John A. Macdonald refused to sign the manifesto, although urged to do so. Many years after, he told his biographer, Mr. Pope, that he had " advocated the formation of the British American League as a much more sensible procedure," and that, under the influence of the League, the annexation sentiment had disappeared (Pope, *Life of Sir John A. Macdonald*, vol. ii. p. 71). He had evidently forgotten that the League Convention was held in Kingston more than two months before the manifesto appeared.

vigorous in its denunciation of Lord Elgin and the policy of the English Government as they ; at times the language of some of their leaders was defiant of the authority of the Government, if not almost seditious in character. But unlike many of their fellow partisans they did not allow the bitterness of defeat to undermine their loyalty to the Crown. When all around them wavered, they rallied staunchly to the British flag. At the critical moment of the struggle, the Grand Master of the Order issued an appeal to the brethren to remember the immemorial loyalty of the Order, and their bounden obligation to maintain the connection between the colonies and Great Britain.[1] " Therefore, my brethren . . . our course is clear and appointed. No matter what may be the clamours of the ignorant, or the projects of the wrong-minded, and still less the craft of the vicious, this outburst of democratic turbulence must be resisted, and all revolutionary projects, whether made under professions of loyalty or otherwise, we are bound by our solemn obligations to oppose."

The decisive conduct of the Grand Master offset to a large extent the inaction of the Tory leaders. When the latter failed to lead, the rank and file of the Orangemen were able to look to their own officers for direction in the crisis. The response to the appeal of the Grand Master was quick and decisive. The London Orangemen presented an address bearing over 900 signatures, deploring the payment of rebels, but stoutly affirming their unswerving devotion to the Crown.[2] The loyal attitude of the Orangemen did much to check the spread of annexation sentiment among the Tories of Upper Canada.

The Governor-General had been anxiously watching the dangerous course of events in Montreal. Although fearful of the outcome, he did not for a moment relax his efforts to maintain inviolable the connection

---

[1] October 19, 1849.
[2] *London Times* (C.W.), November 23, 1849.

between the colony and the mother country. "To render annexation by violence impossible, and by any other means as impossible as may be," was, he declared, "the polar star" of his policy. In a striking despatch to the Colonial Secretary soon after the appearance of the manifesto, he took particular pains to point out the serious responsibility of the English Government for the future of Canada.

"Very much, as respects the results of this annexation movement, depends upon what you do at home. I cannot say what the effect may be, if the British Government and press are lukewarm on the subject. The Annexationists will take heart, but, in a tenfold greater degree, the friends of the connection will be discouraged. If it be admitted that separation must take place sooner or later, the argument in favour of a present move seems to me almost irresistible. I am prepared to contend that with responsible government, fairly worked out with free trade, there is no reason why the colonial relation should not be indefinitely maintained. But look at my present difficulty, which may be increased beyond calculation, if indiscreet expressions be made use of during the present crisis. The English Government thought it necessary, in order to give moral support to its representative in Ireland, to assert in the most solemn manner that the Crown never would consent to the severance of the union. . . . But, when I protest against Canadian projects for dismembering the empire, I am always told the most eminent statesmen in England have over and over again told us that whenever we chose we might separate. Why then blame us for discussing the subject ? " [1]

A part of the alarming success of the manifesto was undoubtedly due to the chagrin of the people of Montreal at the proposed removal of the capital, which touched their civic pride, and, at the same time, threatened still further to affect the social and political

[1] November 16, 1849 ; *Letters and Journals of Lord Elgin,* p. 112.

prestige, and the commercial importance of the city. The circumstances of the time favoured at first the policy of the Annexationists. Their vigorous propaganda took the loyalists by surprise, and for a time appeared to sweep everything out of the way. But the latter soon rallied, and presented a strong united front to their opponents. Instead of winning an easy victory, as they had anticipated, the Annexationists found it necessary to undertake what promised to be a long and strenuous campaign to overcome the sentimental scruples of the great body of loyalists. The prospects were by no means as encouraging after the Government came out so decisively against them. Moreover, the reports which came in from the distant parts of the province, especially Upper Canada, clearly showed that both the public and the press were generally unfavourable to annexation.

Almost at the outset of the struggle the Annexationists found themselves fighting against heavy odds. Scarcely a month had elapsed since the issuance of the manifesto before some of the signers of that document realized their mistake, and began to withdraw quietly from the association. An excellent harvest in Upper Canada gave a fillip to the trade of the province. Business conditions were, according to *The Transcript*, better than they had been for some time past ; the receipts from customs and canal dues were almost 50 per cent. above those of the previous year. The worst of the crisis was apparently over, and the commercial community again took heart. With the slow but steady improvement in trade, evidences of a waning interest in annexation became manifest. The meetings of the local association were but thinly attended, in spite of the efforts of the officers to maintain an active organization. The business instincts of the public again asserted themselves, and this time to the disadvantage of the Annexationists.

The situation was admirably described by the Montreal correspondent of *The London Times*. " I am more confident every day that the late move (annexation) is a bubble which will have burst before next summer, to be blown up again and again at recurring periods of distress. Nine-tenths at least of the Annexationists are so reluctantly. They believe that incorporation with the United States will act in a magical manner on the value of property and labour in Canada, and on commerce ; that it will, in short, restore their own dilapidated fortunes. Show them a revival of prosperity without it, and annexation will be laid on the shelf until the next rainy day.

" The remaining tenth is composed of a few Montreal merchants who have long been Yankees in heart, and have a natural inclination for democratic institutions, and manufacturers who want admission to the American market. Among the former are some of the richest men in Canada, who have been making enormous profits in their several lines of business, and who, disgusted at the falling off of their receipts, throw the blame on the British connection, and erroneously believe that annexation would restore them their beloved gains.

" I believe the prospects of Canada were never as good as they are at this moment. During the autumn, the exports to the United States have been double what they ever were before in the most prosperous year during an equal period, consisting principally of flour, grain, peas for the manufacture of Yankee coffee (this is now a large business), horses, and a large quantity of timber. Next spring, the St. Lawrence will bristle with masts from all parts of the globe. The revenue derived from the canals will not only pay the interest of the debt incurred for their construction, but will yield a considerable surplus." [1]

[1] *The Times*, December 20, 1849.

CHAPTER IV

THE MOVEMENT IN LOWER CANADA

AT this critical juncture, leadership in the Annexation Party was sadly lacking. The leaders of the movement were anxious to avoid even the appearance of treasonable hostility to the Crown. Many of the members of the party belonged " to that new school who think an appeal to arms at any time, not only undesirable, but positively wrong." There was the greater reason for caution in this case, since, in the opinion of some of the inner councillors, " the game " of the Government was to drive the advocates of independence and annexation " into some overt act of treason or sedition, if not into open rebellion, so that they may bring into action the whole apparatus of civil law and military power." If, said the Montreal correspondent of *The New York Post*, " the men who have put themselves at the head of the annexation or independence movement have a fault, it is that of over-circumspection ; they have been, and will be, cautious to keep their agitation within constitutional limits, or, as it has been facetiously termed, on the shady side of the law ' ; they will not expose themselves to the bright flashes of General Rowand's cannon, nor to the brighter flashes of Judge Draper's charges to juries. Nor will the journalists of the party commit themselves ; they are conducted by men who know quite well what they are doing, and how far they can go with propriety ; they do not work on their fellow countrymen by appealing to their passions, in the revolutionary slang of the term, but by appealing to their interests, by placing facts before them, and leaving them to draw their own conclusions." [1]

But the purely polemical character of the policy of the association seriously detracted from the effectiveness of its campaign. After the issue of the manifesto, the Montreal Association had nothing to present in the way of a definite scheme of separation ; they could only repeat with parrot-like persistence the cry for annexation. The very haste and zeal with which they had pressed for pledges to the manifesto produced a reaction. Worst of all, the funds of the association were running low. In half-coaxing, half-despairing tones, *The Courier* pleaded for the sinews of war with which to carry on the campaign of education throughout the province. They must follow, it contended, the example of the English Free Trade Union, by subscribing funds, and despatching speakers all over the colony. But the response to this appeal was not very encouraging. " It would appear," said *The British American*, " that the Annexation Party is in a sickly condition, and if some good Samaritan does not put up the cash, it will die a natural death before six months." [2]

In the hope of reviving public interest in the question, and with a view to rebutting the arguments of their critics, the executive of the association resolved to issue a second address to the people of Canada. The language of the address, like that of the original

[1] *New York Post*, February 16, 1850.
[2] Quoted from *The Globe*, December 6, 1849.

manifesto, was calm and dignified, an appeal to the intelligent self-interest of the public, rather than to the political passion or prejudice of the people. The address, which was signed by John Redpath and the joint secretaries of the association, ran as follows :

ADDRESS OF THE MONTREAL ANNEXATION
ASSOCIATION TO THE PEOPLE OF CANADA

FELLOW COLONISTS,

When those whom we have the honour to represent undertook to recommend to you, in the address to the people of Canada, published in October last, the consideration of the peaceable separation of this province from Great Britain, and its annexation to the United States, they were fully aware of the responsibility which they assumed, and were, therefore, anxious to adopt only such measures as would be perfectly safe for those whose co-operation they sought to enlist. They were ready to suffer whatever odium might for a time be cast on the movers in such a project ; but they were resolved to do nothing which would cause civil commotion, or personal calamity. Prepared to maintain the right of every people to choose that government which they believe most calculated to promote their own happiness and prosperity, they would not assent to any proposition which, followed out, might bring those who thought with them into armed conflict with those who differed from them. Conscious of obeying no other motives than those springing from patriotism, disinterested and sincere, it was yet not without some hesitation that they committed themselves to a course which, although just and lawful, might divide them from many of their fellow subjects, and from associations long endeared to them.

The vast interest at stake—the welfare of themselves, their fellow countrymen, and their posterity—urged them to proceed ; and the favourable reception accorded to the expression of their opinion has shown that they did not make a false estimate of the circumstances by which they were surrounded, nor of the good sense, justice, and liberality of the people of Great Britain. If we refer for a moment to the condemnation passed on the address by certain public writers of this province (who, we are convinced, do not express the sentiments of the great body of the people), we do so in no spirit of triumph. But it is of importance for the advancement of the change we seek, to keep steadily before the public of Canada the fact, that this condemnation has not been confirmed by those in whose behalf it was professedly pronounced. Men in this colony who arrogated the right of speaking for the Government and people of Great Britain declared that we asked an impossibility, something to which Great Britain would never consent, which she would put down at all costs ; even at that of bloodshed. They even urged the infliction of punishment—such as arbitrary power is able to visit—on the guiltless expression of opinion, without waiting to learn if those in whose behalf they would persecute were really offended. . . .

We now stand in a totally different position from that which was occupied by the signers of the original address. The most influential organs of public opinion in the mother country, as well as the understood organs of its government, have spoken with as much distinctness as was possible, in reply to an unofficial demand. We now know with certainty that for which we had before only well-founded belief, that the people of Great Britain acknowledge the right of the inhabitants of this province to choose for themselves, and to establish the government which they deem best adapted to secure prosperity, and comfort the greater number. We here place a few of these declarations on record not as our title to rights which we did not possess before, but as valuable acknowledgments of their existence.

(*From " The London Times," October* 31)

" There was a time when so singular a document as this would have exposed its authors to the penalties of high treason, and the colony in which it was broached to the calamities of civil war ; when every Englishman would have boiled with indignation at the presumption which complained of English dominion, and at the temerity which proposed to carry the presumption of language into action. But those days have passed away. We have been taught wisdom by experience ; and the most valuable, as well as the most costly, of our lessons has been taught by the barren issue of a precipitate conflict with a province, from which remonstrances proceeded to rebellion, and crowned rebellion with independence. . . .

" We should not go to war for the sterile honour of retaining a reluctant colony in galling subjection ; we should not purchase an unwilling obedience by an outlay of treasure or of blood. If, indeed, with colonial dependence or independence there were indissolubly bound up metropolitan prosperity or decay ; if it were tolerably clear that the preservation of our colonial empire would ensure the preservation of metropolitan greatness, and that the latter would wane with the extinction of the former—then such suggestions as the Montreal address contains would find no place in the discussions, no sympathy in the feelings, of the people of England. They would one and all identify their own interests and prosperity with that which their forefathers were content to regard for and by itself, viz. the supremacy of English power. But the difference between them and their forefathers is that they will count and ponder on that more vulgar balance of profit and loss which was forgotten by the generation which hailed the commencement, and lamented the conclusion, of the great American War. Is the retention of Canada profitable ? will its loss be hurtful to England ? is the questions which Englishmen of the present day will put to themselves, as the converse of this question is that which Canadians are already discussing on their side. . . . Meanwhile, ere this question be solved, let us congratulate ourselves on the reflection that the document which we have quoted proves that the political training which England gives to her colonists is one which need neither make them ashamed of her, nor her of them ; and that the future which awaits men thus trained can never be obscure or dishonourable."

(From " The London Times," November 2)

" We retract nothing that we have said on the tone, the temper, and the gravity of the document. By whomsoever it was proposed, by whomsoever concocted, it reflects great credit on the skill, tact, and adroitness of its authors."

(From " The London Weekly Despatch ")

" This movement is a fine and cheering example, which is wonderfully well timed for the world's instruction. Here is no bluster, and bravado ; no vituperations are uttered for past wrongs. No appeal is made to the god of battles. A violent separation is not proposed ; nor even one which shall be involuntary on the part of Great Britain. We are treated like rational beings by those who act like rational beings themselves. The actual tangible loss of the present connection is put in evidence, and, side by side with it, the actual tangible gain of the proposed measure. Canada exhibits her day book and ledger, and asks Lord John Russell to add up the column, and see the account for himself. Revolutions, separation, independence, annexation are words that conjure up the ideas of armed multitudes, troops in hot pursuit, desperate patriots dying for the Queen, and dying for the people, courts-martial and shootings, courts civil, and hangings, sea-fights and land-fights, with a bitterness engendered by the result, whatever it be, that

alienates men's hearts for many a generation. . . .
All these associations, inevitable in European outbreaks, are superseded by these straightforward Canadians. They show how the whole is settled by logic and
arithmetic. The Duke of Wellington is not the least
needed. A common accountant, or his clerk, is all
the extraneous aid the Cabinet requires. Revolution
is tamed and civilized. The Peace Congress may be
congratulated."

(From " The Dundee Advertiser ")

" In all likelihood Canada will cease to be a British
possession, and that in a very short time. There has
been a tendency to this separation for a considerable
time back, and we do not think that the loss of Canada
as a colony is to be regretted. On the contrary, we
are convinced that both the colonists and the British
will be benefited. The operation of free trade will
relieve colonists from the obligation of protective
duties, and they will have no interest in continuing
to submit to the British rule, except in so far as they
require British protection against their enemies. If
Canada be annexed to the United States, she requires
such protection no longer. She will be as independent
of England as America is, and England will be as
independent of her as she is of America. Canadian
produce will find its way to our markets as readily
as ever, and our manufactures to the Canadian
markets. . . .

" We shall simply be saved the trouble and expense
of her government, and these have been of no trifling
nature. We believe our colonies have cost this country
an amount of money which it is impossible to estimate,
in wars, in protective duties, and in expenses of
government. We shall not regret to see more of them
follow the example of Canada and be at the trouble
and expense of maintaining themselves. There is no
doubt but that the majority of the Canadian population
have a right to judge for themselves, and to choose

what government they please. It is said that they are under obligations to us, and that they are, therefore, not free so to choose. We say the sooner we cease from conferring obligations the better for us ; hitherto we have paid dearly enough for maintaining our connection with this colony. We shall now maintain all that is worth preserving—our commercial intercourse— without being taxed for it."

(*From " The Illustrated News "*)

" All these arguments are good as regards Canada ; and could the statesmen of this country believe that they were the sentiments of a large majority of the Canadian people, there can be little doubt but that they would agree to annexation, which, in such a case, would sooner or later be accomplished in spite of them. . . .

" Sooner or later the independence of Canada is sure to be accomplished—as surely as the infants born yesterday will grow into men—unless, indeed, we shall decree all our colonies to be integral parts of the kingdom of Great Britain, and allow them to send members to Parliament by the same right, and for the same reason, that we accord the franchise to London or to Manchester, to Middlesex or to Lancashire. It is possible that by such a course of proceeding, we might preserve some of our larger colonies for a time ; but even with such a participation in British power, we doubt whether we could retain Canada for two generations, or the great continent of Australia for three. Their independence is a question of time ; and it will be well for us at home if we have sufficient wisdom to know when the time has come, and sufficient virtue to reconcile ourselves peaceably to that which is inevitable. To be deprived of Canada by force, and the connivance of the United States, would be humiliation indeed ; but to yield it up of our own free will would be but a sacrifice. We question, indeed, whether it would not be a gain.

" We seize the opportunity to observe that the magnanimous promptitude of the greater portion of the British public to admit our rights, and to appreciate the feelings, and respect the motives which actuated the framers of the original address, calls for the grateful acknowledgments of the people of Canada."

The response of the people of the United States to the address has not been less satisfactory than that from Great Britain. Not only has the press generally declared in favour of receiving Canada into the Union if she seek that admission in a legitimate and peaceable manner ; but one of the states lying immediately on our own border, in the proceedings of its legislature, has pointedly alluded to the fact that the admission of Canada was contemplated by the original Articles of Confederation, and has by the following resolutions declared its desire to see that union effected.

Proceedings of the Vermont Legislature, 1849

" No. 29. Resolutions relating to the annexation of Canada to the United States.

" Whereas by the original articles of Confederation adopted by the States of this Union, it was provided that Canada, acceding to this Confederation, and joining in the measures of these United States, shall be admitted into and entitled to all the advantages of this Union.

" And whereas recent occurrences in the said province of Canada indicate a strong and growing desire on the part of the people thereof to avail themselves of the advantages of the foregoing offer, and to apply for admission among the sovereign States of this Union.

" Therefore, resolved by the Senate and the House of Representatives, that, believing the admission of Canada into this Union to be a measure intimately connected with the permanent prosperity and glory of both countries, the Government of the State of Vermont is earnestly desirous to see such reunion effected, without a violation, on the part of the United States, of the amicable relations existing with the British Government, or of the law of nations.

" *Resolved.*—The peaceable annexation of Canada to the United States, with the consent of the British Government and of the people of Canada, and upon just and honourable terms, is an object in the highest degree desirable to the people of the United States. It would open a wide and fertile field to the enterprise and the industry of the American people ; it would extend the boundaries and increase the power of our country ; it would enlist a brave, industrious, and intelligent people under the flag of our nation ; it would spread wide the liberal principles of republican government, and promote the preponderance of free institutions in this Union. We therefore trust that our national Government, in the spirit of peace and of courtesy to both the British Government and the people of Canada, will adopt all proper and honourable means to secure the annexation of Canada to the United States."

We were always persuaded that the people of Great Britain would consent to allow the separation which we desired, without which consent we would consider it neither practicable nor desirable, provided that separation were demanded by the majority of the people of Canada, but we know that many of our fellow colonists thought otherwise, and were therefore waiting for the judgment of the people of Great Britain, before committing themselves to our movement. We can now confidently call on such persons to dismiss all considerations of that nature, and to apply themselves only to the comparison of our present position with that which we must expect to occupy as a sovereign state of the North American Union. If the change be beneficial, nothing prevents its accomplishment. You

HAVE ONLY TO WILL IT.   Motives for the change were set forth in considerable detail in the original address to the people of Canada.   Nothing has since occurred to make that statement less true.   After all the vain attempts to show that a few expressions were exaggerated, or to disprove some isolated assertions, that representation of our condition remains unshaken. The belief in the more rapid progress of the United States than of Canada does not, indeed, depend upon the evidences of any body of men who may address you to-day.   The contrast is matter of daily, and, to us, of mortifying observation.   It has been related and deplored by every British traveller who has compared the two borders.   All well-informed men, even in England, have repeatedly heard it and read of it. It is past all honest doubt or denial.   We here adduce the evidence of some witnesses—of men uninfluenced by prejudice, except what is in favour of British rule.

(*From " The London Daily News "*)

" To all who are acquainted with Canada, or have read the publications respecting it which have appeared for a series of years back, this (the manifesto) is quite intelligible.   The contrast between the United States side of the boundary line and the Canadian side has been the subject of frequent remark.   A cool and dispassionate man of business, who visited Canada about a month ago, expresses himself on this subject in a letter that now lies before us, as follows :

" I had often read of the contrast presented between the American and Canadian shores (of the St. Lawrence), but I could not have comprehended it in all its fulness unless I had witnessed it with my own eyes. On the one side all is life, activity, and prosperity ; on the other it is like the stillness of death.   Montreal is a very fine city, more like an European town than anything I have yet seen on the American continent ; but there the universal complaint is that their trade is gone.   The mercantile classes seemed to me to be unanimous in favour of annexation ; and one cannot wonder at it, when you find a mere nominal line separating them from the prosperity of their neighbours.''

(*From Lord Durham's Report*)

" Under such circumstances there is little stimulus to industry or enterprise, and their effect is aggravated by the striking contrast presented by such of the United States as border upon this province, where all is activity and progress. . . . I allude to the striking contrast which is presented by the American and British sides of the frontier line, in respect to every sign of productive industry, increasing wealth, and progressive civilization. By describing one side and reversing the picture, the other would also be described. On the American side all is activity and bustle. . . . On the British side of the line, with the exception of a few favoured spots where some approach to American prosperity is apparent, all seems waste and desolate. . . . Throughout the course of these pages, I have constantly had occasion to refer to this contrast. I have not hesitated to do so, though no man's just pride in his country and firm attachment to its institutions can be more deeply shocked by the mortifying admission of inferiority. . . . The contrast which I have described is the theme of every traveller who visits these countries, and who observes on one side of the line the abundance, and, on the other, the scarcity of every sign of material prosperity which thriving agriculture and flourishing cities indicate, and of that civilization which schools and churches testify even to the outward senses.''

(*From Dr. Dixon's Tour in America*)

" I found the country full of complaints and dissatisfaction from one end to the other. The people everywhere, and of all shades of politics, spoke the same language. Their fortunes were wrecked, their commerce destroyed ; their agriculture, the sinews of the colony, enfeebled, ruined. . . .

" On the enactment of Lord Stanley's Bill respecting the admission of Canada flour into this country, a vast outlay in building mills took place, which mills had just begun to work profitably ; but the new policy effectually crushed this trade. I myself saw one of these mills, belonging to one of our friends—a new building of great size, and which must have cost many thousand pounds in its erection—standing still. This I understood was generally the case. . . . In the present state of things, cast off by the mother country, and left to their own resources, with the United States just by their side, possessing vast political power and influence ; a growing credit and monetary resources ; a prodigious mercantile and commercial navy ; an active, industrious, and virtuous people; a Government capable in all respects, and equally disposed to foster, protect, and strengthen all its possessions ;—we say with all these things staring them in the face, the policy of this country has made it the plain palpable interest of the Canadians to seek for annexation. This is as clear as any problem in Euclid."

(From a letter of the great apostle of Temperance, Father Chiniquy, addressed to the Mélanges Religieux of October 19, 1849, *on his return from the United States)*

" I do not exaggerate when I say that there are not less than 200,000 Canadians in the United States, and unless efficacious means are taken to stop their frightful emigration, before ten years 200,000 more of our compatriots will have carried to the American Union their arms, their intelligence, and their hearts. It is no part of my present plan to examine the causes of this deplorable emigration ; but it must be always true that when a people *en masse* quits its country, it is because that unfortunate country is struck with some

hideous plague—is devoured with some cancer. God
has placed in the heart of man love for his country,
and when man turns his back upon his country, and,
with the eye moistened by tears, bids it an eternal
adieu, it is because something essential has been wanting to him in that country. It is because he has
wanted bread, room, or just liberty. I leave others
to say which of the three has been deficient in Canada.
All that I can assure you of is that in the United States
these three essential elements of the life of nations are
found in abundance."

Nor is the decline in prosperity caused by the
reversal of the protective policy of the mother country,
by any means less evident than when the former
address was issued. We need go into no proofs of this
allegation ; they have been recently proclaimed by
those who are opposed to the course we desire to
adopt.

Under these circumstances, encouraged by Great
Britain and the United States to act with freedom in
the exercise of an enlightened judgment, do you see
any other probable means of escape from a position of
acknowledged inferiority, than that which has been set
before you by the advocates of annexation ? Those
who have protested against the Address to the People
of Canada have declared their belief that the evils of
which we complain, and which they recognize, might
be removed by judicious legislation. They are now
told that Great Britain can do nothing to restore our
past advantages.

Thus says the London *Times* on this subject :

" It must be admitted that the latter have grievances, though not all equally oppressive nor all of
the same origin. They have been planted and thriven
under protective laws. Those laws are now abrogated ;
and abrogated—as the people of Canada have the good
sense to see—without a chance of re-enactment. So
far, they suffer, in common with all our colonies, the

effects of a bad and obsolete colonial system. The change, however, is made. The colonists know that what has been done will not be undone, and that the grain crops of Western Canada must compete in the markets of England with the grain crops of the United States, of Poland, and of the whole world. They are suffering from the revulsion."

In this particular, as in every other, the views of those who addressed you in favour of annexation have been fully confirmed.

Is there any brighter hope from any other quarter? Our opponents maintain that present causes of complaint would be removed by the attainment of reciprocal free trade with the United States. It is perhaps too soon to affirm as a positive fact that this advantage cannot be obtained. But it is quite clear that those who lately vaunted most loudly the benefits to accrue from it now despair of securing it. They have already begun to depreciate it as something of very inferior utility.

For the social and political disadvantages under which we labour, no adequate remedy other than that which we advocate has ever been proposed. The most able British writers—those best acquainted with the colony—acknowledge, and at the same time deplore, them as inseparable from the colonial condition, and inevitable while that condition continues.

Our country is of no account in the congress of nations; as individuals we are practically excluded from the honours of the empire, while men who have no permanent interest in our welfare acquire riches and obtain honours on our soil. We have no common objects of national pride and solicitude; but as citizens of the United States, we should attain a nationality worthy of our highest aspirations.

These sentiments have been so well expressed in a late work, *The Colonies of England*, by J. A. Roebuck, Esq., M.P., that we here transcribe his language:

" The career that lies between two men, one of whom

has been born and lives upon the southern shore of the St. Lawrence, and the other on the north of that river, is a striking example of the observation here made. The one is a citizen of the United States, the other a subject of England, a Canadian colonist. The one has a country which he can call his own ; a great country, already distinguished in arms, in arts, and in some degree in literature. In his country's honour and fame the American has a share, and he enters upon his career of life with lofty aspirations, hoping to achieve fame for himself in some of the many paths to renown which his country affords. She has a senate, an army, a navy, a bar, many powerful and wealthy churches ; her men of science, her physicians, philosophers, are all a national brotherhood, giving and receiving distinction. How galling to the poor colonist is the contrast to this which his inglorious career affords ! He has no country—the place where he was born, and where he has to linger out his life unknown to fame, has no history, no past glory, no present renown. What there is of note is England's.

" Canada is not a nation ; she is a colony—a tiny sphere, a satellite of a mighty star in whose brightness she is lost. Canada has no navy, no literature, no brotherhood of science. If, then, a Canadian looks for honour in any of these various fields, he must seek it as an Englishman ; he must forget and desert his country before he can be known to fame."

If all these substantial arguments in favour of annexation remain unchanged, or have been strengthened by lapse of time, you will certainly not be deterred from pursuing the course indicated as desirable, by the arbitrary commands of those who assume to be your masters. Those who addressed you were known to be beyond suspicion of seeking personal emolument from the public funds. They employed no force but that of reason ; they repudiated every means but that, most lawful—the assent of every constituted authority in the state. They desire to fortify, and, where necessary, to create a public opinion in favour of their views, which should be manifested, not on paper merely, but in that authoritative way which the Constitution has contemplated, in giving to the people the right of electing their legislators. They, therefore, did not endeavour to obtain all the names which might have been procured to the document they put forth. They were satisfied, when they had enrolled sufficient adherents without solicitation, to show that they were not a few deluded men, acting without warrant of widespread public thought. How have they been replied to? Their opponents have sent agents through the most populous countries immediately adjoining the city unexpectedly favoured by the removal of the seat of Government. As well there, as in this city, they have employed against us every influence derived from official patronage, and yet how trifling has been their success!

In the absence of argument, persecution has been resorted to by an Executive, affecting to owe its existence to the popular will, against such as dared assert the right, not of British subjects merely, but of intellectual beings—the right of thought and free discussion.

Fellow Colonists, will you submit to have your free political action suppressed by such means? Are your servants to dictate to you the subjects which may engage your attention, and prohibit all others under pain of their interference and censure? We trust not. We feel assured that you will feel more inclined to support those who have been opposed by means which we will not characterize otherwise than as oppressive. We now call on such of you as are favourable to our views to exert yourselves, in order that the great object before us may be speedily attained. All agree in believing that annexation is inevitable—a mere question of time. It is our conviction that there can be no settled policy—no established public credit—no cessation of public strife—no prosperity—until we reach

the state to which we are destined. Let us then unite
to secure it as early as possible.

JOHN REDPATH, President.

R. MCKAY
A. A. DORION } Secretaries.

MONTREAL,
December 15, 1849.

The Annexation Association of Montreal begs to
thank such portions of the Press as have lent their
assistance, for the able aid they have offered. The
association, while it recognizes no exposition of its
views except those which shall be signed by its officers,
feels a deep debt of gratitude to those who have
generously stood up for truth and the people, against
the obloquy which has been cast on both.

This time the address fell flat. Although greeted
with the warmest commendation by the annexation
press,[1] it failed to arouse even a moiety of the interest
of the original manifesto. The mind of the public
was already partially diverted in other directions, and
the address itself was not sufficiently striking to recall
the wandering attention of the populace. It was a
well-considered statement of the faith of the Annexationists, but it contained little new. Its chief interest
lay in the laboured attempt to defend, or rather justify,
the policy of annexation under cover of the declarations
of English statesmen and the opinions of the English
press. The charge of treason levelled against them by
the loyalists disquieted their peace of mind, even though
it did not stir up their consciences to repentance. So
extensive were the quotations from the public press,
especially from the organs of the Manchester School,
that the address was open to the criticism of being a
mere collection of newspaper clippings. The argument
failed to convince the public, for it bore upon its face
the evidence of special pleading. The leaders of the

---

[1] *L'Avenir*, December 21, 1849.

annexation party had somewhat mistaken the temper
of the people ; they had interpreted the discontent of
the public as an evidence of annexation sentiment.
The movement, according to *The Gazette*, was premature
in its conception and impolitic in its activities, and
" those who initiated it had weakened their own cause
by separating from a powerful party who were advocating changes which must be made before their own
scheme of annexation can succeed." [1]

The struggle between the loyalist and annexationist
press was becoming increasingly bitter. Charges and
counter charges were bandied back and forth. On the
one hand, Lord Elgin was accused of attempting to
bribe the Catholic bishops to oppose annexation ; [2] on
the other, the charge was made that the annexation
cause and press were receiving aid from the United
States. In respect to the latter charge, *The Herald*
protested : " We do not believe, nor have we any
reason to believe, that one single farthing has been
subscribed in the city of New York with a view to
aiding the annexation movement." [3] In both cases,
the accusation was indignantly denied, but in neither
case was the denial accepted in good faith by the
accusing party. [4]

The appearance of the manifesto awakened an interest in Quebec little less keen than that in Montreal.
All the papers, both English and French, devoted
considerable attention to the subject, and all with one
exception united in condemning the address in more
or less decisive language. For once the English Tory
papers found themselves in accord with the French
Reform press. *The Chronicle* declared that the time
was not yet ripe for annexation, and that the manifesto
had been launched without due regard to the means
by which the object in view could be accomplished.

[1] *The Gazette*, December 31, 1849.
[2] *L'Avenir*, November 4, 1849.
[3] *The Herald*, December 29, 1849.
[4] *The Gazette* alleged that the funds in question had been raised
for the support of the revolt in Ireland, December 31, 1849.

The peaceful pretensions of the Annexationists were worthless, since the records of history amply proved that separation had never been attained by mere móral suasion. *The Mercury* contended that, in addition to the strong moral ties which bound the Canadian people to the heart of the motherland, there were many material interests which England could not sacrifice without seriously impairing her power and prestige as an Imperial State. She would not consent to the amicable dismemberment of the empire, and to the loss of the fortifications and public works of the colonies upon which she had poured out so much money. The British Empire was not subject to the grant of any Government ; it was held in trust for future generations.

The attitude of the French Liberal papers was equally hostile to a political union. *Le Canadien* ridiculed the false, glowing prospects held out by the Annexationists, who professed, in effect, to be able to change the climate of the country, and to bring Canada within the corn and cotton belt, by the simple process of eliminating the boundary line. It warned its fellow countrymen of the sinister designs of the Annexationists against their race. If they (the French-Canadians) understood the real object of the Annexationists, they would receive the emissaries of the new political creed " à coups de fourche." *La Gazette de Québec* declared " that there was nothing in the actual state of depression in Canada which could not find a prompt and efficacious remedy by the adoption of well-considered legislation, without having recourse to a measure which outraged the feelings of the Canadian people, was revolutionary in character, and tended to dismember the British Empire."

In an able series of articles *Le Journal de Québec* undertook to controvert the whole argument of the Annexationists.[1] It pointed out the striking inconsistency in the tone of the manifesto, and the leading

[1] *Le Journal de Québec*, October 18, 20, 23, and 27, 1849.

articles of *The Courier* ; for, whereas the former was loud in its professions of the most cordial friendship for all the inhabitants of the province, the latter was breathing out threatenings against the French, and advocating annexation as the best means of crushing French ascendency.   Peace and goodwill, it ironically remarked, were the hypocritical watchwords of all revolutionaries.   The commercial condition of the province was, it contended, by no means as bad as the manifesto represented.   The existing economic depression was felt as severely in Europe as in Canada, and was, at worst, merely temporary, for there were already signs of returning prosperity.   Owing to over-speculation, the distress in Montreal was particularly acute, but the conditions in that city were not representative of the province at large.   In clamouring for annexation, the Montreal merchants were failing in courage and patriotism, and were pusillanimously seeking to throw off on England the blame for their own weakness and folly.

Notwithstanding the opposition of the press, the Annexationists of Quebec were by no means daunted or discouraged, but proceeded to organize an association on similar lines to that in Montreal.   A circular was distributed throughout the city calling for a meeting of all the friends of annexation at the Hotel St. George.[1]   From thirty to fifty persons assembled, not all of whom, however, were Annexationists.   Mr. M. H. Dubard,[2] the chairman of the meeting, and Mr. M. Bonner, of *La Gazette de Québec*, played the most prominent part in getting the organization under way.   An annexation address was prepared, and subsequently circulated throughout the city.   About five hundred signatures in all were obtained.

The canvassers appear to have been careless or over-

---

[1] October 17, 1849.
[2] *Le Journal de Québec* described him as an irresponsible stranger, whose views had always been opposed to the interests of his compatriots

zealous in their work, for many persons at once came forward to protest that their names had been placed upon the list without their knowledge or authorization. The majority of the signatures, according to *L'Ami de la Religion*, were collected in the backward quarters of the city by the most deceitful means. According to report, quite a number of ignorant French-Canadians were induced to sign the address by the alluring representation that their debts to the Government would be cancelled in case of annexation. However, the names of many excellent citizens were found upon the list, although but few, if any, were persons of outstanding influence and character in the community.

The Annexationists were so much encouraged by the success of this canvass, and by the receipt of a letter from Papineau, urging an immediate separation from Great Britain, that they determined to make a demonstration in force. An attempt was made to secure the Parliament building for a public meeting, but the mayor refused to allow the building to be used for that purpose. This little contretemps proved an excellent advertisement for the meeting. The rally at St. George's Hall, in point of attendance and public interest, was a great success; but owing to the presence of a considerable number of loyalists, who persistently interrupted the proceedings, the meeting was turned into a veritable Donnybrook Fair. Both nationalities were represented on the programme; Dr. Brady presided, and M. Aubin acted as *pro tem.* secretary; Messrs. Alleyn and Soulard were the chief French orators, while Mr. Gordon, of the British American League, spoke on behalf of the English community.

A series of resolutions were adopted, declaring: (1) That the general discussion of the subject of independence and annexation was worthy of the attention of the citizens of Quebec. (2) That in view of the commercial, political, and social difficulties of the province, the importance and increasing needs of the country, and the small interest which England had taken in the welfare of the colonies, this meeting expressed its firm conviction that a peaceable separation from the motherland with a view to annexation to the United States was indispensable to the tranquillity and prosperity of Canada. (3) That English statesmen would willingly accord independence, if desired by the majority of the Canadian people. It was further resolved to form a local association to promote the object in view, and to secure the return to Parliament of members favourable to the cause of annexation. A committee of fifty-one persons, representing the English, French, and Irish sections of the population, was appointed to draw up a constitution for the association.

When the first resolution was proposed, according to *Le Journal de Québec*, it was rejected by a large majority, though the chairman declared it carried. The loyalists attempted to capture the meeting ; but, owing to the non-appearance of their speakers, they were forced to content themselves with loudly cheering for the Queen. The meeting broke up in great confusion. In order to avenge themselves on their opponents, the Rouges attacked the house of Mr. Couchon, the local Reform member. At a large mass meeting in the suburbs of St. Roch's, the following Sunday, the struggle between the supporters of Papineau and Lafontaine again broke out. A resolution in favour of annexation was carried with difficulty.[1]

In the meantime the loyalists of the city had been equally active. The officers of the militia signed an address condemning the manifesto, asserting their loyalty to the Crown, and their readiness " to stand forward in defence of the glorious Constitution under which they had the happiness to serve." In order to counteract the annexationist address, and to attest the strength of pro-British sentiment in the city, a counter protest was prepared, and thrown open to

---

[1] According to *The Montreal Courier*, three thousand persons were present, and the resolutions were carried unanimously.

the public for signature. The response was eminently satisfactory ; without even the formality of a canvass, upwards of 1,000 names were secured ; in the French ward of St. Roch alone, over 300 names were appended to the document.

The success which had attended the annexation movement aroused the righteous indignation of Bishop Mountain, who feared that the interest of the Anglican Church might be imperilled by a union with a non-episcopal country. Although but seldom participating in politics, he felt constrained by a sense of duty to draw up a pastoral letter to the clergy and laity of the diocese, entitled : *Thoughts on Annexation in Connection with the Duty and Interests of Members of the Church of England, and as affecting some Particular Religious Questions.* The address revealed the bishop in the dual rôle of the ecclesiastic and the politician, the High Churchman and the man of worldly wisdom ; it afforded a splendid exposition of the principles of a High Church Tory who, amid all his sacerdotalism, was not forgetful of the material advantages which flowed from ecclesiastical preferment, and refused to surrender them without a struggle.

At the outset, the bishop called upon all Churchmen to bear in mind the scriptural injunction : " My son, fear thou the Lord and the king, and meddle not with them that are given to change." He indignantly repudiated the charge that the clergy were loyal solely because they feared that they might lose their emoluments by annexation. But, notwithstanding this repudiation, he proceeded to demonstrate in his own person that the Church was not indifferent to merely worldly considerations. The material position of the Church in Canada was, in his opinion, greatly superior to that of the Episcopalian Church in the United States. Annexation would involve the most injurious consequences to the Church, in the loss of its ecclesiastical authority and the prestige of the English connection and establishment ; it would occasion the sacrifice of the endowments of the Church, in particular the withdrawal or cancellation of the clergy reserves for the maintenance of the clergy. The Church would be forced to fall back upon the system of voluntary support in effect in other religious organizations. From a religious point of view, also, annexation would be most objectionable in introducing the curse of slavery into Canada.

" True," he concluded, " there is the same Episcopal communion in the United States, but it is not the national Church of England with the peculiar characteristics and appendages of that establishment which have gone far to mould the national mind and manners, and to stamp upon Englishmen an impress which is received even by unwilling hands as a striking mark in every part of the world. Pause, then, before you throw up your title and distinction as Englishmen. English Churchmen, hold your hand, and think twice, before you sign away your interest in the land of your fathers and its institutions, before you pledge that hand to those who would begin the dismemberment of the empire." Even if the industries of the country were depressed for the time, and even though there were difficulties in their colonial relations affecting their private interests, nevertheless they might " find it a precipitate and ill-advised, as it certainly was an unjustifiable, step to rush into this experiment of annexation." Changes, depression, and political turmoil were not confined to Canada, but were also common to the American States. Under these circumstances, it was better, both from a religious and political standpoint, for Churchmen to remain content with their present status, rather than to seek annexation.

Shortly after these events, there occurred a splendid opportunity of testing the strength of annexation sentiment in the city. The appointment of Mr. Chabot as Commissioner of Public Works created a vacancy in the city's representation. Urged on by

L'Avenir, the Annexationists determined to oppose the re-election of the hon. minister, provided a suitable candidate could be secured. Fortunately for the party, a popular and influential citizen, Joseph Legaré, who had contested the Riding in the Papineau interest at the late general election, was ready to enter the lists again. At a meeting of the Annexationists at which about 200 persons were present, the situation was thoroughly canvassed, and it was resolved to support Mr. Legaré, on condition that he would openly declare himself an Annexationist.[1]

In response to this demand, Legaré came out in favour of annexation in his election address. The prospect of an annexation victory appeared very promising. At the late general election Mr. Legaré had received a majority of the French-Canadian votes, and there was every reason to believe that, on this occasion, he would poll the full strength of the Papineau Party and of the English Annexationists, and in addition would receive the support of a considerable number of Tory irreconcilables who would vote for any candidate in opposition to the Government. If he could capture one-third of the English voters, his election was deemed to be assured.[2]

At the nomination proceedings, the friends of Legaré were in a decisive majority, and Mr. Chabot was forced to withdraw and leave the meeting to his rival. The struggle became daily more intense. The annexation campaign was very adroitly conducted by Messrs. Aubin, Fréchette,[3] and Lee, the local leaders of the party. A special appeal was made to the working-men and the discontented Irish, to rally to the support of a true democratic candidate. The Annexationists, however, were placed at a decided disadvantage by the lack of a local organ, as *L'Indépendent Canadien* had

[1] December 23, 1849.
[2] *L'Avenir*, January 4, 1850.
[3] Messrs. Aubin and Fréchette were former residents in the United States.

been forced to suspend publication not long before. The Montreal annexationist papers, especially *Le Moniteur Canadien* and *L'Avenir*, did their best to supply this deficiency by devoting special attention to the affairs of the district. The latter journal appealed to the material interests of the citizens of Quebec by adroitly suggesting the possible removal of the capital to Upper Canada. With annexation, however, Quebec would be made the permanent seat of government of a newly formed state ; and, moreover, would inevitably become a great ship-building centre, and *entrepôt* of trade for the western states of the Union.[1]

The Montreal Association likewise realized the cardinal importance of the election. If the seat could be won, the whole province would be convinced of the strength of the movement, and it was believed would soon follow in the wake of Quebec. It was accordingly resolved to lend financial assistance to the Quebec Annexationists, upon receiving assurance of the reasonable probability of Mr. Legaré's election. The assurances were evidently satisfactory, for, soon after, several hundred pounds were sent to Quebec for judicious distribution in the annexation interest.[2]

The Reform press and Party were putting up an equally aggressive fight on behalf of the new Commissioner. They adroitly sought to give the campaign a semi-religious character by representing the annexation movement as an insidious attack upon the Catholic faith. At the same time, they appealed to the Tory loyalists not to carry their hostility to the Government to the extreme of voting for an Annexationist ; but, on this one occasion, to prove their loyalty to the Crown by supporting the ministerial candidate. For the moment, the position of the Tory Party in Quebec was one of superior power and great responsibility. The electoral contest had resolved itself into a struggle between the Government and the Papineau Party,

[1] *L'Avenir*, December 28, 1849.
[2] *The Montreal Gazette*, January 30, 1850.

now reinforced by the English Annexationists, with
both of the contending parties urgently appealing for
the support of the independent electorate.

The Tories did not feel strong enough, or deem it
expedient, to put up a candidate of their own ; but they
held the balance of power, or at least appeared to do
so. They could crush or give a fillip to the annexation
movement. They had a splendid opportunity of
vindicating the reputation of the party for loyalty,
which had been so much aspersed by the recent proceedings of their political friends in Montreal. But
they missed the opportunity. Some of the ultra-
Tories resolved to defeat the Government at all costs.
The local leaders of the party, such as Munn and
Gilmour, ostensibly opposed any participation in the
annexation campaign, but they failed to take any
action to check the seditious efforts of many of their
fellow partisans. Of the Tory papers, *The Chronicle*
and *The Gazette* adopted a neutral attitude in the
contest, but *The Mercury* threw its influence on the
side of the annexation candidate.

The election proved a much greater victory for the
Government than even the most ardent Reformers had
expected ; for Mr. Chabot was returned by a majority
of about 800, almost double that of the general election
in 1848. Every ward in the city, and every poll but
one, gave a plurality to the Commissioner of Public
Works. The French-Canadian section of the city
polled an almost unanimous vote in favour of the
Government candidate. On the other hand, Mr. Legaré
ran slightly ahead of his opponent among the English-
speaking population.

A scrutiny of the ballots brought out the fact that a
considerable number of Tories followed *The Mercury's*
advice to vote against the Commissioner of Public
Works. Thanks to the efforts of John Maguire, the
Irish Reformers were kept in line, though the majority
of the Irish voters were captured by the appeals of
the Annexationists to their anti-English feelings. The

handful of Scotch electors, true to their Liberal traditions, voted as usual for the Reform candidate ; but
the majority of the English voters, who constituted a
much larger element of the electorate, cast their ballots
on the other side.   To the French-Canadians was due
the honour of vindicating the loyalty of the Canadian
people.   " The partisans of law and order," declared
L'Ami de la Religion, " have had to struggle against
the Annexationists, against those who possessing
nothing have nothing to lose, and against the intrigues
of certain Tories," who, in their hatred of the French,
were willing to join forces with the enemies of the
Queen.   The result of the contest, it concluded, marked
the triumph of the principles of a constitutional monarchy over the principles of republican institutions.

The splendid victory of Mr. Chabot tempted two of
the local Tory journals to forget their previous benevolent neutrality, and to claim a share in the triumph.
But they were not prepared to recognize the result as a
vindication of the Government.   The election, according to *The Gazette*, " could not be considered as an
approbation of the Ministry, but rather as a demonstration of public opinion against annexation."   Although not displeased at the defeat of the Annexationists, *The Chronicle* regretted that Legaré had not
been brought out as a straight opposition candidate, in
which case, it believed, the chances of his election
would have been much better.   On the other hand,
L'Avenir, though disappointed, was by no means
dejected over the result.   The defeat was due, in its
opinion, to the dominating influence of the priests over
the French population, and the liberal use of money by
the supporters of the Government.   It pointed with
pride to the poll of 1,200 votes for Mr. Legaré as conclusive evidence of the vitality of the annexation
cause.[1]

The validity of these various explanations was
naturally attacked by the ministerial journals.   They

[1] *L'Avenir*, February 12, 1850.

denied *in toto* that the return of Mr. Chabot was due either to corrupt or ecclesiastical influences, and ridiculed the contention that Legaré would have polled a larger number of French-Canadian votes as a Tory candidate. The election was, according to *Le Journal de Québec*, a triumph for the Government and the anti-Annexationists alike. As the question of annexation was made the dominant issue in the election, it claimed that it was but just to add to the loyalist vote the names of all those electors, who by the non-exercise of their right of franchise had declared in effect in favour of the maintenance of the existing British régime.[1]

The result of the election was a severe disappointment to the Montreal Annexationists, some of whom were inclined to indulge in captious criticism of the mode in which the election had been conducted.[2] Mr. Legaré, *The Courier* declared, was not a candidate of the party, and the association should never have recognized him as such. In case of a future vacancy in any constituency, it should be the duty of the Executive of the association to select or ratify a candidate, and then support him by all honourable means. *The Gazette* drew from the defeat the lesson of the necessity of unifying the forces of the opposition. It appealed to the British Annexationists to drop the question of annexation for the time being, and to join with their Conservative brethren and the progressive French party in overthrowing their common foe—the Reform Government. But the appeal was fruitless. The Annexationists determined to continue the struggle more aggressively, if possible, throughout the province.

In the Three Rivers District, the attempt of the

---

[1] *Le Journal de Québec*, January 31, 1850.

[2] The Montreal correspondent of *The New York Post* wrote: " Our party managed the affair very badly ; they should have been satisfied to know that Legaré was an annexationist in principle, but they should not have put him forward ostensibly on that ground ; had they not done so all the British party would have voted for him as against the Government."—*The New York Post*, February 15, 1850

Annexationists to obtain a favourable hearing resulted in failure. A meeting at St. François, Yamaska, which was regularly called by the local magistrate, at the instance of the Annexationists, unanimously adopted a resolution, " that this parish deems it its duty to declare publicly its determination to aid in maintaining the connection with Great Britain." *Le Journal des Trois Rivières*, the chief ministerial organ of the district, declared : " At first we did not think it necessary to oppose the movement, but now that the question has become a live one, it appears to us urgent, even indispensable, that there should be demonstrations and assemblies in all parts of the country against annexation." The French-Canadians, especially, should seize the occasion to disprove the reflections so often cast upon their loyalty by their opponents, and to show their appreciation of the rights which the Crown had granted them, and their fidelity to the flag which guaranteed those rights, and protected them.

In no part of the province outside of Montreal did the annexation movement meet with such favour as in the Eastern Townships, especially among the English population. As a small and isolated minority in the midst of a large French population, they were keenly sensitive of the danger of the political ascendency of an alien race, whose social and religious life was essentially different from their own. The sense of social isolation had produced a feeling of ultra-loyalty to the British Crown and British institutions. The passage of the Rebellion Losses Bill was looked upon as a personal humiliation and a base betrayal, since it dealt a severe blow to their superior prestige, and placed a premium upon the disloyalty of their political opponents. The action of the English Government was especially resented by the local Tories as an unjust return for their lifelong devotion to the Crown.

But the commercial factor, as we have seen, was even more powerful than the political grievance in developing the desire for annexation. The situation of the district along the American border necessarily produced a social intimacy and a close commercial connection with the neighbouring states. The fruitfulness of the soil and the energy of the people had won for the district an enviable reputation for comfort and prosperity. But the withdrawal of the English preference, and the closing of the American market, dealt a crushing blow to the local farmers. Through no fault of their own they were reduced from comparative affluence to poverty. They were the victims of artificial circumstances over which they had no control. Their hearts were filled with resentment and despair.

Thanks to these favourable conditions, the annexation movement spread like wildfire throughout the whole district. The County of Sherbrooke took the lead. A requisition was drawn up, and signed by over one thousand of the inhabitants, of all three nationalities,[1] endorsing the Montreal manifesto, and calling upon Mr. A. T. Galt, the local representative, for a public expression of his views. Much to the disappointment of the loyalists, who had counted upon his fidelity to the Crown,[2] Mr. Galt threw aside his former professions of loyalty, and came out boldly for annexation.

In a long and somewhat laboured letter, Mr. Galt set forth in the darkest colours the unfortunate political and economic conditions of the province, for which he held the colonial régime primarily responsible. The colonial status was admitted by English statesmen to be " one of tutelage merely," from which they would gladly release the people of Canada, when the latter so desired. " It will be a far nobler cause for pride in Great Britain to have educated such a vast nation in the proper enjoyment of freedom, than to possess for

---

[1] The list was said to contain the names of about seventy American citizens.

[2] *The Quebec Gazette* had prophesied that Mr. Galt would give his constituents some " good English advice."

ever the nominal control of the whole continent as discontented and suffering colonies." Canada, he argued, had reached a position where it " was essential for its advancement that it should be independent."

" To make Canada great, there must be opened to her inhabitants those elements of emulation and pride which will call forth all their energies ; the dissensions of her citizens must be terminated by abolishing distinctions of race ; they must be made to feel that they form part of one great country, and that its destinies are entrusted to their guidance. Were it possible for Canada to become an integral part of the British Empire, still, its position is such as to blend its interests more naturally with the United States and to make the former connection less desirable. But knowing as we do the Constitution of Great Britain, and the varied interests which govern its legislation, it is not a question of choice whether we shall be incorporated with Great Britain, or with the United States, but, shall we remain a dependency of the former, or become an integral part of the latter country ?

" The permanent interests of Canada, its present state, and its future prospects all point to the adoption of annexation ; and unless it be the case, contrary to my belief, that we now possess all the means of development as a people that are essential for prosperity, we may expect to see the country languish, and latent discontent ever on the eve of breaking out, until our independence be acknowledged. A union with the United States will give Canada a place among nations ; the accumulated wisdom of their legislators will become our own ; we shall share in the triumph of their unparalleled progress ; we shall reap the fruits of that political skill which has thus far shielded their institutions from harm ; our interests will be watched over, and our industry protected and encouraged, by their wise commercial policy ; and, although no longer dependent on Great Britain, we shall feel that we have served her well in ensuring that harmony between the two countries which is now constantly in peril from conflicting interests."

In reply to the arguments of the British connectionists to the effect that annexation would increase the burden of taxation of the province, and despoil it of its public works and public lands, he contended that annexation would reduce the cost of living, and relieve the colony of its public debt and the expense of administering its public lands, and entitle it to a share of the public works and increasing revenue of the United States. In conclusion, he pointed out that " the safety of the country " demanded " that the legislature should direct the movement." No local agitation or sectional demand could exert any influence on the English Government.

In virtue of his superior ability, personal integrity, and business connection, as managing director of the British American Land Association, which owned extensive holdings throughout the district, Mr. Galt was probably the most influential man in the Eastern Townships. His open avowal of annexation convictions carried great weight with the general public, and especially with the tenants of the company and the commercial class ; moreover, the sound and substantial arguments he advanced in favour of annexation were calculated to appeal with telling force to the business instincts of the people.

The accession of Mr. Galt encouraged the Montreal association to press forward its campaign among the agriculturists of the district. Public meetings were called wherever a small band of sympathizers could be gathered together. Speakers were sent out from headquarters to canvass the community, address public gatherings, and organize local associations. To the Hon. Robert Jones and Mr. Charles Laberge was committed the mission of spreading the doctrines of annexation among their fellow countrymen. The agents were wisely chosen. The Hon. Robert Jones was a popular member of the Legislative Council, who enjoyed more than a local reputation on the hustings, while his colleague was an active worker in the Papineau Party, and a successful public speaker. The task of Mr. Laberge proved the more difficult undertaking, for the French habitants were much less favourably inclined towards the new ideas than their more progressive English neighbours.

The campaign started off auspiciously. As the result of a series of successful meetings, local associations were formed at Durham, St. George d'Henryville,[1] St. Athanase,[2] Bedford,[3] and Clarenceville.[4] At all these various gatherings resolutions of the same general order were adopted : (1) approving of the Montreal manifesto ; (2) pledging the support of the meeting to such candidates only as were avowed Annexationists ; (3) charging the deplorable condition of the province to its colonial status, and alleging, in effect, that it would be more advantageous to England to have a prosperous ally than a ruined colony ; (4) declaring that legal means should be adopted to obtain the consent of the English Government to a peaceful separation and annexation to the United States ; and (5) affiliating the local branch with the Montreal association. The commercial condition of the province received special consideration at the Clarenceville meeting. Additional resolutions were there adopted declaring : (1) "That their sentiments of respect and filial affection towards Great Britain remained unchanged," but that the reversal of the commercial policy of the empire forced them "to seek to ameliorate their social, political, and commercial condition by a peaceful separation from the motherland, and by annexation to the United States"; (2) That by annexation Canadian products would gain free entry into the American market, which would

---

[1] *L'Avenir*, November 27, 1849.
[2] December 5, 1849.
[3] The meetings at Bedford and Clarenceville were held in response to local requisitions. At the latter place the call was signed by over two hundred persons (*L'Avenir*, December 28, 1849).
[4] December 22, 1849.

more than compensate for the loss of the English preference; and (3) That the existing condition of colonial
dependence upon English manufactures was injurious
to the progress of mechanical arts in the province.

At all these meetings the chief interest in the proceedings was manifested by members of the English
community. They were chiefly instrumental in the
organization of the local associations, and, in the
majority of cases, all the officers and members of
the committees were of the English race; even in
the branches in which the French were represented
on the directorate, they played but a subordinate part
in the conduct of affairs. The two races refused to
amalgamate; even the common commercial interests
of the two nationalities were not sufficiently strong to
overcome the inherited suspicion of the French population on the one hand, and the feeling of superiority
of the English on the other.

But not all the annexation meetings met with the
same measure of success. In some instances the
attempt to form local associations turned out to be
complete failures,[1] owing either to the small attendance,
or to the unfriendly attitude of the audience. But, as
a general rule, the loyalists of the Eastern Townships
offered but little opposition to the annexation propaganda. Save for a few loyal addresses from the
officers of several French-Canadian battalions, and a
declaration of loyalty from the Tories of Melbourne,
the Annexationists had matters their own way. For
a time it appeared as though they had swept the
district.

The Annexationists of the County of Stanstead soon
followed the example of their friends in Sherbrooke and
drew up a requisition calling upon Mr. McConnell to
declare his views in regard to annexation. The plan
again worked successfully, both in securing the signatures of a large number of the leading residents of the
Riding, and in eliciting a favourable response from the

---

[1] At Hinchinbrook, Belle Rivière, and Stanstead.

local member. In an open reply to the requisition, McConnell declared : [1]

"I have given it my utmost attention, and, after due consideration, do not hesitate to avow—deeply feeling the responsibility which I hereby incur—that I desire (to quote the words of the Montreal Address) a friendly and peaceful separation from the British connection, and a union upon equitable terms with the North American confederation of sovereign states.

"The first and principal reason arises from the present state of the country and our destitution of any adequate means to effect these changes and improvements which the interests of the country imperatively demand."

He severely criticized the policies of both political parties in Canada, and particularly condemned the change of fiscal policy in the motherland. Since England had revolutionized her colonial policy, it was useless to look to her for help. "Our interests and theirs are totally incompatible."

"While the political bonds which cement us to England are dissolving by the mere action of circumstances, those ties which are eventually to link us to the great confederation of our neighbours, are becoming more and more apparent." Throughout half the year the ports of the St. Lawrence were closed, and the inhabitants of the province were dependent upon the favour of the United States for the importation of American and other foreign goods. In case of the importation of European articles, the Canadian merchant and consumer found himself subjected to the payment of double duties, those imposed by the American tariff, and those collected under the Canadian Customs Act. At the same time, a high tariff was set up by the United States against Canadian products, while American goods were admitted into the English market upon equal terms with colonial products.

[1] January 1, 1850. Copy of letter, *Montreal Gazette*, January 14, 1850.

Under these discriminatory conditions, it was impossible for the Canadian merchant and producer to compete with his favoured American neighbours. The remedy, he concluded, was not to be found, either in a return to the policy of an imperial preference, or in the adoption of a reciprocity agreement with the United States, as was proposed in certain quarters, but in annexation. It was no longer considered disloyal to advocate a separation from Great Britain, and he was prepared to debate the question upon the floor of the House.[1]

With the advent of the New Year, the annexation campaign was pushed forward with renewed vigour. A grand rally was held at St. Athanase in Rouville County, at which about a thousand persons were present. A deputation from the Montreal Association went down to take part in the proceedings.[2] Additional interest was lent to the gathering by the presence of Dr. Davignon, the local member, and a body of personal friends and supporters. The action of the Doctor in signing the protest of the members of the Legislature against annexation had already called forth a vote of censure from some of his constituents,[3] and it was anticipated that on this occasion another attempt would be made to condemn his pro-British stand. The mayor occupied the chair. Messrs. Jones and Laberge were the principal speakers. The latter declared that the meeting had been convoked for two different purposes : first, to consider if annexation were advan-

---

[1] In a series of articles in reply to the letters of Galt and McConnell, " An Englishman " set forth the following objections to annexation : (1) That peaceful separation was impossible ; (2) That England would not agree to dismember the empire ; (3) That separation would entail a long civil war ; (4) That annexation would only aggravate racial difficulties ; (5) That the withdrawal of the British troops would throw the cost of defence and maintaining civil order upon the local revenue ; (6) That annexation would be expensive to all classes of the community ; (7) That England would grant elective institutions for the asking ; (8) That Canadians should create subordinate machinery of government and learn to run it before venturing to alter the constitution.

[2] Including Messrs. Jones, Laberge, Penny and Papin.

[3] Resolution of meeting at St. George d'Henryville.

tageous, and if so, how to obtain it; and second, to give Dr. Davignon an opportunity to explain his position.

By way of introduction, he described at some length the nature and workings of the United States Constitution, and then appealed to the audience to determine whether it would not be better for the Canadian people to elect their own Governor, rather than to have one selected for them by a distant sovereign who was ignorant of the needs of the country. He severely criticized the high salary of the Governor-General as compared with that of the Governors of the American States, and in conclusion emphasized the social, political, and commercial advantages which would result from annexation. An opportunity was given Dr. Davignon to speak, of which he gladly availed himself. The annexation movement, he pointed out for the benefit of his compatriots, had originated with the Tory Party, and had taken on a distinctly anti-French character. He denied the right of the Mayor to convoke such an assembly merely on the ground that the County was said to favour annexation. Not only was the County not in favour of it, but even in those parishes where meetings had been held a majority of the inhabitants were opposed to it. Moreover, he contended that the persons in whom the people had most confidence were in no way connected with the movement.[1]

At this point, the audience became so unruly that Dr. Davignon was forced to sit down, and he and his friends withdrew from the meeting.[2] After this purging of the assembly, the Annexationists proceeded to pass a series of resolutions, censuring the local member,

---

[1] Mr. Laberge alleged that Dr. Davignon stated in his speech that MacNab was the leader of the annexation party, and that W. Molson had declared that the object of the association was to crush the French-Canadians.

[2] *L'Avenir* reported that two-thirds of the audience remained. *La Minerve* alleged that the anti-Annexationists formed the more respectable part of the audience, and that the majority of the Annexationists were Tories. Both of these statements, however, were denied by *L'Avenir*.

attributing the depression of trade to their colonial status and the free-trade policy of England, and declaring that a peaceful separation was necessary to promote the mutual good and prosperity of Canada and the parent state. The people of Canada, according to the third resolution, could rely upon England's sense of justice to grant them independence. The destiny of the colony, when once independent, was to become an integral part of the United States. Annexation would assure to them all the advantages without the expense of independence ; it would furnish a market for their products, develop a national industry, set up a new and democratic form of government, enable them to take a leading part among the nations of the world, open up to Canadian ambition a worthy field of opportunity, now unfortunately closed, guarantee the maintenance of an established social order—" the first consideration to the prosperity of a people "—promote a simple, prompt, and less costly system of administration, and, as a consequence, introduce immigration and capital into the country to develop its vast resources.[1] From the standpoint of the Annexationists, the meeting was a great success. Dr. Davignon, according to the Montreal correspondent of *The New York Post*, was in a hopeless minority at the assembly, and stood no chance whatever of being returned to Parliament at the next election.[2]

At the same time the loyalist friends of the local member, made up of a few English gentlemen and a considerable number of the local seigneurs, organized an independent meeting under the chairmanship of Major Campbell,[3] at which resolutions were adopted, refusing to join in the annexation movement, the only result of which would necessarily be " to introduce fresh miseries " into the country.

The following day, several magistrates and militia

[1] *L'Avenir*, January 25, 1850.
[2] *The New York Post*, February 1, 1850.
[3] The Major was not a resident of the parish.

officers, all but two of whom were of English descent, addressed an open letter to the Provincial Secretary in which they asserted that they possessed a constitutional right to discuss the actual state of the country, and to take measures to improve its present sorry condition by peaceful means. They not only expressed approval of the Montreal manifesto, but boasted of the part they had taken in supporting that address. As a mark of their appreciation of the labours and sacrifices of the fathers of the movement, they tendered the resignation of their respective offices. They were unwilling, they declared, to retain their positions, when so many of their fellow Annexationists had been peremptorily dismissed from the public service as unworthy to hold any office of honour or profit under the Crown.[1]

The movement rapidly spread to the neighbouring counties. A visit of the Hon. R. Jones to the County of Missisquoi led to the organization of a branch association at St. Armond, all the officers of which were of the Anglo-Saxon race.[2] In addition to the usual resolutions, approving of the manifesto, and deploring the political and commercial ills of the country, a resolution was adopted condemning in strong terms the prescription of freedom of speech in the dismissal of many officials against whom no charge was laid save in respect to their political opinions in favour of annexation. The striking similarity of the resolutions of the various annexation meetings afforded good ground for the allegation that they were previously prepared by the Montreal association, and accepted in due course by the various audiences, without pretence of careful consideration.[3] The whole campaign in the Eastern Townships was, it was claimed, not spontaneous in origin or character, but was directed from headquarters in Montreal.

[1] *The Mirror*, February 1, 1850.
[2] *L'Avenir*, February 15, 1850.
[3] *The Pilot*, January 26, 1850.

In the County of Huntingdon, a requisition was drawn up, and signed by about a hundred persons, mainly of French extraction, calling for a meeting at St. Edouard, to discuss the question of annexation.[1] An invitation was extended to Papineau, Holmes, De Witt, and other leading Annexationists of Montreal, as also to Dr. Savageau, the local Liberal member, to be present, and take part in the proceedings. Notwithstanding the active opposition of several of the local French clergy, who solemnly warned their congregations from the pulpit against having anything to do with the annexation movement, a large audience of about five hundred persons responded to the call. Letters were read from Messrs. Papineau, Papin, and others expressing their regret at being unable to attend.

In his communication, Papineau declared that at first the Government was of the opinion that the manifesto was a passing ebullition of a small minority of the citizens of Montreal, and that the movement could be easily snuffed out by the use of the prerogative ; but the Ministry had since had occasion to modify that opinion. The manifesto was not a mere temporary outburst of feeling, but an expression of the sober second thought of the general public. The movement was no longer confined to Montreal and some of the Eastern Counties, but was rapidly winning its way throughout the whole province. Not only had a majority of the Montreal papers come out in favour of annexation, but the circulation of these papers had greatly increased at the expense of the ministerial press. He was especially pleased at the demand for annexation from his British fellow citizens, since their influence would have more weight with the English Government than the petitions and protests of an equal number of French-Canadians. The overwhelming strength of the Ministry in the Legislature was no criterion of their strength at the polls, and he was convinced that at the next election a majority of the

[1] January 28, 1850.

electorate in both Upper and Lower Canada would declare for annexation. The recent addresses of their French compatriots in the United States afforded them the most convincing proof of the commercial advantages of annexation. Their fellow countrymen had prospered under the free institutions of the great republic, and why should they not share in the same advantages, when they were invited so to do by their own brethren ? The earnest appeals and representations of their compatriots could not fail to carry conviction to any honest heart.

Now was the time, he concluded, to press forward the demand for separation, since the greater part of the English press sympathized with the aspirations of the colonies for independence. The reply of Mr. Papin admirably epitomized the ideals of the Rouge Party in regard to annexation. The cause of annexation, he declared in an outburst of republican enthusiasm, " is none other than the cause of progress, civilization, education, democracy, and liberty."

The meeting was one of the most successful in the Eastern Townships in respect to both numbers and enthusiasm. Several of the leading local magistrates and officers of militia occupied seats upon the platform, and the speeches of the representatives of both nationalities were of an unusually high order.[1] Mr. Lanctot, an exile of 1837, stated that, although he had always believed that annexation would be advantageous to Canada, and that the sooner it was accomplished the better it would be for her, nevertheless declared that, if it should require force for its attainment, he would be one of the first to oppose it. He was convinced, however, that forcible measures would be unnecessary ; for, now that the English people had attained the boon of free trade, they would the more readily grant liberty and independence to the colonies.

The speech of Mr. Dorion set forth in glowing colours the contrast between the political and commercial

[1] Messrs. Jones and De Witt were the chief English speakers.

advantages of annexation on the one hand and the degradation of the colonial status on the other. The Act of Union had inflicted a heavy civil list upon the province, altogether out of proportion to the administrative expenses of the American states. He condemned the colonial principle of a nominated English Governor, as incompatible with the democratic spirit of the time. Since the loss of the colonial preference, there were no longer commercial reasons for maintaining the imperial connection. The superior transportation facilities of the United States placed the Canadian producers at a decided disadvantage in competing in the English market. The farmers of the province were now forced to seek in the United States a new market for their products ; but unfortunately that market was closed by a high tariff wall, and the recent message of the President had recommended that the duties on agricultural products should be still further increased. Annexation alone would ensure to them an open market, and a higher price for their products. But there was a further reason of a religious character for desiring annexation. The system of ecclesiastical tithes was subjected to especial criticism.

So long as Canada maintained her colonial status, there was no hope, Mr. Dorion concluded, of securing the abolition of that unjust burden upon the piety of the people, or of obtaining the redress of their many other grievances of a similar character. The attack upon the clergy was carried even further by the following speaker, Mr. Lanctot of Laprairie. The habitants, he asserted, were suffering from the burden of tithes, the oppression of the seignorial system, and the woeful lack of educational facilities. They were in a humiliating state of backwardness as compared with their American neighbours.

To the minds of the young French Radicals the only hope of freeing their countrymen from the ascendency of the Church lay in annexation to the United States. The progressive democracy of the great republic had

freed their fellow countrymen who had taken up their
residence across the lines, and it was believed that
those same influences would sweep away the anachron-
ism of a religious establishment and an European feudal
system, which still lingered on in Quebec.

Notwithstanding the opposition of M. Caissé, *curé* of
St. Jacques le Mineur, and a couple of his friends, the
several resolutions were carried by overwhelming
majorities, not more than a dozen voting against them.
The resolutions embodied an interesting combination
of the principles of the manifesto and the tenets of the
Rouge Party.[1] To the customary articles deploring
the serious condition of the country, commending the
Montreal address, censuring the action of the Ministry
in dismissing the annexation officials, and appealing
for a generous union of the English and French popu-
lations to promote their common interests, there were
added several new resolutions of different tenor, expressing approval of the great moral benefits which
would result from elective institutions, demanding the
abolition of the tithing system and seignorial tenure,
and calling for the payment of jurors. Pleasure was
expressed that Mr. Savageau had not signed the
Legislative protest against annexation. He was requested, however, to make known his views upon the
question, and in case his opinion was unfavourable, to
hand in his resignation.

The temerity of the Annexationists, in calling upon
the local member to declare for annexation, roused
the loyalists of the Riding to action. An address to
Mr. Savageau was drawn up, and signed by over 1,200
persons, including many of the magistrates, militia
officers, and other prominent citizens of the county,
stating that as, in their judgment, the great majority of
the electors were opposed to annexation, they sincerely
hoped that he would not comply with the demand of
the Annexationists, but would retain his seat. In
conclusion, they protested strongly against the in-

[1] January 28, 1850.

temperate and inconsiderate agitation of the Annexationists. Mr. Savageau declared in reply that the address was the best proof that the country was opposed to annexation.

It was most inopportune, in his opinion, to start their agitation at the very moment when England had handed over to them the management of their own affairs. They should seek to perfect the existing Constitution, rather than to agitate for the uncertain advantage of a political union with the United States. Moreover, the attitude of the English Government was not such as to warrant the pretension that the colonies would be willingly surrendered. The only effect of continuing the agitation would be to create a division in the ranks of the Liberal Party, before their political leaders had had an opportunity of giving the new Constitution a fair trial. The commercial outlook of the province was growing brighter. A reciprocity agreement for the admission of Canadian products into the United States would soon be secured, and the repeal of the Navigation Laws would further tend to stimulate trade. The remaining social and political advantages which the Annexationists held out could be secured equally well by Canadian efforts and through their own institutions. The primary duty of the moment was to rid the country of some of the existing burdens and difficulties; then perhaps at some future time, when the colony had developed into a mighty state, some of the advantages of annexation which were not to be found in the existing circumstances might be made manifest.[1]

---

[1] *La Minerve*, February 25, 1850.

CHAPTER V

THE MOVEMENT IN UPPER CANADA

IN Upper Canada, the manifesto awakened the keenest interest, but met with almost universal condemnation ; only here and there were found a few disaffected spirits bold enough publicly to defend or avow its principles. Upon receipt of the address in Toronto, the loyalists of the city at once took steps to repudiate any sympathy with the annexation movement. Some such action, it was felt, would be highly desirable in view of the false con-

ceptions which unfortunately had won general acceptance in both England and the United States, that
the Canadian people were ready for annexation. As the
prevalence of this misconception was impairing the
credit of the country, there was the greater reason for
presenting to the world the clearest evidence of the
weakness of annexation sentiment, and the strength of
loyalist feeling in the commercial centre of Upper
Canada. A requisition for a public meeting in support
of the British connection was quickly circulated, and
signed by a large number of citizens.[1] At a small
private caucus, attended by leading members of both
political parties, a declaration of protest against
annexation was drawn up and adopted, and a committee appointed to secure signatures to the same.[2]
The declaration ran as follows :

" We, the undersigned inhabitants of the City of
Toronto and the Home District, having learned from
the public press that a document has been circulated
for signatures in the City of Montreal advocating the
annexation of Her Majesty's Province of Canada to
a foreign state, desire, without reference to local or
provincial politics, to record our solemn protest against
any such proceeding—to deny emphatically the truth
of many of the statements on which that document is
based, especially that which asserts the general depression of the province, which we believe to be grossly
exaggerated, if not exclusively applicable to Montreal
—to declare our unwavering attachment to our connection with Great Britain—the high value we place
upon our position as British subjects, and our firm
determination to resist all attempts at trifling with our
allegiance, or transferring us from the mild and just
rule of our Gracious Sovereign to the United States of
America or any other foreign state."

When the committee began to circulate this petition,

---

[1] *The Globe*, October 16, 1849.
[2] Mr. W. B. Jarvis was chairman and A. Morrison secretary of
the meeting.

they at once experienced difficulty in securing signatures, owing to the objection of many of the citizens to those clauses of the address which minimized the existence of widespread commercial depression, and praised the just and beneficent character of English rule. Many staunch supporters of the British connection, especially among the Conservatives, absolutely refused to sign the declaration in that form, while others attached their signatures under protest, and only for the purpose of asserting their loyalty.

Prominent among those who refused to sign the address, on account of its objectionable language, was the local Conservative member, Mr. W. H. Boulton. As soon as his decision became known, he was immediately called upon by four of his most prominent constituents, including J. Hillyard Cameron and J. Hagarty, to make a public statement of his views on annexation. In complying with this request, Mr. Boulton explained that his attitude was due solely to his objection to the phrasing of the address, and not to its object. He " utterly condemned " the course of the Montreal Annexationists, and proclaimed his " unswerving attachment to the British connection." But, nevertheless, he proceeded to attack the fiscal policy of Great Britain, which was responsible for the existing depression, because it placed the agriculturists of Canada at a serious disadvantage in competing with their American neighbours. There were, in his opinion, but three possible remedies for the country's ills : first, reciprocal free trade with the United States ; second, a protective tariff ; third, the abolition of all import duties and shipping charges. The last of these three policies would, he believed, prove most advantageous to the interests of Canada.[1]

To meet these objections to the form of the declaration, another meeting of the committee was called, at which it was determined to issue a revised address, which would, it was hoped, prove acceptable to the

[1] *The Colonist*, October 26, 1849.

whole body of loyalists. The amended address read as follows : [1]

" We, the undersigned inhabitants of the City of Toronto and the Home District, in allegiance to Her Majesty, Queen Victoria, do hereby solemnly protest against a movement recently made in the City of Montreal, for the annexation of the province to the United States of America.

" However great may have been the depression, commercial or otherwise, under which the province has laboured, and however much mistaken or injurious the policy and conduct which the mother country has pursued toward us, we still unhesitatingly declare that there is nothing in what has occurred, or now exists, to warrant an attempt so revolutionary in its character, and so repugnant to our feelings, as that which seeks the dismemberment of the glorious empire of Great Britain, by transferring this colony to a foreign power.

" Confident in our resources and energies, and still relying on the will and ability of England to do us justice, we have no desire to seek any remedy for political or commercial evils by other than constitutional means."

The judgment of the committee was confirmed by the hearty enthusiasm with which all classes of citizens came forward to sign the new declaration, copies of which were placed in the banks and prominent business-houses, for public subscription. Liberals and Conservatives joined hands in the common cause, notwithstanding the efforts of a section of the ultra-Conservatives to prevent united action. At the head of the list were enrolled the names of the chief municipal officials, the local parliamentary representatives, the members of the judiciary, and the most prominent merchants and professional men of the City. In the list of signatures are to be found the names of the Hon. Robert Baldwin, Chief Justice Robinson, Mr. Justice Sullivan, the Hon. Chancellors Blake and Jamieson, three members

[1] *The Colonist*, October 30, 1849.

of the Legislative Council, Gordon, Allan, and Widmer, and four of the Lower Chamber, John H. Cameron, W. B. Robinson, Henry Sherwood, and J. C. Morrison. So great was the zeal of the committee, that several of the members put aside their private business in order to attend to the matter in hand. Signatures poured in rapidly.[1] At the end of the first day, 500 names were appended; on October 25, 1,500 were reported; by November 13, the number had risen to 3,600; and by the 20th of the month, a grand total of 4,447 was attained.[2] The verdict of Toronto was clear and overwhelming in its repudiation of annexation.

The majority of the city papers were equally emphatic in condemning the action of the Montreal malcontents. Although strongly holding to the view that the maladministration of the Government was responsible for the growth of annexation sentiment, *The Patriot* warned its readers against encouraging the movement in any way.[3] Annexation, it contended, would not save the people of the province from the evils of low prices, French domination and Liberal tyranny. It called upon all branches of the League in Upper Canada to take prompt action to prevent the spread of the agitation. They should not allow their disgust with the Baldwin Ministry to lead them into an attitude of hostility to the British connection. There was the greater reason for maintaining their loyalty, since the English Government had repeatedly asserted that, so far from desiring to cast off the colonies, it was most anxious to retain them. It was the duty of the Tory

---

[1] *The Patriot* declared, however, that it could only account for the slowness with which signatures were received by the fact " that it is difficult to induce men to tolerate as allies those whose past actions and principles they hold in abhorrence." It was of the opinion that a separate party declaration should have been made by the Tories.

[2] The first sheet of 200 names was stolen.

[3] *The Patriot* of October 12, 1849, contained a very uncomplimentary article on the condition of Canada as compared with the United States.

Party to stand fast to its political principles, until they were vindicated at the next general elections, for there was little doubt that the disgusted public would take the first opportunity of hurling the existing administration from office, and of restoring to power those leaders who were truly representative of loyal British feeling.

In a subsequent editorial it discussed at length the various arguments of the Montreal manifesto. The manufacturing interests of the province, it contended, could be promoted as well by a Canadian as by an American protective tariff. It further maintained that the rapid increase of the public debts and expenditures of the United States would involve a heavier burden of taxation on the people of Canada in case of union ; that the American judiciary and magistracy were both poorly paid and inefficient ; that the price of foodstuffs was fixed by English quotations, and was not dependent on the American market ; that by means of the bonding privilege the farmers and merchants of Canada were placed upon an equality with their neighbours across the line ; that agriculture in Upper Canada was superior to that of any part of the United States ; that American capital was so fully employed in American industries that it would not seek investment away from home ; that the slavery issue would inevitably disrupt the American union ; that the general moral tone of society in the United States was greatly inferior to that in Canada ; and finally, that the proceedings of Congress were no less disgraceful than those of the Provincial Legislature.[1]

The Colonist greeted the Montreal manifesto with a cry of anguish : " The discussion of annexation is wormwood and gall to us." Montreal, it asserted, was not the Paris of Canada, and could not dictate the political feeling of the country ; she had yet to convert the people of Upper Canada to the new political faith. Neither should she forget that, although the minds of

[1] *The Patriot*, January 19, 1850.

the public might be won by reason, they would never be changed by violence.   Montreal, it averred, was subject to great fluctuations of opinion, of which the manifesto was only a fleeting and whimsical expression ; in time the old feeling of loyalty would again return with full force.   But *The Colonist* soon recovered its mental equilibrium, and prepared to consider the address in a fair and reasonable manner.   The manifesto, it assured its readers, " will perhaps prove after all not so terrible an affair as it seems at first.   But no acquaintance can reconcile us to the deformity of some of its features."   The address, it continued, " is not consistent with itself, though it may suit well the heterogeneous catalogue of signatures appended.   It contains statements irrefragably true, mixed with others wildly erroneous, and the latter kind we believe largely to predominate.   There seems to be so much variety in the reasoning, as if it were to give to every signer the chance of a consistent ground for his consent. The main facts to be gathered from the proceeding are that Montreal is suffering in all its interests an unparalleled and hopeless depression such as to make almost desperate chances desirable ; and that endurance has disappeared, since loyalty, its best support, was so roughly handled of late."   Much of the reasoning of the manifesto was, *The Colonist* contended, not only inconsequential, but implied a precipitation of passion which was far removed from the annexationist professions of equanimity and goodwill.   But the public would not be deceived by mere verbal representations, when the actions of the Annexationists were so much at variance with their peaceful protestations.[1]   The manifesto had undoubtedly awakened much excitement among all classes of the population ; but, according to present appearances, it would not gain much support among the people of Upper Canada ; for, in the judgment of the latter, " the remedy is far worse than the disease."

[1] *The Colonist*, October 16, 1849.

Towards the signers of the address, *The Colonist* urged that only the most temperate language should be used, since in the existing intensity of feeling any undue excess of passion would promote, rather than check, the spread of the annexation movement.[1] The folly of the Montreal agitators might in the end prove beneficial to the country in more than one way, especially by revealing to the Canadian people the real identity of the policies of independence and annexation, and by arousing the people of England to a realization of the danger of the Whig policy of dismembering the empire. Under the guise of granting independence to this colony, the Cobdenites were, in fact, handing it over to the United States.[2]

The appearance of the manifesto aroused the fighting spirit of *The Globe.* It was not content to oppose the annexation movement by merely defensive measures, such as the organization of protest demonstrations, and the adoption of resolutions of loyalty; it called upon the Government to dismiss peremptorily every official, Reform or Tory, who had signed the Montreal address.[3] But it did not rely on coercion alone to stop the movement; for, at the same time, it appealed to the judgment of the public by publishing a series of articles dealing seriatim with the claims and pretensions of the Annexationists.

It appealed to the chivalry of the Canadian people; it pleaded with them not to be guilty of the base ingratitude of demanding separation at the very moment when England had so generously granted to the colony

[1] *The Colonist*, October 23, 1849.
[2] At the same time there was running in *The Colonist* a series of articles by " Agricola " strongly supporting a protective policy, and warning the people against annexation. There seemed in the opinion of the writer " to be little self-reliance amongst the advocates of annexation; having lost their old nurse, they would fain have the leading-strings handed over to the United States." Annexation and reciprocity would merely open the Canadian market for American exploitation. Canada, he concluded, should develop an independent fiscal policy of her own.
[3] *The Globe*, October 20, 1849.

the most liberal form of government; it denied *in toto* " that there are in this country any symptoms of rapid decay, or of slow decay either, except in Montreal, or that the withdrawal of protection by the home Government, accompanied as it has been by complete commercial freedom, is at all likely to be permanently injurious to us "; it refuted the allegations with regard to the financial embarrassment of the Provincial Government and the various civic corporations. The depression in Montreal, it contended, was local, the result of changing economic conditions, by which that city was losing its grip upon the import and wholesale trade of the province. It specifically denied that the real estate market in Canada was worse than in the similarly situated, newly developed regions of the United States, or that the circulating capital of the country was becoming less, or that the banks were not in a sound and prosperous condition; it claimed, on the contrary, that the credit of the Canadian Government was superior to that of the American States, as was evidenced by a lower rate of interest upon its funded debt.

It ardently maintained that, since 1783, Great Britain had done more for the civilization of the world than the boastful democracy of the United States, and it denounced the policy of the latter in abetting the slave trade at the very time when England was exerting all her energies to suppress the iniquitous traffic in human souls. It countered the contention that Canada was devoid of manufacturing industries, by pointing out that the absence of manufacturing was due to the more profitable employment of capital in agricultural and other pursuits; a similar deficiency of railroads in Canada, as compared with the United States, was due to the superior means of water transportation which Providence had bestowed upon the province. It questioned the validity of the argument that a free entry into the American market was essential to the prosperity of the Canadian farmer, since the price of agricultural products, especially corn, was determined for the agriculturists of both countries by the quotations of the English market.

But no part of the argument of *The Globe* was so skilfully handled as its reply to the favourite contention of the Annexationists, viz. that the colonies could not permanently remain under the British flag. The grant of colonial autonomy, it pointed out, had effected a political and constitutional revolution in the organization of the empire by which Canada and the other self-governing colonies would be enabled to work out their own political destinies within the empire, as integral and independent members of the group of sister federated states. In short, on political, ethical, and economic grounds, annexation would prove injurious to the best interests of Canada.[1]

In a critical view of the political situation, *The Examiner* stated that the most striking effect of the manifesto upon the public mind was the absence of the usual violence of temper with which the question had been previously discussed. This spirit of moderation was undoubtedly due, in part, to the temperate tone of the manifesto, which avoided an appeal to the passions of any section of the public. Notwithstanding the efforts of Baldwin to stop the spread of annexation sentiment within the Reform Party, the movement threatened to disrupt existing party ties, and might even lead to a fusion or recasting of the various political factions throughout the province, such as had apparently taken place in Montreal, where the force of annexation sentiment had proved sufficiently powerful to triumph over the blind passions and the partisan and racial rivalries which had distracted the inhabitants of that city for many years past. It was a difficult matter for the Government to deal with the agitation. The Annexationists had appealed to reason and not to

[1] *The Globe*, October 20, 23, 24, etc., 1849. On November 17 *The Globe* contained a satirical parallel between the American Declaration of Independence and the manifesto of " John Redpath & Co."

force ; they could not be cast into prison, nor be denied the constitutional right of petition. The suggested dismissal of all annexation officials, however much deserved, would not prevent the spread of annexation views ; it might, on the contrary, promote the very object it was designed to checkmate, by arousing a feeling of sympathy towards the victims of the Government's displeasure.

As a public document, the manifesto, in the opinion of *The Examiner*, was open to grave criticism. It did not cover the whole case. "It was a programme rather than an argument." The assumed advantages of annexation were drawn in glowing colours, but no attempt was made to develop a plan of separation. The moment that this was attempted, great practical difficulties would be discovered. The English Government could not deal with a petition of a minority without violating constitutional principles. The Annexationists could not make any real advance, until they had converted the majority of the Canadian electorate to their opinion. And, even in the latter case, the difficulties of the Annexationists might be more serious than ever ; for if England should refuse to accede to the demand for separation, which was not improbable, a continuance of the agitation would inevitably lead to a political revolution.

Nor had the Annexationists afforded any information in regard to the terms on which separation should take place. For example, what arrangements were to be made in regard to the imperial guarantee of the provincial debt, the Crown lands of the province, the surrender of the right of fiscal legislation, and the repayment of the expenditures of the British Government upon the public works of the province ? To the commercial and material conditions of the colony was traceable " the accelerating causes and the continuance of the annexation movement." An outburst of disappointed partisan passion had awakened the agitation ; " the continued denial of reciprocity by the

Americans was likely to keep it alive." The primary question of the day was how to secure reciprocity in the face of the selfish policy of the United States. If it could not be won by persuasion, it might possibly be obtained by coercion, by inducing the British Government to place countervailing duties on American products equal to those which the United States imposed on Canadian produce.[1]

In reviewing the situation one week later, *The Examiner* declared that the annexation movement was making no perceptible progress. The Montreal manifesto had met with greater condemnation than praise ; the onslaught upon it had been vigorous, the defence but feeble. It was evident that annexation feeling was but half formed, and needed time to gain strength and marshal its forces. In Upper Canada, it was " as yet without courage to give it voice and utterance " ; it was timid and non-committal, or covered itself under a simulated reverence for the motherland. On the other hand, the loyalists, according to *The Examiner*, expressed a more ardent affection for the Crown than they really " believed or felt."

The Montreal manifesto, by reducing the question of annexation to a mere matter of dollars and cents, and by appealing to no higher passion than self-interest, was not calculated to produce an electrical effect. It came as a surprise to the public ; and, as a result, awakened a bewildering medley of curiosity and excitement. The proposal was too far-reaching to be quickly or readily understood. The convictions of the people could not be changed in a day ; nor would their ancient loyalty yield to anything short of overwhelming argument. " The manifesto proved nothing, changed nothing ; all it did was to open the question, and this it did unskilfully. It made no converts. It brought out parties who were already convinced, and thus formed the nucleus of a party." Moreover, the Canadian public should not forget that political con-

---

[1] *The Examiner*, October 24, 1849.

ditions in the United States " would tend to keep the question of annexation of any more territory, North or South, in abeyance for some time," since any attempt to bring about the annexation of Canada would disturb the balance of power in Congress, and stir up the slave-holding states to demand a dissolution of the Union.

The state of English public opinion was likewise uncertain. Some definite knowledge of British sentiment was a necessary condition precedent to an intelligent discussion of the complicated issues involved in a change of allegiance; but, as yet, neither the Cabinet nor the press had expressed an opinion on the question of separation or annexation; and until some official statement was forthcoming as to the attitude of the Government, it was premature and foolish for the Annexationists or the public to seek to determine the political future of the colony. The provincial Government was placed in a delicate situation. A sentiment favourable to annexation was spreading throughout the province in spite of the measures of the Government, but *The Examiner* was firmly convinced that the adoption of a wise and well-considered commercial policy "would do much to calm the storm." [1]

The Mirror, a Radical Irish Catholic organ, greeted the manifesto with cordial interest. It boasted that it was the first journal in Canada honest enough to announce that the annexation movement was a fact, not a mere speculation. The agitation could no longer be laughed at. "It was a fine and natural expression of a great national want. It was a demand of men who feel their own capabilities and their own disadvantages, and who dare claim the right of exerting the former and ridding themselves of the latter." It ridiculed the co-operation of *The Globe* and the Hon. H. Sherwood, a local Tory leader, in working up sentiment against annexation. It was, indeed, unfortunate for

The Examiner, December 26, 1849.

the British connection that its continuance should be jeopardized by the support of such friends. One-half of the first two dozen signers of the Toronto protest were overpaid officials, whose patriotism was measured by their pockets, and who dreaded the effect of annexation upon their salaries. The Montreal Tory Annexationists, it continued, would now have an opportunity of testing the sincerity of their Western allies. The former were men of progress, but they never made a more fatal error than when they united with the Upper Canada Tories. The latter merely " spouted annexation to frighten the English Ministry and Parliament; the former thought the matter out." [1]

Towards the English nation, *The Mirror* adopted the bitter and hostile tone of the Fenian press. It countered the anti-slavery arguments of the Reform papers by the bold declaration that the position of the Southern negro under the American flag was preferable to that of the Irish subject under the curse of English rule. *The Mirror*, however, showed a decided penchant for the independence of Canada, in preference to annexation. " For our part we can see nothing at all to be boasted of in our beggarly connection with Great Britain. On the contrary we see much in it of which we are heartily ashamed; we had rather see our country the humblest independent state in Christendom, than the liveried lackey of the greatest empire on earth. We feel too proud of Canada to hold her as the dependent of any nation. For this reason, we feel some repugnance even to annexation, which savours somewhat of a state of vassalage." [2] It predicted, however, that annexation would come in due time, but it questioned the wisdom of the Annexationists in endeavouring unduly to hasten the day of consummation.

The Independent, as was to be expected, greeted the

[1] *The Mirror*, October 19, 1849.
[2] *Ibid.*, November 2, 1849.

manifesto with the heartiest approval.   Notwithstanding the apparently hostile attitude of the people of Canada West, it believed that at heart there was a widespread sympathy with annexation.   The tone of the press of Upper Canada would doubtless disappoint the expectations of the Eastern Annexationists, but the latter should remember that the condition of affairs in the two sections of the province were quite dissimilar. In Lower Canada, the evils of the colonial régime had been most quickly and severely felt ; and, as a natural consequence, had produced an independence and aggressiveness of opinion, and a fusion of political parties far in advance of anything to be found as yet in the more backward districts of Canada West.   The opposition to annexation in Upper Canada arose primarily out of the peculiar position of the political parties, rather than from a desire to perpetuate the imperial bond beyond the time when it would be to the interest of the colonies to sever it.

Unfortunately for the province, the press of the Western District implicitly followed the behests of the party leaders ; only *The Examiner* and *The Mirror*, particularly the latter, had evidenced a spirit of political independence in the matter.   But, notwithstanding the timidity of the press, a majority of the people of the West, it claimed, were friendly to annexation, provided it could be brought about with the approval and goodwill of England.   Two-thirds of the old Reform Party were Annexationists at heart, though they did not care to avow it openly as yet.[1]   In Baldwin's own Riding, a careful canvass of the electors had revealed that at least one-half of the voters, including all of the men of importance, were favourable to annexation.   In the ranks of the Tory Party, many Annexationists were to be found, and the number was rapidly increasing.   The Canadian-born Tories frankly admitted that annexation was necessary to save the country from economic ruin, but the majority of them

[1] *The Independent*, November 2, 1849.

preferred to wait a while before taking any overt action. Throughout the Western peninsula, *The Independent* concluded, " a good half of the population were Annexationists," and a part of the remainder were at least favourable.[1] Taking it all in all, the situation in Upper Canada was most encouraging.

As an offset to the revolutionary teaching of *The Independent*, the Church revived the Laudian doctrine of indefeasible allegiance. In a spirit of loyalty, worthy of the most sycophantic ecclesiastic of the days of the Stuarts, it declared that the object of the manifesto " could not be carried into effect without going into opposition to the plainest and most solemn declarations of the revealed word of God." But, however acceptable such tenets might be to the High Church Tories, they only served to awaken the scorn and ridicule of the Reform press, and to drive the Clear Grit Party further in the direction of the United States.

The Liberal yeomen of York were not far behind the citizens of Toronto in asserting their loyalty to the British flag, though, unfortunately, they gave their declarations a distinctly partisan character. At a meeting of the Reformers of the Riding, an address to the Hon. James Price, the local member, was unanimously adopted, requesting him, in view of the dangerous complications of the time, to reconsider his intention of withdrawing from public life. One of the paragraphs of the address bitterly arraigned the policy of the Tory Party, " who do not scruple in the violence of their attacks to talk of separation, annexation, and other utopian and treasonable schemes, with the insidious design of entrapping the Reformers with the bait, and detaching from the ranks of the Liberal Party a sufficient number of supporters to ensure their downfall." [2] Shortly after, at a great Reform meeting at Sharon, a resolution was adopted, " That this meeting has no sympathy with those designing men

[1] Quoted from *L'Avenir*, December 21, 1849.
[2] *The Globe*, October 18, 1849.

who, after committing acts which we shudder to record, now adopt schemes of sedition and of separation from that country, which they have long affected to revere ; and this meeting hopes that all friends of good reform will keep away from such individuals." At the same time a resolution was agreed to in favour of reciprocal free trade with the United States.

In the Hamilton and Niagara Districts, public sentiment, though deeply tinged by party politics, ran strongly against annexation. According to report, an annexation association was formed in Hamilton, but it kept its light very carefully concealed under a bushel. No record of its proceedings was ever given to the public ; nor does it appear to have taken any active part in working up annexation sentiment in the community. That such a sentiment existed in certain quarters was unquestioned ; but, with one exception, it found little sympathy in the press of the district. *The Journal and Express*, a Clear Grit paper, opened its columns to the discussion of the question, but the editor carefully refrained from lending any countenance to the movement in the editorial page. According to *The Hamilton Spectator*, many causes had contributed to the movement ; but first among these stand misgovernment, extravagance, and the holding out of a premium to rebellion." [1]

Lord Elgin, it declared, had done more to alienate the loyalty of the country than all the agitation of the Annexationists. The movement had suddenly arisen in Montreal out of contempt for his person and policy, and not from any general feeling of discontent with the British connection. Although the people of Upper Canada deeply sympathized with the citizens of Montreal, they could not join with them in seeking to dismember the empire. They preferred to remonstrate against the misrule of " the Grey family compact," rather than to threaten the motherland with separation. " The proceedings in Montreal, if persevered in,

[1] The meeting was presided over by Captain Irving, M.L.C.

can only end in defeat, disgrace, and ruin. . . . From Upper Canada the agitation will meet with stern, uncompromising opposition." Instead of securing admittance into the American Union, the Montreal Annexationists might only succeed in repealing the Act of Union ; for, rather than be forced into a political union with the United States, the people of Canada West would join hands to bring about a division of the province, and the Montreal agitators would then find themselves worse off than before—a miserable minority at the mercy of an overwhelming majority.

A city contemporary, *The Spirit of the Age*, came out strongly in favour of separation. "Travellers from Europe have generally remarked on the backwardness observed in the British provinces as compared with the adjoining states of the Union. The people of Canada are fully impressed with the fact that such is the case to a large extent. A spirit of inquiry, however, is abroad as to the causes which keep us so far in the rear in the onward march of improvement. The trammels of prejudice and fashion no longer reign supreme in the Canadian mind. Men are beginning to perceive that their vital interests must not be sacrificed at the shrine of party, or for the sake of a fanciful or exploded theory. Whatever others may think, we are of the opinion that a dependent position holds out but poor inducements to enterprise, or the practice of self-reliance." [1]

Both the Gore and Niagara District Councils unanimously adopted resolutions condemning the Montreal manifesto, and pledging their fealty to the Crown. The resolution of the latter body went on to declare that they were ready by all means in their power " to suppress any attempt at separation, no matter from what source it might originate." [2] In the town of Niagara, a loyal address was drawn up, and signed by upwards of 200 inhabitants, including W. H. Dickson,

---

[1] Quoted from *The Examiner*, October 17, 1849.
[2] *The Globe*, November 17, 1849.

the local Reform member, the District Judge and Sheriff and chief local officials, protesting against the manifesto, professing their attachment to British institutions, and appealing to the public to do everything possible to allay the agitation. Only a small group of American citizens and a few headstrong Tories declined to sign the address.[1] The Grimsby branch of the League joined in the chorus of censure.[2] Lord Elgin, who was making a tour of the district at the time, paid a just tribute to the self-sacrificing loyalty of the inhabitants in making the protest. "They have done so," he declared, in a letter to the Colonial Secretary, " (and many other District Councils in Upper Canada have done the same), under the impression that it would be base to declare against England at the moment she has given a signal proof of her determination to concede constitutional government in all its plenitude to Canada. I am confident, however, that the large majority of persons who have thus protested firmly believe that their annexation to the United States would add one-fourth to the value of the produce of their farms."[3]

The St. Catharine's Journal,[4] the organ of Hamilton Merritt, frankly admitted that many of the allegations of the manifesto in regard to the depression of Canadian trade as compared with that of the United States were undoubtedly true, and acknowledged that such a condition of affairs could not long continue without producing a revolution. Nevertheless, it refused to countenance the annexation movement in any way. A reciprocity treaty with the United States would, in its judgment, afford to the Canadian people much greater advantages than annexation ; and, thanks to the hearty co-operation of the motherland, such an

---

[1] *The Globe*, October 29, 1849.
[2] *The Pilot*, November 6, 1849 ; *British Parliamentary Papers Relating to Canada.*
[3] Lord Elgin, *Letters and Journals*, p. 104.
[4] Quoted from *The Mirror*, November 2, 1849.

arrangement would soon be consummated. It was folly, it declared, to throw away the great public works of the colony, and their political freedom, by such "a childish, petulant mode of proceeding" as the manifesto proposed.[1] Unlike some of its contemporaries, the *Journal* did not seek to decry the movement, for fear that it would grow in strength, nor propose the adoption of repressive measures to snuff it out; it preferred, on the contrary, freely to discuss the issue with the Annexationists, in the belief that the decision of the public would undoubtedly favour the maintenance of the imperial relation.

At the same time, it deprecated a blind attachment to the parent state at the expense of Canadian interests. "Whilst we would strive to prevent our friends from taking any active part in favour of annexation, we would also save them from pledging themselves to sustain any administration favourable to the British connection. There is a humiliation in such a position that we would fain see the Reformers saved from. We are the advocates of British connection, but it is not the all in all with us. We view it but as a means to an end, and that end is the prosperity of Canada. This, we are satisfied, can be best accomplished by a continuous connection with England. . . . Our creed may not be orthodox, but we are free to say that we believe first in patriotism, and then in loyalty. Now we don't hold with those whose first item is loyalty, and whose second is patriotism." The conduct of England towards the colonies had been generosity itself; she neither levied imperial taxes, nor exacted payment for naval and military protection. "Would this be the case," it inquired, "if we were annexed? Let us not be duped by disappointed men, who a few

[1] Mr. William Kirby, author of *Chien d'Or*, issued a bitter philippic against the Annexationists. ",I trust to arraign you before my judging countrymen, to prove your falsehood, malignancy, and treachery, and convict you before heaven and earth, as the most reckless, causeless, unreasoning, and selfish batch of revolutionists that ever disgraced the calendar of political crime."

months ago were the bitter opponents of every Liberal measure, but now forsooth, when they have no chance of the loaves and fishes, are ready to run into the arms of the neighbouring republic." [1]

The St. Catharine's Constitutional, a newly established organ of the Conservative Party, declared in an early issue : " The old landmarks of party are in a great measure done away with, and the all-absorbing question now is whether we shall remain an integral portion of the empire of Great Britain, or whether, forgetting the holy tie by which we are bound to her, we shall seek an alliance with a neighbouring republic. Enterprising, acute, and energetic—but still a republic, and a republic that sanctions a traffic in the bones and sinews of human beings. We must unequivocally pronounce in favour of British connection, and we fearlessly inquire ' Why separate ? ' " [2]

Equally unsympathetic was the reception of the manifesto in the Western peninsula. London won the distinction of taking the lead in opposition to annexation. In response to a requisition of about sixty freeholders, a meeting was called by the Mayor to express the loyalty of the city, and its hostility to a political union with the United States. [3] A respectable-sized audience assembled, and the following resolutions were unanimously adopted : (1) That we view with surprise and regret the late movement in Montreal suggesting a separation from the mother country, and advocating a union with the United States ; (2) That our allegiance to our beloved Queen and our attachment to the British Empire are subjects of principle and feeling, and are not to be weighed in the scale of uncertain interests and speculations ; (3) That a calm comparison of the alleged advantages and disadvantages of the proposed scheme shows that it is not desirable on the grounds urged by its advocates.

[1] Quoted from *The Examiner*, December 26, 1849.
[2] Quoted from *The Montreal Gazette*, January 9, 1850.
[3] October 19, 1849.

The two principal speakers were the Hon. J. G. Goodhue and Mr. John Wilson, the local member.   In moving the second resolution, the former declared that the attempt to disrupt the empire would, if successful, be disastrous to the credit of the colony.   The movement was the more reprehensible since England was not endeavouring to force any objectionable measures or policy upon them ; but, on the contrary, had granted to the province the largest liberty of action.   Although the authors of the manifesto professed to pursue only peaceable means of attaining annexation, nevertheless the movement might fall into more revolutionary hands, and prove dangerous to the welfare of the country.   The growth of the agitation could be best retarded by an early and general expression of pro-British feeling throughout the province.   In the face of a hostile public the idea of annexation would, he concluded, soon be abandoned.

The speech of Mr. Wilson was devoted almost entirely to a review and careful analysis of the economic conditions of the country out of which, in his judgment, the annexation movement had originated.   Montreal, he explained, was bearing the brunt of the commercial depression.   Thanks to her splendid situation, she had long been accustomed to wield the commercial sceptre over Canada, but with the establishment of ports of entry in the principal cities of Upper Canada, and with the opening of the American market, she had lost her monopoly of the import and distributing trade.   The merchants of Canada West now found that they could procure their supplies to better advantage at American ports and through local wholesale houses than at Montreal.   The business of the colony as a whole had not decreased, but only so much of it as flowed through the mouth of the St. Lawrence.[1]

Turning then to the consideration of the fiscal policy of the motherland, he maintained that, notwithstanding the artful plea of the Annexationists that the policy

[1] A similar view was expressed by Mr. A. Hope.

of free trade would ruin the Canadian farmers, the latter would not grudge the English labourers the boon of cheaper food. They would not be one whit the poorer because many of their fellow citizens were better fed. He denied the validity of the contention that annexation would restore the prosperity of the country by the introduction of manufacturing industries from across the line ; on the contrary, in the opinion of the speaker, it would ruin the existing manufactories by flooding the market with the free products of the United States. He was not prepared to renounce his allegiance in order to gain the material advantage of an increase in the price of lands. In conclusion, he ridiculed the claim of the manifesto that annexation would save Canada from the peril of Anglo-Saxon complications and from the danger of French domination. A transfer of allegiance would not avert the possibility of war, nor change the position of the two races. The French would still cling to their own race, land, and religion.

At a similar public meeting at Stratford, shortly after, resolutions were adopted in condemnation of the manifesto, declaring that any measure for the dismemberment of the empire was opposed to the present and future interests of the colony, and praying the Legislature to relieve the grievances from which the province was suffering. An address of similar import was circulated among the citizens, and received many signatures.[1]

The Western papers, almost without exception, showed no sympathy with the annexation propaganda. " What ! " exclaimed *The London Pioneer*, " is it come to this ? that for paltry pelf we are prepared Esau-like to sell our birthright as Britons—to sever our connection with the land of our nativity, and to dissolve our interest in that glorious history to which we have been accustomed to point with pleasure and pride—and not only to sever that connection, but to

[1] *The Pilot*, November 15, 1849.

link ourselves to a confederacy whose principal boast is that they successfully resisted Britain's power, and whose aim is to be considered its rival in the world ? " [1] *The Times*, the local Conservative organ, bitterly resented the attempts of the Liberal press to fasten the stigma of disloyalty upon the Tory Party. On behalf of its fellow partisans of the Western District, it distinctly repudiated any connection or sympathy with the Montreal Annexationists. [2]

The opportunity of scoring their opponents was too tempting for the Reform press to resist ; and, with but few exceptions, they used their advantage in true partisan fashion. *The Canadian Free Press*, for example, arraigned the Tory Annexationists in the most unsparing terms. " The history of the Annexation Party is remarkably instructive. But a few months ago, it boasted of its loyalty, and professed the most ardent attachment to the mother country ; now it is making every effort to shake off its allegiance to the Crown of Britain, and to unite itself with a republic which it has for years held up to scorn. The project of annexation is ushered in under the worst possible auspices—those of the Montreal mob, and the twaddlers of the League. Had it come from any other quarter, it might have had a better chance of a favourable hearing—its coming from Montreal will be fatal to it." [3]

The Huron Signal, likewise, affected to treat the annexation movement as the product of a treasonable conspiracy of a few disappointed place-hunters and speculators of Montreal. Although, it declared, the farmers and business men of Upper Canada were suffering from hard times, it did not believe that the Canadian public, on the average, were in any worse position than their American neighbours, nor that an appeal to their material interests alone would suffice to induce them

---

[1] Quoted from *The Globe*, October 27, 1849.
[2] *The Times* (C.W.), December 14, 1849.
[3] Quoted from *The Pilot*, November 6, 1849.

to throw off their allegiance. "We feel satisfied that even with the consent of the British Government, it would be impossible to induce a majority, or even a respectable minority, of the people of Upper Canada to agree to a union with the United States. We are too proud of our national individuality to consent to be swallowed up, or become a mere insignificant integer of an unwieldy republic."

Of somewhat similar tenor was the declaration of faith of *The Dumfries Recorder*, as set forth in its prospectus. "That the present cry for annexation raised by a few disappointed hack politicians, at whose hands this fertile country has already suffered so much, must be regarded as not only insane, but absolutely wicked, in every way injurious to the trade, credit, and prosperity of the country ; that the connection with Great Britain ought to be maintained, not merely on account of old associations, or a sense of reciprocal favour, but from a clear perception of mutual benefit." The attitude of *The Guelph and Galt Advertiser* was much more reasonable. It undertook to prove by a series of cogent arguments, and a long array of statistics, that Canada was more prosperous than the United States, and that annexation would seriously endanger the material well-being of the province. On the other hand, as we shall presently see, one or two of the Clear Grit papers were inclined to coquette with the United States, as a means of getting rid of the privileges of the Anglican Church.

Public opinion in the Midland District was divided on the subject of annexation, though the great majority of the electorate were undoubtedly opposed to it. In response to a requisition, a public meeting was held at Cobourg to express disapprobation of the annexation movement.[1] The leading members of both political parties participated in the demonstration, and there was a marked harmony throughout the whole proceedings. A series of resolutions was agreed to, condemn-

[1] October 30, 1849.

ing the Montreal manifesto ; vindicating the loyalty of the colony ; urging the co-operation of the Imperial and Colonial Governments for the relief of the existing depression of trade ; declaring that the credit of the colony could be restored by the adoption of a policy of rigid economy and sound legislation, by the elimination of bitter partisanship, and a general submission to the principles of constitutional government ; commending the action of Baldwin and Hincks in opposing annexation ; and thanking the motherland for her expenditures on the public works of the colony. A committee was appointed to draw up an address in consonance with the foregoing resolutions.[1]

A similar meeting at Belleville was attended by one of the largest audiences ever assembled in that city. For the moment, Reformers and Conservatives forgot their party differences ; prominent Tories such as H. Corby and G. Benjamin, Warden of the County and Grand Master of the Orangemen, joined hands with their political opponents, Dr. Hope, and Bella Flint, the local Reform member, in opposing the further progress of annexation. Resolutions were unanimously adopted, proclaiming the unswerving loyalty of the people to the Crown and to British institutions, and condemning the proposal of a political union with a country whose government was " stained with the unnatural crimes of slavery and repudiation."

A few of the papers of the district wavered for a moment in their allegiance, but the majority stood fast by the British connection. *The Cobourg Star*, the editor of which was a prominent member of the League, expressed the fear that should the scheme of a federal union of the provinces, which would again be discussed at the approaching convention of the League, " be found impracticable, no other means than annexation can be pointed out which will satisfy the people."

According to *The Kingston Chronicle and News*, the leading local organ of the Tory Party in the Bay of

[1] *The Globe*, November 6, 1849.

Quinte section, the policy of Cobden had undermined the loyalty of the people of the colony. But, it urged, the material advantages of annexation should not lead them to dissolve the imperial tie ; it was " still incumbent on the Annexationists to prove that the British connection was absolutely incompatible with the prosperity of the province." This was more particularly the case, since most of the advantages of annexation could be obtained by a reciprocity treaty with the United States, the prospects of securing which were excellent, in case the Democratic Party were victorious at the next elections, as now appeared most probable. For the time being, the policy of the League was, in the opinion of *The Chronicle*, most suited to the commercial conditions of the country, and best calculated to maintain the British connection. " If it should fail to restore prosperity to the country, then we shall be prepared to adopt any course which, on mature consideration, shall be deemed necessary to so vital an object, even though that course should involve annexation." But, it concluded, annexation should be accepted only as a last resort.

The British American came out emphatically against annexation. The City of Montreal, it declared, had been taken with the annexation mania, as a result of provincial misgovernment. " A change of men will not now satisfy the Montrealers ; a change of measures they now look upon as useless ; but it remains with Upper Canada to decide whether they will doff the garb of loyalty and don that of republicanism. They may agitate as they will, and hire as many lecturers as they please ; but, when the day of trial comes, they will find that the loyalists of Canada will be ready to do their duty." " We have no faith," it continued, " in annexation. We believe that republicanism and its institutions are totally unsuited to the habits and tastes of the great majority of Canadians." It had also little faith in the saving virtue of English protection. If the Government would cease to look out for the partisan interest of its office-holders, the agitation for annexation would, it concluded, soon disappear.

According to *The Kingston Whig*, the prospects of the Annexationists were most encouraging. " During a recent absence from home, the editor passed through a dozen villages in Upper Canada, and the sole topic of conversation among all classes and parties was annexation. Nay, in the good city of Kingston, loyal old Kingston, the stronghold of Conservatism, *par excellence*, nine-tenths of the people are annexationists ; and if any practical benefit could arise from signing any manifesto, they would cheerfully do it. But they possess common sense ; and, knowing that without the consent of Great Britain all attempts at annexation must be worse than useless, they wisely bide their time." [1]

The Kingston Argus came out frankly in favour of annexation.[2] The bold and clear-cut manner in which it proclaimed its principles contrasted markedly with the doubtful hesitancy of many of its contemporaries. The latter, it declared, either shrank from the task of directing public opinion, or, as in the case of the Ministerial press, complacently accepted the advantages which accrued from the party being in office. " For ourselves, we have to say that we have long looked forward to the ultimate annexation of these provinces to the United States as a thing inevitable. So many of the most loyal men among us have held the same opinion, that our conviction has not yet been shaken, and passing events tend to strengthen it. The time of its accomplishment is not far distant ; whether it is agreeable to our feelings personally, we shall not take into consideration. It would be ungrateful in the extreme to forget our fatherland and all we owe to it, but it would be baser still to allow our private feelings and interests to interfere with the duty we owe to the land we live in."

[1] Quoted from *The Burlington Daily Sentinel*, October 31, 1849.
[2] *Ibid.*, November 1, 1849.

On the other hand, *The Herald* and *The Age*, which represented the interests of the local Reformers, concurred in the opinion that the annexation cry " was a mere cloak to effectually prostrate the Reform Party." Although, according to *The Age*, the manifesto did not exhibit on its face a partisan spirit, nevertheless, both from its origin and the character of its support, the address ought reasonably to be attributed to the disappointed and baffled hopes of a clique, " which, having been beaten in the fight over the Rebellion Losses Bill, now turned their attention to more dangerous designs." In any case, the motives of the authors were open to grave suspicion. There was, it contended, a striking inconsistency in the language of the manifesto in professing the greatest deference to the wishes of England in regard to separation, and in painting such a graphic picture of the woes of the country as a result of imperial policy. What, it demanded, would the Annexationists do, if the English Government should refuse, as was most probable, its consent to annexation ?

Very similar was the language of *The Peterborough Despatch.* " That the document is an emanation of disappointed Toryism, none will pretend to deny, although we are prepared to admit that in some particulars it is exceedingly plausible. It will, we imagine, be granted that this move is purported to have originated in the passing of the Rebellion Losses Bill, and further that the object sought by the individuals connected with the proposed measure is neither more nor less than that attributed to the men who have been so often designated Rebels and Traitors by the MacNabs and Cayleys of Canada. Here, then, we have the consistency of the scions of the old compact. In one case they hang and shoot men for using lead to attain a certain object, while they themselves avow that they are about to attempt the realization of the same object, through the means of soft sawder. Don't they wish they may get it ? "

The general consensus of opinion in the Eastern

District of Upper Canada was equally opposed to annexation, though here and there voices were raised in
its support. The old prejudice of the United Empire
loyalists against the American people and republican
institutions had largely disappeared, but the inhabitants were not yet prepared to exchange their citizenship.[1] At the session of the Grand Jury in Bathurst
Township, Lanark, a protest was drawn up against the
Montreal manifesto. The inhabitants of the Township, they declared, had no sympathy with the annexation movement. The jurors, who were evidently
staunch Reformers, added the rider that there was
nothing to fear, but everything to hope from a continuance of the British connection, so long as the
existing Government remained in office to conduct the
affairs of the colony according to English constitutional
principles.[2] At a subsequent meeting of the Lanark
and Renfrew Reform Association, a resolution was
adopted, incorporating into the objects of the Association a declaration in favour of the British connection.

The editor of *The Brockville Recorder*, a Liberal
paper, bore testimony to the fact that in a trip through
a portion of Leeds and Bathurst, he had met with but
one Annexationist. Although the farmers were complaining of hard times, they were comfortable in their
homes and politically contented. *The Cornwall Free-
holder* accused the Tories of secretly sympathizing with
the Annexationists. "Even in this truly loyal district
we have heard of some of the old Tory compact who
are even now holding offices of emolument under the
Government, exulting over and secretly extolling the
treasonable document; and, were it not for the half-
pay consideration, we have no doubt they would step
forth in their proper garb—their assumed loyalty cast
aside—as traitors to their sovereign. Such men should
be narrowly watched by the Government. We distinctly tell these political incendiaries that the day of

---

[1] Letter from W. A. Buell, *The Globe*, November 20, 1849.
[2] October 26, 1849.

retribution is not far off. The Reformers of Upper Canada have no sympathy with these men—they have got all the liberties that rational men can desire, and they revere that magnanimous nation which has so promptly conceded to them the management of their own affairs in the shape of responsible government."

The Brockville Statesman, the organ of Mr. Gowan, and the leading Tory paper of the district, advised its readers to have nothing to do with the annexation movement, but to look to the League as the only legitimate exponent of the principles of the Conservative Party. The approaching convention of the League would pass judgment upon the question of annexation; until then it was the duty "of every true man to remain stationary but steady."

In the Ottawa valley, according to *The Bytown Packet*,[1] the local Liberal organ, public opinion ran strongly against separation. It expressed the opinion that "the people of Montreal are ready for any mischief. They are, however, powerless; for upon this question, as upon every other question, the great majority will declare against them. This move, originating as it did with the Montreal Tory merchants, is too apparently selfish to command any degree of attention in the Upper Province; and in the Lower the parties with whom it originated are well understood and treated with contempt accordingly. On the whole, the affair is too contemptible just now to attract much notice."

The movement, it admitted, however, might create a new party which would find "many converts among the discontented, vicious, and disappointed class who fancy themselves men of a new idea." The Annexationists were but deceiving themselves and the country at large in pretending that the home Government was anxious to get rid of the colonies. England would not agree to annexation, whatever some of her statesmen might say to the contrary. She was still deeply

[1] *The Bytown Packet*, October 20, 1849.

attached to the colonies, and necessity alone would cause her to throw them off. Whatever the attitude of the Canadian Tories might prove to be, it would be exceedingly imprudent for the Reformers to join in a separationist movement at the very moment of the grant of responsible government.[1] Under these circumstances, it concluded, the annexation movement was both impracticable and uncalled for. *The Bytown Gazette* likewise indulged in some biting sarcasm at the expense of the people of Montreal. The inhabitants of that fair city had taken up a new fad: they had now gone mad on the subject of annexation. But, it remarked, " We never put great faith in the great Canadian emporium of shopkeepers, and in the present instance less than ever."

Throughout the Eastern District, the one lone champion of the annexation cause was *The Prescott Telegraph*, a Reform journal of pronounced Radical tendencies. The manifesto, it declared, was its own best defence. " We must confess we never saw so many plain incontrovertible facts put into so small a compass. . . . In truth we are a poor spiritless unenterprising population, without means to help ourselves, and destitute of the energy to improve, if we had the means." Torn by dissensions and domestic conflict, the country presented a humiliating picture of misery and discontent. " For our part, we see no hope, unless all parties will agree to drop their differences, and meet upon some neutral ground; that ground has been marked out in the annexation address." That a change of allegiance would come some day was evident to all reflecting persons in England and the United States, as well as Canada. " In the present position of affairs, it may be that that change can take place as well now as at any future time, particularly if it can be accomplished without bloodshed." England was weary of the expense and discontent of the colonies, and was anxious to get rid of them, if the act could be

[1] *The Bytown Packet*, November 10, 1849.

accomplished in a friendly and honourable fashion. But, it added by way of caution, Canada should not think of severing the tie unless it could be done with mutual satisfaction. But the wails of *The Telegraph* were as the voice of one crying in the wilderness ; they failed to strike a sympathetic chord throughout the district.

For some time subsequent to the Kingston Convention, the League was not much in evidence. Negociations were set on foot by a committee of the League with various persons and organizations in the Maritime Provinces, with a view to interesting them in the calling of an interprovincial conference to consider the question of a federal union. But at first, largely owing to the indifference and suspicion of the colonists by the sea, these efforts did not meet with much success. The rapid progress of the annexation movement, and the secession of many of their prominent members, stirred up the officers of the League to greater activity ; for it was realized that unless some measures were speedily taken to promote the objects of the association, it would be difficult to justify, or even to maintain, its existence.

Notwithstanding considerable opposition, a portion of which was due to a suspicion on the part of some of the St. John papers that the League was seeking to draw the Maritime Provinces into a political union with the United States, arrangements were at last concluded with the Colonial Association of New Brunswick for a conference at Montreal. The latter body sent two delegates, the Hon. John Robertson and C. Simmons, to meet the representatives of the League—Messrs. Gowan, Crawford, Wilson, Montgomerie, and Gamble. As the conference unfortunately convened at the moment when the citizens of Montreal were in a state of great excitement over the annexation manifesto, its proceedings attracted but scanty notice from the press and public.[1] In truth, the inhabitants

[1] October 13, 1849.

of the city had very little faith in the object of the conference. As a result of its deliberations, the conference unanimously adopted a series of resolutions setting forth : (1) That the commercial ills of the colonies were due to the fiscal policy of England in depriving them of preference in the British market without securing for them an equivalent fiscal advantage elsewhere; (2) that the colonies would inevitably be ruined, if Great Britain did not restore the colonial preference, or else procure for Canadian products an entrance into foreign markets, especially into the United States, on terms of reciprocity, "one or the other of which policies is considered indispensable to the continuance of our present political connection with Great Britain." [1]

As the conference committee was now ready to report, a call was issued for a second convention to meet in Toronto, the beginning of November. The success of the annexation movement forced the League to determine its future policy in the light of recent political developments. All the old issues of the last convention were at once revived. In the various branches of the League, the questions of annexation and elective institutions were most carefully canvassed, and upon these two issues the election of the delegates was generally fought out. Some of the League leaders were wavering in their political faith ; some were suspected of annexation proclivities because of their advocacy of the popular election of public officials ; while others stood fast by the ancient principles of the Tory Party.

Just prior to the assembling of the convention, Mr. J. W. Gamble, a prominent member of the progressive wing of the party, came out with an open letter in which he advocated the adoption of the policy of protection. Although personally opposed to annexation on political grounds, he admitted that, from a commercial standpoint, a political union with the United States would be more advantageous to the

---

[1] *The Globe*, November 8, 1849.

colony than the existing humiliating position of "hewers of wood and drawers of water to Great Britain." Annexation, he argued, would undoubtedly introduce American capital into the country and afford protection to Canadian industries against outside nations ; but, at the same time, it would only effect a change of masters by subjecting the industries of the province to the domination of the United States in place of Great Britain.[1]

The Leagues of Western Canada pronounced clearly and emphatically against annexation ; some of the branches specifically instructed their delegates to oppose it on the floor of the convention should the issue be there raised.[2] The Grimsby League adopted a resolution expressing "their abhorrence of annexation, and repudiation of the doctrine of abjuring one's country from capricious or other motives." But from Lower Canada, a few well-known Annexationists were chosen as delegates. The selection of Toronto as the seat of the convention placed the Annexationists at a distinct disadvantage, for they were called upon to defend their cause in the very centre of pro-British feeling. The situation was rendered even more difficult for them by reason of the fact that several branches, which were unable to provide for the expenses of local delegates, selected citizens of Toronto as their representatives. In truth, the influence of Toronto was most markedly felt throughout the proceedings of the convention.

In November the convention assembled with upwards of sixty delegates in attendance. As at Kingston, the delegates were a heterogeneous body of men, representing almost all shades of political thought—ultra-Tories, Liberal Conservatives, a few stray Radicals, and several Annexationists. Additional interest was lent to the proceedings from the fact that the convention was expected to consider the recent manifesto, and determine the future attitude of the League towards annexa-

[1] *The Colonist*, October 30, 1849.
[2] *The Guelph and Galt Advertiser*, November 1, 1849.

tion. It was thought by some of the Tories that a
reaction had set in against both the Government and
the Annexationists, from which the League might profit.
" The sacrifice of French interests," *The Colonist* declared, " by the removal of the Government from
Montreal, and the scorn which the Ministerial press had
thrown upon the annexation movement, had alienated
a multitude of their staunchest supporters," while the
rashness of the proceedings of the Montreal Annexationists had had a similar effect upon many of the
members of that party. By judicious diplomacy, and
the adoption of an attractive programme, it was believed that many of the disaffected might be won over
to the League. There was the greater reason for hope
in this respect, since several of the most prominent
members of the League, as Gowan, Gamble, Prince, and
Wilson were not only Liberal in their political views,
but were also on cordial terms with many of the
Annexationists.

The question of annexation was the most absorbing
topic before the convention. The delegates apparently
could not avoid debating the question ; it was dragged
into the discussion of almost every matter from elective
institutions to a federal union of the provinces. The
convention, in this regard, merely reflected the state
of public opinion ; as in the country, so in the convention, annexation was the leading issue of the
day.

The subject came up at the very opening of the
convention in a series of resolutions, the first of which
recited that " exciting and irritating political questions
involving the dismemberment of the colony from the
empire " were " engendering discontent, discord, and
fierce political animosities," and called for the adoption
of judicious measures to allay the social and political
unrest of the people. Everywhere, Mr. Gamble declared, in introducing the resolutions, the people were
talking of annexation and independence, and the
Government seemed powerless, or unwilling, to punish

the press which was promoting the agitation. Although he regretted the publication of the manifesto, he hoped that the question of annexation would be thoroughly discussed by the convention. The leaders of the League, he announced, " regarded it as a *dernier ressort*, and were not going to buck the question." But the friends of annexation at once took exception to the language of the resolution, as unjustly reflecting upon the character of the movement in Montreal ; and, notwithstanding the protestations of Mr. Gamble to the contrary, they pressed for the excision of the objectionable clause. Mr. Crawford of Brockville voiced the protest of the dissentients against the disrespectful language of the resolution, which was calculated to irritate the feelings of the Annexationists, and " to cause several gentlemen belonging to the convention to withdraw."

The manifesto was a calm and moderate document, and not a revolutionary instrument. Such ill will as was evidenced throughout the province did not exist between the pro- and anti-annexationists, but rather between the two old political parties. Every man with whom he had conversed regarding the subject had admitted " that the time for annexation would come," and now, he believed, was the proper time to discuss, and, if possible, determine the question. Messrs. Macdonald of Ganonoque and Hamilton of Beverley joined in the protest against the censure of the Annexationists. The former declared that the remedy proposed by the manifesto " was probably the only one that the country would finally adopt," while the latter considered it inadvisable to condemn the movement when the convention itself was divided upon the question. Some of the delegates were fully convinced that annexation would never come ; others regarded it as a *dernier ressort*; and still others were of the opinion that it was near at hand. For his part he did not care to discuss the question of loyalty to the British flag at a time when the farmers of the country were suffering from the British connection, while their American neighbours were prosperous.

In moving a substitute resolution, " that these colonies cannot remain in their present commercial and political state," Mr. Gowan expressed the opinion that annexation sentiment was growing rapidly throughout the province. The Ministerial press, in trying to put down annexation by crying up the prosperity of the country, were building " on a foundation of sand." The question of separation was now a mere matter of pounds, shillings, and pence. Since England had put the question on that basis, by the abrogation of the protective system for purely selfish reasons, it was not unpatriotic for Canada to consider the subject from the standpoint of her own special interests. The depressed condition of the province was a sorry contrast to the prosperity of the United States. He did not elaborate the deplorable state of Canadian industry and agriculture from any desire to influence the convention in favour of annexation, but in order to prove the necessity for a change in the commercial policy of the motherland.

In seconding the amendment, Mr. Murney of Belleville stated that he had thought at first that the question of annexation should have been shelved as at the Kingston Convention, but that he had yielded his opinion in response to the general demand of the delegates for a free and frank discussion of the whole situation of affairs. The manifesto, he regretfully admitted, had met with sympathy from many who had not as yet expressed themselves openly. " The feeling was spreading faster than they were aware of, and he hoped that they would do something to stem the current." Mr. Wilson of Quebec expressed the opinion that the delegates would not now be hearing so much about annexation, if the previous convention had been permitted freely to discuss the subject. Personally his sense of loyalty was second to that of the interests of his family. There was every probability that the people of Canada would demand a political union with

the United States, unless England reversed her fiscal
policy, for the sentiment in favour of annexation was
spreading rapidly, particularly in the West. He
agreed with the view of Mr. Gowan, that the convention
should discuss the issue upon a purely business basis.

The primary importance of the commercial side of
separation was further emphasized by Mr. Duggan of
Toronto, who demanded that England should show
due consideration of Canadian interests in the determination of her fiscal policy. Many Canadians, he
admitted, wished for annexation ; personally he did
not, " but it was forced upon him " by the unfriendly
action of the motherland. This phase of the discussion
called forth another speech from Mr. Wilson, even more
Radical in tone than any of his previous utterances.
Although he professed a sentimental preference for the
British flag over the Stars and Stripes, and severely
attacked the unfairness of the manifesto in failing to
show the reverse side of the picture, which annexation
would entail in the loss of revenue, the sacrifice of the
public lands of the province, and the increase in public
expenditures, he frankly avowed that, if England did
not do Canada justice, he was prepared to fight. An
amendment by Mr. O'Brien to the effect that, if Great
Britain did not herself provide a market for Canadian
products, or secure the admission of Canadian products
into the markets of foreign countries, or of the United
States under favourable conditions, Canada " would
be compelled to seek the welfare of her own people "
irrespective of the interests or opposition of England,
was lost upon division. In order to avoid a confusion
of issues, the Gamble and Gowan resolutions were
thrown into the melting-pot, and recast in a considerably modified form, which happily proved acceptable
to the whole body of delegates.

The question of annexation again claimed the chief
attention in the discussion of the resolution in favour
of a federal union of the provinces. Such a union,
it was felt by practically all the speakers, including

Mr. Gamble, the author of the resolution, and President Moffatt, was the only means of avoiding annexation. The very existence of the League, it was admitted, was endangered by the defection of so many of its members. A truly national policy was required to fire the imagination of the Canadian people. An intercolonial convention ought, in the opinion of Mr. Gamble, to be called at once, for Canada " was on the verge of a revolution." Several of the delegates expressed grave doubt as to whether England would voluntarily surrender the North American colonies to the United States, but the majority of the speakers were of the opinion that she might be willing to grant independence to Canada, either as a separate state, or, preferably, as a member of an intercolonial federation.

The annexation issue was again raised upon a resolution of Mr. Wilson in favour of an elective Legislative Council. Upon this resolution, the convention, for a time, threatened to split asunder ; the progressive and conservative wings of the convention lined up in battle array. It was urged by the representatives of the new Tory democracy that the adoption of the elective system would be an effective offset to the radical propaganda of the Annexationists in favour of the more popular institutions of the United States, especially in view of the fact that those doctrines were taking a firm hold on the growing democracy of Canada. To the ultra-Tories, on the contrary, the principle of popular election was a dangerous American innovation, incompatible with the British Constitution. The resolution, it was feared, presaged a political revolution ; it marked the first step towards republican institutions—a step which would inevitably result in time in the incorporation of Canada into the United States. An amendment by Mr. Murney expressing disapproval of any change in the existing Constitution, and coupling therewith a condemnation of the Montreal manifesto, was lost upon division.

So manifest was the interest of the convention in the

subject of annexation, that the leaders of the League were convinced that to attempt in any way to suppress or limit the discussion of the question, as at the former convention, would only breed discontent, and further the cause of annexation. Moreover, it was politically advisable for the League not to outrage the suscepti- bilities of any of its supporters, or drive them out of the party into the camp of the Annexationists. President Moffatt urged upon the delegates the wisdom of culti- vating the most cordial relation with the Annexationists with a view to joint action against the Government at the next general election. As the delegates were over- whelmingly pro-British in sentiment, there was little danger to apprehend that the debate would be con- verted into a propaganda for annexation. At the same time, some of the loyalist members thought it advisable to commit the convention to the maintenance of the British connection.

A resolution was accordingly introduced by Mr. Miller : " That it is a matter of regret to this conven- tion that the subject of a separation of this colony from the motherland and annexation to the United States of America has been openly advocated by a portion of the press and inhabitants of this province : and this convention unhesitatingly records its entire disapproba- tion of this course, and calls upon all well-wishers of this country to discountenance it by every means in their power." In presenting the motion, Mr. Miller stated that, if there had been one, there had been twenty delegates who were opposed to the discussion of the question of annexation, because they wished that the impression should go abroad that the convention was neutral upon the matter. They desired the Public to draw the conclusion that annexationist sympathies were strongly in evidence in the Conservative Party, and that the convention, if not favourable to separa- tion, was at least not opposed to it. Should such an opinion gain general currency, it would, in his opinion, seriously operate against the League. The revolutionary spirit was abroad throughout the world. Although the Annexationists professed the most peaceable aims, there was not the slightest chance of the peaceful consummation of their policy. " They were dissolving the bonds of society, and revolutionizing the country, not for the purpose of maintaining the great principles of civil and religious liberty, but for the mere chance of commercial advantage."

The chief argument of the Annexationists was the commercial one—the loss of the imperial preference, and the advantage of the American market. But annexation, he contended, would sacrifice Canadian farmers to the American cotton, tobacco, sugar, and manufacturing interests. He denied the allegation that the English Government and people were desirous of throwing off the colonies. The views of the leaders of the Radical Party in England in regard to separation, upon which the Annexationists based their erroneous representations, were uttered at the time of civil war in Canada. In the face of a colonial rebellion, they had nobly declared that they would not hold the colonies in subjection against their will; but, on the contrary, would grant to them the fullest liberty of determining their own political future in relation to England. But such a position, he maintained, was fundamentally different from that of the Annexationists. Another argument of the Annexationists, "supported, he was sorry to say, by a portion of the Conservative Party," was to the effect that, as a union with the United States was a mere matter of time, the sooner steps were taken to that end, the better it would be for the province. But he believed that time would develop a sense of deeper attachment to the motherland : the old loyalty of 1812 would break out again with renewed vigour. The peaceful plea of the manifesto betrayed " a Judas loyalty which proffered the kiss of affection to the Sovereign as an emblem of its treason." In conclusion, he assured the delegates that the resolu-

tion was presented with no intent of stirring up a
division in the convention, but in order that the League
might stamp the annexation movement with its disapprobation.

Mr. Rolland MacDonald of St. Catharine's, whose
appearance was greeted with loud cries of " Question ! "
delivered a ranting pro-British address, amid the restless confusion of the delegates. The Annexationists,
he declared, should not be too thin-skinned. He did
not believe that there was a single member of the convention who was prepared to support annexation, out
and out, though there were several who were suspected
of leaning that way. Many of the signers of the
manifesto were loyal Britishers at heart, and would
still fight for the maintenance of the British connection :
some had appended their names " on account of pique,
and many in order to compel Great Britain to take
notice of our position." These he desired to reclaim
by holding out the hope of the future greatness and
prosperity of the country. He accused the supporters
of the principle of popular election of playing the
game of the Annexationists, and charged the Government with insincerity in not opposing the election of
Mr. Perry.

The greater prosperity of the United States was, he
claimed, fictitious, an inflated result of heavy borrow-
ings of English capital. Was Canada to revolt, he
asked, because she had been granted freedom of trade,
the abrogation of the Navigation Laws, and the right
of self-government, for which she had long contended ?
By annexation they would lose the control of their
public lands, customs revenues, postal system, and the
English grant for troops and fortifications ; on the
other hand, their taxes would be quadrupled, and they
would be burdened with a part of the United States
debt. Why should they wish for annexation to a
country which spoke of them with contempt, and
which, moreover, did not want them until the slavery
issue had been settled ? Great Britain would never

consent to surrender the colonies voluntarily, since by
so doing she would reduce herself to the rank of a fifth-
rate power in the world. Two of the annexation papers
in Montreal and Toronto were, he alleged, supported
by American funds intended for the Irish rebellion.
But the people of Canada were loyal to the core, and
could not be corrupted by foreign gold ; their allegiance
was not a mere matter of monetary advantage, and
they would not barter their British inheritance for a
mess of pottage. Even though England should agree
to independence, the Canadian public would not consent to convert their province into a slave state. He
called upon Reformers and Tories alike to " clear their
skirts of the Annexationists," and to unite in pressing
upon the British Government the necessity of procuring
for Canadian products an entrance into the American
market.

Mr. Gamble rose to clear himself of the charge of
annexation sympathies which had been lodged against
him by the previous speaker ; but almost at once
launched into an embittered attack upon the British
Government. England, he contended, had placed the
empire upon a materialistic plane, and had branded
the loyalists of Canada as spurious patriots. The
arguments of the Annexationists could not be answered
by mere rhetorical appeals to the British flag, such as
they had just listened to. Mr. Mack of Montreal expressed the opinion that both the resolution and the
accompanying speeches were uncalled for, as the
loyalty of the League was too well known to require
vindication. The chief danger of annexation arose, in
his judgment, out of the old scorn of the English
Government towards the colonies, and the fatuous
policy of the Manchester School.

At this point, an amendment was proposed by Mr.
Hamilton : " That it is wholly inexpedient to discuss
the question of annexation at this convention, the
loyalty of whose members cannot be questioned, and
amongst whom, as a body, there is found no individual

to advocate any such obnoxious principle." Only a firm expression of opinion on the part of the convention would, he urged, force the English Government to realize that any further delay, or refusal to remedy the legitimate grievances of the colony, might lead to annexation. The convention was quite justified, in his opinion, in using the threat of annexation as a means of coercing England into a compliance with their demands. The Canadian farmers would not suffer much longer without seeking relief in a union with the United States. If the resolution of Mr. Miller was adopted, the idea would prevail that no matter what England did, or failed to do, Canada would remain staunchly loyal to the bitter end. The League should not forget the insults that the British Government had heaped upon them. They were not called upon, Mr. George Duggan added, to trumpet forth their undying loyalty, but should rather seek to find some remedy or remedies for the evils from which they were now suffering. But these clever attempts to divert the attention of the delegates from the main resolution, by arousing the smouldering embers of resentment against the motherland, did not succeed.

The delegates shared the opinion of Mr. G. Duggan that, however much the expediency of the introduction of the original resolution might be questioned, the convention could not amend it, without creating the false impression that the League was in sympathy with annexation. The amendment was accordingly defeated by an overwhelming majority, only four or five delegates venturing to support it. The Miller resolution was thereupon agreed to unanimously.

The convention revealed very clearly that the question of annexation had grown in interest and importance since the Kingston Convention. Notwithstanding the defection of many of the Annexationists from the party, there was still a considerable leaven of annexation sentiment in some branches of the League, especially in Lower Canada. But the convention was too strongly

British in feeling for the few isolated representatives of pro-American sentiment to venture to advocate their cause openly, save as an ultimate resort, in case that all their remedies failed to restore prosperity to the colony. The overwhelming majority of the delegates were unswervingly loyal, though a few were free to admit that the question of annexation was worthy of consideration ; they refused, however, to have anything to do with it, so long as there was a reasonable hope of saving the country in any other way. A few of the ultra-loyalists, Colonel Playfair for example, would not admit that annexation was a proper subject for discussion. The decisive vote of the convention settled the question of annexation for all time, so far as the general body of the League was concerned. The annexationist members saw the folly of waging a losing battle against such heavy odds, and desisted from any further agitation within the League.

Immediately after the close of the convention, Mr. T. Wilson of Quebec addressed an open letter to Mr. John Redpath, in which he deplored a continuance of the annexation campaign, as threatening serious injury to the interests and prosperity of Canada, and as weakening the hands of those who were seeking to improve the constitution of the country. He deeply sympathized with his many fellow citizens who had been reduced to insolvency by the unjust fiscal legislation of England, but he was convinced that the adoption of the policy of the League in respect to elective institutions, and the protection of Canadian industries, would rescue the province from its distress. " For annexation the people are not yet ready, and the discussion of the question is premature and imprudent, and, if persisted in, can only lead to commotion and civil war." For these reasons, he appealed to Mr. Redpath, as President of the Montrea association, to drop the annexation issue for the time being, until the policy of the League had been tried. " All are agreed that we cannot remain as we are, and many that annexation may be necessary, but only as a last step." They should, therefore, wait to see what the future had in store, before rushing hastily into an advocacy of annexation.

The response of Mr. Redpath was a scathing intimation to Mr. Wilson to mind his own business, and not meddle in the affairs of other persons and organizations. In conclusion, he remarked : " I do not despair of yet seeing you a good annexationist (criminal though the idea may appear to you at present) after you have seen the futility of the various nostrums which are now occupying your attention." This brief but pointed correspondence marked the final breach of the League and the Annexation Party. The latter, through its President, decisively refused to sell out to its quondam friends, or to compromise its principles in any way. The flag of annexation was nailed more tightly than ever to the masthead of the association.

At a subsequent meeting of the Montreal branch of the League, the Hon. George Moffatt stated that he deemed the expression of an opinion on the annexation movement premature at present, but thought that the Annexationists might have continued to act with them. He did not say that annexation might not finally come to be a matter for consideration and debate, but the time had not come yet. When that time did come, he would consider it entirely as a Canadian question. " But we ought first to ascertain what Great Britain could and would do for us." Should England, however, refuse to adopt a policy under which Canada could prosper, " then we must consider an alternative." In conclusion he severely criticized the policy of Great Britain in respect to free trade and the Navigation Laws.

Mr. Backus, who avowed himself an Annexationist, saw no incompatibility in belonging to both the League and the annexation association, but several of the other members expressed themselves as strongly opposed to annexation. In the ensuing election of officers, the former annexationist officials were dropped from the slate, and a pronounced pro-British Executive, with Hon. George Moffatt as President, and Messrs. Gugy, Allan, Fisher, and Mack as Vice-Presidents, was chosen in their stead. With such a board of officials, there was little opportunity for the future propagation of separationist tenets in the Montreal branch of the League. There might indeed be a hankering desire on the part of some of the members for an alliance with the Annexationists, but there was no longer any question of the loyalty of the League.

Several of the Leagues in Upper Canada likewise took occasion to register " their most decided disapprobation of all attempts being made to sever these British-American provinces from the mother country, with a view of joining the republican United States of America." [1]   The Cambden Branch expressed the hope " that the convention, when it meets again, will use every exertion to suppress such an iniquitous measure." Among the Conservatives of Upper Canada, the consensus of opinion was tending more strongly every day against any interference with the colonial relation.

One phase of the annexation movement in Upper Canada has been reserved for separate consideration, namely, its relation to the Clear Grit Party. The general election, as we have seen, had returned an overwhelming majority of Reformers to the House of Assembly. As long as the struggle for responsible government was being fought out, the Baldwin-Lafontaine Ministry commanded the united support of the party. But with the triumph of the principles of English Liberalism, the former division in the ranks of the party again reappeared. The joint leaders of the Government were too cautious in temperament and too conservative in policy to please the more radical element of the Reformers. The latter were daily growing more impatient at the moderation of the

[1] *British Parl. Pap.* (Papers relating to Canada, 1850).

Government, and its apparent disinclination to deal with the burning political and ecclesiastical issues of the day.

Mr. George Brown of *The Globe* essayed in vain the difficult rôle of endeavouring by friendly criticism to stir up the Ministry to action, and, at the same time, of curbing the restless spirit of the militant democratic wing of the party. The patience of the Clear Grits was at last exhausted. The Hon. Malcolm Cameron, the most prominent member of the group in the Assembly, threw up his position in the Government, as a protest against the failure of Mr. Baldwin to settle the question of clergy reserves. Throughout the province many of the local Radical leaders, such as Peter Perry, Caleb Hopkins, Dr. John Rolph, and William MacDougal of *The Examiner*, assumed an attitude of open hostility to the Government. Although not formally withdrawing from the Reform Party, the Clear Grits practically set up an independent political organization with a distinct party press. The principles of the party were derived almost exclusively from the democracy of the United States. Their chief demands were for the secularization of the clergy reserves, the retrenchment of public expenditure, the reform of the judicial system, and the adoption of popular elective institutions. But to none of these proposals did the Government lend an attentive ear.

With the grant of responsible Government, Baldwin regarded his constitutional labours as practically complete. But to the Clear Grits, Ministerial responsibility was not an end in itself, but merely a means for the attainment of the ultimate democratic ends of the party. They could not help but contrast the material prosperity, religious freedom, and liberal institutions of the United States with the industrial depression, and the undemocratic political and ecclesiastical régime at home. They were weary of the long unending struggle against the forces of privilege within the province, backed up by the sovereign authority of the petty tyrants of Downing Street. So long as Canada remained a dependency of a distant empire, and subject to the rule of the Colonial Office, there appeared, to many of the Radicals, to be but small prospect of the attainment of their political demands.

Much had been expected from the advent of the Reform Ministry to office, but events had proved that even their own political leaders had fallen a prey to the fatal influence of English officialism. In their bitter disappointment over the failure of the Government to relieve their grievances, the thoughts of many of the extremists naturally turned towards the possible emancipation of the colony from the control of the powers at Westminster, and its contingent incorporation in the United States, in case that relief could not be secured by any other means. " Recent events," said *The Examiner*, " tell us that responsible Government, as it now exists, is an illusion, a mockery, and a snare—only Downing Street law under a new name. We must have a Government that is really representative and responsible, if we ever hope to attain to a state of public tranquillity. If we cannot have it while a colony, we shall unequivocally labour to obtain and secure it through our independence as a state." [1]

Throughout the summer and fall of 1849, the Clear Grit press, especially *The Toronto Examiner* and *The Hamilton Provincialist*, was carrying on with much success a guerilla warfare against the Government. Their indictments of the extravagance and inefficiency of the administrative and judicial branches of the Government reflected the bitter disappointment and chagrin of many of the public at finding that their taxes were in no wise diminished in consequence of the depression of trade ; while their demand for elective institutions was warmly welcomed by the growing democracy of the country, who had long been weary of the bureaucracy of the old régime. But the fundamental grievance of the party was the maintenance of

[1] *The Examiner*, June 26, 1850.

the clergy reserves. All other grievances could be patiently borne for a time without exciting a demand for separation, but the burden of a system of ecclesiastical privilege, which was inseparably bound up with the imperial connection, tried the loyalty of the progressive Reformers to the breaking-point. " If," declared *The Examiner*,[1] " the Imperial and Colonial Governments want to create a universal shout from Gaspé to Sandwich for annexation to the Republic, they have only to tell the people that the clergy reserves are to be held intact by imperial power. . . . The remedy to which every eye will then be directed will most unquestionably be annexation to the United States." A similar opinion was entertained by *The Provincialist* and other Clear Grit organs.

The Radical press throughout the province was doing everything in its power to force the Government to deal with the allied questions of the rectories and the clergy reserves. The majority of the party still believed that the evils of the country could be best relieved by the united efforts of all the Reformers rather than by creating a schism in the ranks, or by advocating such an extreme policy as annexation ; but, at the same time, they intimated in unmistakable terms that Mr. Baldwin must carry out their election pledges in respect to the clergy reserves, under pain of disrupting the party, and forcing the Clear Grit members into an attitude of opposition to the British connection.[2]

The whole question was brought to an issue in the bye-election in the third Riding of York. Mr. Peter Perry, the prospective candidate of the Reformers, was a prominent member of the Clear Grit wing of the party, which was exceptionally strong in the constituency. Although he had made no public declara-

---

[1] *The Examiner*, November 14, 1849.
[2] *The Hamilton Provincialist* of November 7, 1849, declared that it was still opposed to annexation, if Baldwin would carry out his promise to deal with the clergy reserves.

tion on the subject of annexation, his views were generally understood to be favourable to a union with the United States. The scattered Annexationists of the Riding and the organs of that party claimed him as an adherent, if not a member, of their own group. This anomalous situation of affairs called forth, as we have seen, the masterful letter of Baldwin in which he disavowed the Annexationists and all their friends.

Mr. Perry was informed, in effect, that the Government would not recognize an annexation candidate as a member of the Reform Party. Notwithstanding the personal character of this communication, Perry vouchsafed no reply. Shortly after, a deputation of his constituents waited on him to invite him to become a candidate for the Riding. One of the members of the deputation—a British connectionist—took occasion to question the prospective member in regard to his views on the subject of annexation, with which his name had recently been very freely connected.[1] The answer of Mr. Perry was distinctly non-committal. He gave his word that, if elected, he would not advocate annexation during the coming term of service, and further pledged himself to resign his seat, in case his opinion as to the present inadvisability of an annexation propaganda should undergo a change. Annexation, in his judgment, was not an immediate issue in this election. He assured the deputation that the electors would be given a full opportunity to discuss and vote upon the question before its final determination by Parliament. This answer was apparently satisfactory to the deputation, for Mr. Perry was duly adopted as the candidate of the party.[2]

But *The Globe* was by no means satisfied with the equivocal attitude of Mr. Perry. By his recent conduct, it declared, he had practically ranged himself with the opponents of the British connection, and for this reason alone his election should be opposed in the

[1] *The Toronto Globe*, November 1, 1849.
[2] *Ibid.*, October 30, 1849.

most strenuous manner. This was not a question of party, for all loyalists should unite in frowning down the annexation movement.[1] A few days later, however, *The Globe* considerably modified its belligerent tone. It was now content to call upon Mr. Perry to define his position more clearly, in justice to the Reform Party, since there was reason to fear, from the boastings of the Annexationists, that he was not faithful in his allegiance to the Crown.

The agitation of *The Globe* stirred up the ultra-loyal Reformers of the Riding to consider the possibility of putting a candidate in the field against Mr. Perry. A meeting was accordingly called, at which delegates were present from four of the five townships of the east Riding, to choose a candidate in the Reform interest. A motion to the effect that Mr. Perry be adopted as the nominee of the party found no seconder. A deputation was appointed to wait upon Mr. Perry and present the Toronto anti-annexation manifesto for his signature. In case of his refusal to sign the same, Mr. William Clark, a prosperous local farmer, was asked to accept the nomination of the convention, and the delegates pledged themselves to do everything in their power to secure his return to Parliament.

In accordance with their instructions, Messrs. McMaster and Hall, the representatives of the convention, waited upon Mr. Perry ; but the latter firmly refused to sign the desired declaration, on the ground that it would tend to suppress the free discussion of a question which was worthy of the consideration of the people of the province. Annexation, in his opinion, was the ultimate destiny of Canada, but he did not think that the time had yet arrived for it. He renewed his pledge that he would oppose the policy of annexation, if the question were brought up in the coming Parliament. Retrenchment and reciprocity with the United States would, in his judgment, best serve the interests of the public for the present. Mr. Perry was

[1] *The Toronto Globe*, October 23, 1849.

a shrewd politician. He clearly saw that no person could be elected in the Riding as an avowed Annexationist. Annexation sentiment in Upper Canada was as yet, according to his own declaration, "without sufficient moral courage to give free voice to its political convictions." He had no intention of blocking his political future by a premature declaration of faith ; but, at the same time, he stood ready to espouse the cause, as soon as it gave promise of ultimate success.

The successful opportunist tactics of Mr. Perry placed *The Globe* in a most embarrassing position. It would gladly have opposed his candidature tooth and nail, but his personal strength in the Riding was such that it was extremely inexpedient to oppose his election, and so court almost certain defeat. It felt itself in honour bound to support Mr. Clark, as an anti-annexationist candidate, but it did not wish further to antagonize the Clear Grit element in the party by an uncompromising opposition. There was already grave danger of an open disruption in the ranks of the Reformers, and it was feared that an internecine struggle in the third Riding might spread to the remainder of the province, and not only accentuate the existing differences between the two wings of the party, but might also, in the event of the defeat of the Ministerial candidate, deal a dangerous blow to the prestige of the Government, and even endanger its position. Under these circumstances, it adopted a coaxing tone towards Mr. Perry and his supporters, in the hope of avoiding an open conflict on the question of annexation. The situation was relieved, however, by Mr. Clark's declination of the proffered nomination, which left a clear field to Mr. Perry.

The Clear Grit press had been following the contest with peculiar interest. Mr. Perry was fighting the battle of the party with singular adroitness and success, and they could well afford to enjoy the discomfiture of their erstwhile friends, and the happy turn of events in their favour. *The Provincialist* took the keenest de-

light in poking fun at the hapless struggle of *The Globe*
in endeavouring to extricate itself from a humiliating
position.   *The Examiner* supported the candidature
of Perry, whether as an Annexationist or otherwise, in
view of the favourable effect it would undoubtedly have
upon English public opinion.   *The Journal and Express* warmly commended the action of Perry in refusing
to sign the counter-manifesto.   No candidate, it declared, ought to pledge himself in regard to future
issues, since he was responsible only for his present
course of conduct and not for distant contingencies.
The Long Point Advocate took strong exception to the
pronouncement of Baldwin that the Ministry, if defeated, were prepared to support any Government
or party in opposition to annexation.   Rather than
sustain, it declared, a Tory Government, even though
favourable to the British connection, " the Reformers
generally would prefer independence or annexation."

The embarrassment of the Government occasioned
much glee in the Conservative ranks.   The conduct of
Perry was regarded as a personal rebuff to Baldwin,
and as a severe blow to his authority as a political
leader ;   it afforded conclusive evidence of the rapid
breaking up of the Reform Party.   Tory journalists
accused the Executive of postponing the issue of the
writ for the third Riding until it was considered safe to
hold the election.   The Government, *The Colonist* exclaimed, had shown its weakness in the face of treason.[1]
Under the circumstances, it was considered the part
of wisdom not to put a Tory candidate in the field,
but to allow the two factions of the Reformers to fight
it out.

The writ of election was issued soon after in due
course.   On nomination day, Colonel Thompson presented himself as a candidate ;   but, on finding merely
a handful of voters in his favour, discreetly decided to
withdraw.   Mr. Perry was thereupon declared elected
by acclamation.   The result of the election was natur-

[1] *The Toronto Colonist*, November 13, 1849.

ally represented by the annexation press as a splendid triumph for their cause.   *The Independent* claimed that Perry was prepared to make himself the champion of independence and annexation at the next general election.   It expressed its cordial approval of his decision to oppose any immediate action in regard to annexation, since, in the opinion of *The Independent*, it would be most ill advised to force the question prematurely upon Parliament.   Similar considerations of political expediency, it explained, had guided the action of the Annexationists at the recent League convention in determining not to bring the matter to an issue in that body.   At the present time, it boasted, there were not less than fifteen members of Parliament who were in the same position as Mr. Perry, and the coming bye-elections in Megantic and Norfolk would doubtless increase that number.   Such, it concluded, were the splendid results of two brief months of agitation.

L'Avenir, likewise, confidently asserted that there were a large number of Reformers in Upper Canada who were heartily sick of the imperial connection, and would gladly welcome a change of allegiance.   The Clear Grits, in truth, were striving to gain the same end as the Annexationists, though by somewhat different means.   When the reforms, now so eagerly sought by the Clear Grits, were once obtained, " England," it concluded, " would hesitate even less than now to give up Canada. . . . The Annexationists, therefore, should support the Clear Grit Party and their principles with all their might." [1]

The position of the Radical wing of the Reformers was extremely critical.   The rank and file of the party were undoubtedly loyal at heart, but, at the same time, deeply dissatisfied with the existing condition of affairs.   There was indeed grave danger that this dissatisfaction at the continual postponement of reforms might develop into an open hostility to the British connection.   The election of Peter Perry was

[1] *L'Avenir*, April 13, 1850.

truly symptomatic ; it revealed alike the strength of the Clear Grit Party and their political tendencies.

At this crucial moment there appeared an interesting series of letters from the exiled leader of the party, William Lyon Mackenzie, in which he warned his former followers against the perils of annexation.   His sojourn in New York had wrought a disillusionment.   American democracy, as it presented itself in the form of political corruption, crass materialism, and human slavery, filled his soul with righteous indignation.   He was convinced that the vaunted liberty of the United States was merely a sham ;   that neither the grandiloquent principles of the Declaration of Independence nor the unctuous guarantees of the American Constitution assured to the private citizen the same measure of civil and political freedom as was enjoyed by the humblest Canadian subject under the British Constitution and the much-maligned Act of Union.   The growing agitation in favour of separation afforded him an excellent opportunity of conveying to his former Canadian friends and adherents his opinions in regard to annexation.   In an open letter to *The Toronto Examiner*, he stated that, although he was not prepared to oppose the reported rapid strides of annexation sentiment, nevertheless, had he been able to settle in Canada "every effort man could make would have been made by me, not only to keep Canada separated from this country, but also to preserve the British connection, and to make that connection worth preserving.   Failing in that, I would have quietly left the scene, when I could not be useful." [1]

The voice of Mackenzie still exerted considerable influence over the Clear Grit Party, many of the older members of which were numbered among his former followers, and some of whom still looked upon him as their political chieftain.   The timely advice of Mackenzie, together with the resolute stand of Baldwin and Cameron, served to restrain the rash tendencies of the

[1] *The Examiner*, January 31, 1850.

extreme section of the party. The tone of the Clear Grit press gradually veered round from an ultra-friendly to a more critical attitude towards the United States, and, in the end, to a loyal support of the British connection. The gradual revival of trade, the untoward turn of American affairs, and the more favourable prospect of provincial reforms, all contributed to allay the spirit of disaffection among the Clear Grits.

CHAPTER VI

THE DECLINE OF THE MOVEMENT

THE hopes of the Montreal Annexationists were greatly stimulated by the favourable tone of some of the leading English papers, especially those of the Manchester School. *The Morning Advertiser* went so far as to declare that the Government had come to the conclusion that the severance of the imperial tie, in the case of Canada, would be beneficial to the mother country, and that it would lay proposals to that effect before Parliament at the coming session. The Radical pronouncement of Mr. Cobden at Bradford afforded special encouragement to the Montreal Association. In this celebrated speech, he distinctly advocated the extension of the largest measure of self-government to the colonies with a view to their ultimate independence at the earliest possible moment. He called for the immediate withdrawal of any further military or ecclesiastical aid to the colonies, by which simple economy an annual sum of £15,000,000 would be saved to the imperial treasury. "I want to see this country abandon the mere political connection between the colonies and herself, and trust to our common literature, our common language, which will give to the Saxon race unity throughout the world if they do nothing now to prevent that understanding."

In the colonies, the views of Cobden carried scarcely less weight than in England. In Canada, he was justly looked upon as one of the most influential leaders in English political life. By the Reformers, in particular, he was held in the highest honour for his liberal and enlightened statesmanship. His views in respect to the colonies were admittedly Radical, but it was confidently believed by many of the colonists that they would be accepted by the Whig Government in due course of time. If Cobden had been in Canada, *The Courier* triumphantly declared, he and his friends would have signed the manifesto. What Canada wanted was not so much retrenchment or elective institutions as freedom of trade with the United States, which could only be secured by annexation. The colonial system might, it concluded, be bolstered up for a time, but annexation would come at last.

But the roseate hopes of the Annexationists in respect to the attitude of the British Government were doomed to disappointment. In matters of colonial policy, Cobden did not voice the opinion of the English Government or nation. A man of different calibre and different principles was at the head of the colonial office. Earl Grey, the Secretary of State for the Colonies, was a Liberal Imperialist. He favoured the extension of the principles of self-government to the colonies, but was firmly convinced of the paramount necessity of maintaining the integrity of the empire. A man of strong and imperious will, though of liberal sentiments, he did not hesitate in his administration of colonial affairs to play at times the part of a just but benevolent dictator. The didactic despatches which he was accustomed to address to the colonies were a true reflection of his firm political convictions in matters of colonial policy.

The Colonial Secretary had been following the despatches of Lord Elgin with a keen and critical interest. The growth of the annexation movement afforded him an excellent opportunity of intervening in Canadian affairs ; and on this occasion he intervened with more than his accustomed force and authority. In a despatch to the Governor-General of January 9, 1850, he clearly and decisively set forth the determination of the English Government to oppose the annexation movement with all the forces at its command. After acknowledging the receipt of many loyal addresses from various colonial bodies, His Lordship declared :

" With regard to the Address to the people of Canada in favour of severing the province from the British Dominions, for the purpose of annexing it to the United States, which forms the subject of the 3rd of these despatches, I have to inform you that Her Majesty approves of your having dismissed from her service those who have signed a document which is scarcely short of treasonable in its character. Her Majesty confidently relies on the loyalty of the great majority of her Canadian subjects, and she is therefore determined to exert all the authority which belongs to her, for the purpose of maintaining the connection of Canada with this country, being persuaded that the permanence of that connection is highly advantageous to both.

" Your Lordship will, therefore, understand that you are commanded by Her Majesty to resist, to the utmost of your power, any attempt which may be made to bring about the separation of Canada from the British Dominions, and to mark in the strongest manner Her Majesty's displeasure with all those who may directly or indirectly encourage such a design.

" And if any attempt of this kind should take such a form that those who are guilty of it may, according to such advice as you may receive from your law advisers, be made responsible for their conduct in a court of justice, you will not fail to take the necessary measures for bringing them to account."

The despatch of Earl Grey aroused the keenest interest among the Canadian public, as the first official expression of the policy of the home Government towards the annexation movement. It was severely condemned, and in turn as warmly commended, according to the political views of the critics. Some of the annexation journals vented their spleen upon the Colonial Secretary in a most offensive manner. They indignantly repudiated the veiled accusation of treason, flaunted his mild menaces of coercion, and flung back at his lordship the charge of seeking to stifle freedom of thought by the employment of dictatorial methods. *L'Avenir* and *The Herald* were especially outspoken in their criticism of the tone and subject-matter of the despatch. The former professed to see in the despatch a mere reflex of the false representations of the Governor-General to the effect that he had crushed the annexation movement.

The Annexationists were not surprised at the reply since they had no expectation of a favourable opinion from the English Government, until the provincial legislation should adopt resolutions in favour of a union with the United States. It expressed the conviction that the Canadian people would not meekly submit to the dictation of Downing Street, as recommended by the ministerial press.[1] *The Herald* sarcastically remarked : " We may surely be permitted to say that it is not for England, and far less for Lord Grey to tell us that the permanence of the connection is highly advantageous to us, but to convince us that it is so." It practically denied the right of the motherland to a voice in the determination of the future of the colony. " The Annexationists," it concluded, " are not children to be bullied by misrepresentation and falsehood."

The remaining annexation journals were much more discreet in their utterances. The criticism of *The Courier* was couched in moderate language. " Lord Grey's opinion is good so far as it goes ; it is the opinion of an individual—nay, for argument's sake, we will grant that it is the opinion of the Imperial Ministry; but neither Lord Grey, nor the administration of which he is a member, are the Parliament or people of England, and it is to them that the people of Canada must look for a decision in this matter."

But the despatch of the Colonial Secretary had gravely shaken the overweening confidence of *The Courier* in the inevitableness of annexation. " We do not say," it continued, " that a contingency may not arise which will prevent, or rather render unnecessary, any further agitation for Canadian independence and its consequence—annexation. If our commercial affairs be set right—by the passage of a Reciprocity Act in the Legislature of the United States, and under the recent alterations in the Navigation Laws ; if England consents to surrender the Civil List, and to allow us to reduce the salary of the Governor-General to something like an American standard, or if not, to defray his salary herself, as is demanded by the people of Jamaica ; if she allows us to make other reductions which are necessary ; if she grants us an entirely elective Legis-

[1] *L'Avenir,* February 15, 1850.

lature, and consents to a general expansion of the elective principle, and, in fact, gives us entirely the management of our internal affairs; why then, it is possible that we may find it to our advantage to cease the present agitation." The great majority of the Annexationists, it concluded, were as loyal as their pro-British opponents, and more so than the Government which had driven them into the advocacy of a political union with their neighbours.[1]

The criticism of *The Witness* was even more interesting. It deplored the tone and style of his lordship's despatch, as unworthy of a British minister. The people of Canada were as capable of judging their own interests as the gentlemen of Downing Street, and they strongly resented the language of menace and the threats of coercion which had been addressed to them. There was, it asserted, "a splendid opportunity to evince the sincerity of men's professions." The Annexationists had professed their adherence to the principle of peace, and, however much their views might be misrepresented, they ought not to resort to menaces in return. "Rather let there be a public and renewed adhesion to the amicable and peaceful principles they have already announced," and a disclaimer of all attempts to accomplish their ends by means of violence. "If," it concluded in a sanctimonious strain, "Annexationists calmly and patiently commit their cause to Him who ruleth all things, and doeth all things well, He will, if He sees fit, easily bring it about with the consent and goodwill of all parties, for He has the hearts of all men in His hands; and if He does not see meet to bring it about thus, surely no one should attempt to bring it about otherwise."

On the other hand, the loyalist press received the despatch with the heartiest commendations. The Annexationists, *The Gazette* declared, had been entirely mistaken as to the state of English opinion. The agitation, it admitted in a conciliatory tone, had done

[1] Quoted from *The Pilot*, February 7, 1850.

much good within certain limits, especially in revealing to the public the dangerous situation of the country's affairs. But unfortunately some of the annexation leaders and papers had gone too far in attacking the English Government. Now that the attention of the British authorities had been attracted to colonial affairs, it behoved the Annexationists to unite with the League to secure the necessary reforms in colonial government. The despatch, *The Pilot* gleefully declared, placed the Annexationists in a bad fix. The leaders of that party, especially Messrs. Rose and Johnston, would now have an opportunity of putting into effect their open declarations that they would acquiesce in the decision of the English Government. The despatch should give a *coup de grâce* to the annexation cause. The manifesto, it concluded, could not now secure one-half the signatures which were originally obtained.[1]

The French ministerial press very cleverly attempted to interpret the despatch as an expression of the personal will of the sovereign. *La Minerve* discussed the despatch under the caption, " La Reine contre l'annexion." *Le Canadien* warned its readers that the Annexationists had carried their agitation too far to be stopped by the refusal of the English Government to accede to their demand for separation. " Pas de duperie dans une affaire aussi sérieux ; que chacun sache, et soit bien averti que, si nous demandons l'indépendance, il faudra que nous l'ayons bon gré, mal gré, et au prix d'une guerre avec le métropole, si elle rejecte notre demande." A similar opinion was re-echoed in *Le Journal de Québec*. " To convince two million people that their happiness, moral and material, can only be obtained by independence, to impress this strongly on their convictions, and then to pretend that they will stop peaceably and resignedly before a refusal, is to give the lie to history and to one's own conscience." The religious papers were quick to use

[1] *The Pilot*, February 5, 1850.

the despatch as a fitting text with which to admonish the faithful to remember their true allegiance to the Crown. *Les Mélanges Religieux* voiced the opinion that the Annexationists should now drop their agitation in deference to the wishes of the Queen ; any further agitation would give the appearance of open disloyalty and rebellion.

The despatch of the Colonial Secretary had a very clarifying effect ; it swept away many of the obscurities and misconceptions under cover of which the Annexationists had sheltered themselves, and successfully carried on their propaganda. The language of the despatch was too plain-spoken to be misinterpreted ; henceforth the Annexationists could not pretend that the English Government was either favourable or indifferent to the separation of the colonies. The despatch brought the affairs of the party to a crisis. Should they, according to their open professions, acquiesce in the decision of the Colonial Secretary, or should they turn revolutionaries ? This was the vital issue which they were called upon to decide. Some of the members of the party were admittedly Simon Pure republicans, others were personally hostile to Great Britain, but the great majority of the party still retained the kindliest feelings towards the motherland, and were strongly averse to any form or even the appearance of revolutionary activity.

The despatch afforded the moderate element of the party a favourable opportunity of withdrawing from the association, on reasonable grounds, and with a good grace. In view of the unexpected turn of affairs, quite a number of the members saw fit quietly to drop out of the ranks. But the leaders of the party were strong-minded men. Having set their hands to the plough, they were not inclined to turn back at the appearance of new obstacles. Some of them had borne the censure and penalties of the Governor-General, and all of them had stood the personal criticisms of their fellow country-men without flinching ; they were not now to be intimidated by the disapproval or menaces of the Secretary of State.

For some time past the direction of the affairs of the association had fallen into the hands of the Executive Council. On this occasion, they did not even trouble to call a meeting of the members to discuss the new situation, but determined to act for themselves, in the name of the association.[1] A bold but somewhat laboured manifesto was the result. *The Council* went even farther than *The Herald* in affecting to treat his lordship's opinion as a mere personal whim without the sanction of the British nation ; they adroitly maintained that it would be a dangerous principle to permit the use of the Queen's name to suppress the lawful discussions of any public question in the colony ; and they demanded, in effect, that the English Government should stand aside, and permit them to carry on their propaganda without official opposition. This interesting document ran as follows :

To the People of Canada

The Annexation Association of Montreal feel it incumbent on them to address you in reference to the following despatch from Earl Grey, purporting to contain the views of Her Most Gracious Majesty on the question of the peaceable separation of Canada from Great Britain and its Annexation to the United States. [Here follows Earl Grey's despatch.]

The Association have carefully reconsidered their two addresses, and they do not find in them the language of menace or sedition ; but a calm, dispassionate statement of social evils under which Canada suffers, and a remedy, by constitutional means, suggested for consideration. It is to the people of Canada that these statements have been made, and it is for you to decide whether the remedy proposed is one that is advantageous or worthy of being referred to the

[1] *The Gazette* insinuated they feared to convene the association because so many of the members disapproved of their policy.

British nation for their assent. It is impossible for this Association to regard the expression of Earl Grey's opinion as conveying the decision of the British nation. Even should the British Parliament support his lordship, we conceive that their action will be premature, until the question has been constitutionally brought before them as approved by a majority of the representatives of the Canadian people. The Association deny the right of the Colonial Secretary to offer, by anticipation, the decision of the British Government on a question that is not constitutionally before them ; and they further desire to point out the danger that may hereafter arise, if the principle be once admitted that the Queen's name and authority can be introduced to suppress the lawful discussion of any political question in the colony. The British people have a proper and constitutional opportunity of expressing their assent or dissent to any colonial measures, and it is a subject of painful surprise to this Association, that Earl Grey should have encroached on the rights of Her Majesty's Canadian subjects, in venturing to decide that any question was unfit to be brought by them before their representatives. The Association are necessarily ignorant of the terms in which the Governor-General brought their address under the notice of the Colonial Secretary, and how far those terms justify his lordship in giving a character to their proceedings which they have distinctly denied from the outset. The Association now reiterate that they seek the attainment of their object only with the free and willing consent of Great Britain, that they never will urge the subject by other than calm appeals to the reason and intelligence of their fellow subjects—first in Canada, afterwards in England—and that they have no sympathy with any who hold other sentiments than these.

While reasserting the position the Association have assumed, they feel that the language of the Colonial Secretary requires from them the discharge of a further and a higher duty, in denying all right, on his part, to attempt to punish men for.the assertion of opinion.

The free discussion of all subjects is a right inherent in every man under a free form of Government, and the power to advocate, by constitutional means and moderate counsels, changes of any description is the great safeguard against violence and rebellion. The moment an attempt is made to coerce the free expression of public opinion, the most sacred right of the people is attacked, and the groundwork laid for any and every stretch of despotic power. The Association ask their fellow citizens whether, in all they have suggested or done, they have not most carefully avoided advocating aught that could in the slightest degree infringe the laws, or warrant the interference of Executive Authority. And, feeling that their course has been temperate and legal, they deny the right of Earl Grey to use towards them the language of his despatch, or to interfere in their discussions of any subject affecting the interests of Canada. The Association, therefore, intreat their fellow subjects not to allow any feeling of hostility to the policy of those who now address them, to blind them to the consequences of admitting the position assumed by Lord Grey ; but to look only at the great principle involved.

Let the people of Canada, to whom the Association addressed themselves, decide whether the course of Earl Grey is in accordance with the constitution granted to them, and whether his approval or disapproval ought to affect the legal discussion of any subject intended to be brought before the Legislature of this country.

Let them say whether Responsible Government is only a name, or is intended to assume that freedom of opinion, dear to every British subject. To you, then, the people of Canada, we appeal ; and we ask whether we shall be compelled to brood in silence over the evils this country labours under, or whether we have the right temperately to discuss those evils and their cure, free from the threat of punishment, and independent alike of the interference and control of any others than those who are constitutionally responsible to you. In conclusion, the Association would remark, that the subject of discussion has been obscured by the mode adopted for checking the expression of public opinion, and this Association in the broad assertion of an undeniable right, maintain that they will not be diverted from the legal and constitutional course which they have adopted, in full reliance that whenever the question is brought before Great Britain, by our responsible ministers, their application will be treated with that respect and consideration which its magnitude and importance demand. In the deliberate adoption of this course, the Association conceive that they are defending one of the greatest bulwarks of their country's liberties, and they claim the support of all true friends of Canada, whatever be their views of the policy the Association seek to promote.

JOHN REDPATH, President.

R. McKAY ⎱
A. A. DORION ⎰ Secretaries.

The patent weakness of the manifesto exposed the Annexationists to the open attacks of the loyalist press of the city. The latter did not fail to point out, with manifest glee, that the much-advertised great popular movement had become a mere cabal. " This comedy," *Le Canadien* declared, " which has lasted for some time, has degenerated into a miserable farce, and does not now well possess the merit of exciting a laugh." The address had been concocted in " a hole and corner," where the officers of the association, a mere fraction of the original sixty, " met in solemn conclave to decide upon the destinies of Canada." The pro-British papers pointed out with telling force the flagrant inconsistency of the original submissive professions of the association and their subsequent defiant attitude towards the English Government.[1]

[1] *The Pilot*, February 9, 1850.

The quibbling arguments of the manifesto were assailed with gentle ridicule.[1] Must the English Government wait, *The Gazette* inquired, until the Annexationists had convinced the people of Canada of their policy, before venturing to express an opinion on a matter which was vital to an empire? To question the official character of his lordship's despatch was in effect to attack the fundamental principle of responsible government. "We are of the opinion," *The Gazette* concluded, "that many persons will pause before taking the ticklish path," which the association are now treading. *The Pilot* charged the Annexationists with knowing full well that the despatch of the Colonial Secretary truly reflected the mind of Parliament, and that the House of Commons would heartily support the efforts of the Government to suppress the spirit of restlessness in the colonies. Notwithstanding the specious appeal of the manifesto to the inalienable right of liberty of thought, there could be no question, it declared, of the undoubted authority of the Crown to punish its colonial subjects for seditious utterances, or overt acts of treason. To these deep home-thrusts the Annexationists could only reply by reasserting the purity of their motives, and the strictly constitutional character of their agitation. The public, however, were inclined to look to their recent proceedings, rather than to their professions, for evidence of their motives and policy.

Just at this moment there appeared the authoritative declaration of Lord John Russell in the House of Commons, in partial confirmation of the despatch of the Colonial Secretary. In the course of an able exposition of the colonial policy of the Government, the Premier reviewed the situation of Canadian affairs with special reference to the disturbances over the Rebellion Losses Bill, and the more recent political discontent. After a vigorous defence of the conduct of Lord Elgin, he turned to the consideration of the annexation

---

[1] *The Gazette*, February 11, 1850.

movement. " I have, however, seen bitter complaints on this subject, and I have seen that some persons have even gone the length of proposing that, instead of remaining subjects of Her Majesty, the Province of Canada should be annexed to the United States. To that proposal, of course, the Crown could give nothing but a decided negative ; and I trust that although such a suggestion has been made, that from the character of several of the gentlemen who are members of the association, it is not their intention to push their project of joining a neighbouring state to the ultimate result of endeavouring by force of arms to effect a separation from Great Britain ; but that, knowing the determined will of the Sovereign of this country, and of her advisers, not to permit that project to be carried into effect, they will acquiesce in the decision of the Crown. I wonder at the same time that any persons who profess loyalty to the Sovereign should have entertained a project which, if unfortunately any international difference occurred between this country and the United States of America, might have placed them in the position of raising their arms against British authority, and of fighting against the British flag." [1]

But notwithstanding the firmness of this declaration, the principles of the Manchester School still dominated the mind of the Premier ; for, in concluding his speech, one of the most powerful of his long political career, he frankly acknowledged that he looked forward to the day when the great self-governing colonies should assert their independence. " I anticipate indeed with others, that some of the colonies may so grow in population and wealth that they may say : ' Our strength is sufficient to enable us to be independent of England. The link is now become onerous to us, the time is come when we think we can, in amity and alliance with England, maintain our independence.' I do not think that that time is yet approaching. But let us make

[1] *Hansard*, 1850, vol. 108, p. 551.

them as far as possible fit to govern themselves—let us give them, as far as we can, the capacity of ruling their own affairs—let them increase in wealth and population ; and, whatever may happen, we of this great empire shall have the consolation of saying that we have contributed to the happiness of the world." [1]

The speech of Lord John Russell awakened an interest in Canada second only to the recent despatch of his Colonial Secretary. The royalist press drove home with telling force his stern rebuke of the Annexationists, while the latter appealed with equal confidence to the concluding paragraph of the Premier's speech, as affording the most complete justification of their conduct. Each party, in fact, selected so much of the speech as it found to its satisfaction, and used that as a text for its polemics.

To the Governor-General, the speech of the Prime Minister brought the gravest anxiety. In a despatch to the Colonial Secretary, Lord Elgin subjected the speech of the Premier to the keenest political analysis. This despatch alone, we feel safe in saying, would entitle His Excellency to a place in the list of great imperial statesmen. In no other document do we find set forth more clearly the liberal principles upon which he hoped to build up the empire.

" Lord John's speech on the colonies seems to have been eminently successful at home. It is calculated too, I think, to do good in the colonies ; but for one sentence, the introduction of which I deeply deplore—the sting in the tail. Alas for that sting in the tail ! I much fear that when the liberal and enlightened sentiments, the enunciation of which by one so high in authority is so well calculated to make the colonists sensible of the advantages which they derive from their connection with Great Britain, shall have passed away from their memories, there will not be wanting those who will remind them that, on this solemn occasion, the Prime Minister of England, amid the plaudits of a full

[1] *Hansard*, vol. 108, p. 567.

senate, declared that he looked forward to the day when the ties which he was endeavouring to render so easy and mutually advantageous would be severed. And wherefore this foreboding ? or, perhaps, I ought not to use the term foreboding, for really, to judge by the comments of the press on this declaration of Lord John's, I should be led to imagine that the prospect of these sucking democracies, after they have drained their old mother's life-blood, leaving her in the lurch, and setting up as rivals, just at the time when their increasing strength might render them a support instead of a burden, is one of the most cheering which has of late presented itself to the English imagination.

" But wherefore, then, this anticipation—if foreboding be not the correct term ? Because Lord John and the people of England persist in assuming that the colonial relation is incompatible with maturity and full development. And is this really so incontestable a truth that it is a duty not only to hold but to proclaim it ? Consider for a moment what is the effect of proclaiming it in our case. We have on this continent two great empires in presence, or rather, I should say, two great imperial systems. In many respects there is much similarity between them. In so far as powers of self-government are concerned it is certain that our colonists in America have no reason to envy the citizens of any state in the Union. The forms differ, but it may be shown that practically the inhabitants of Canada have a greater power in controlling their own destiny than those of Michigan or New York, who must tolerate a tariff imposed by twenty other states, and pay the expenses of war undertaken for objects which they profess to abhor. And yet there is a difference between the two cases ; a difference, in my humble judgment, of sentiment rather than substance, which renders the one a system of life and strength, and the other a system of death and decay. No matter how raw and rude a territory may be when it is admitted as a state into the Union of the United States, it is at once, by the popular belief, invested with all the dignity of man-hood, and introduced into a system which, despite the combativeness of certain ardent spirits from the South, every American believes and maintains to be immortal.

"But how does the case stand with us ? No matter how great the advance of a British colony in wealth and civilization ; no matter how absolute the power of self-government conceded to it, it is still taught to believe that it is in a condition of pupilage from which it must pass before it can attain maturity. For one I have never been able to comprehend why, elastic as our constitutional system is, we should not be able, now more especially when we have ceased to control the trade of our colonies, to render the links which bind them to the British Crown at least as lasting as those which unite the component parts of the Union. . . . One thing is, however, indispensable to the success of this or any other system of Colonial Government. You must renounce the habit of telling the colonies that the colonial is a provisional existence. You must allow them to believe that, without severing the bonds which unite them to Great Britain, they may attain the degree of perfection, and of social and political develop-ment, to which organized communities of free men have a right to aspire.

"Since I began this letter I have, I regret to say, confirmatory evidence of the justice of the anticipations I had formed of the probable effect of Lord John's declaration. I enclose extracts from two newspapers, an annexationist, *The Herald* of Montreal, and a quasi-annexationist, *The Mirror* of Toronto. You will note the use they make of it. I was more annoyed, however, I confess, by what occurred yesterday in council. We had to determine whether or not to dismiss from his office a gentleman who is both M.P.P., Q.C., and J.P., and who has issued a flaming manifesto in favour, not of annexation, but of an immediate declaration of inde-pendence as a step to it. I will not say anything of my own opinion on the case, but it was generally contended by the members of the Board that it would be impossible to maintain that persons who had declared their intention to throw off their allegiance to the Queen, with a view to annexation, were unfit to retain offices granted during pleasure, if persons who made a similar declaration with a view to independence were to be differently dealt with.

"Baldwin had Lord John's speech in his hand. He is a man of singularly placid demeanour, but he has been seriously ill, so possibly his nerves are shaken—at any rate I never saw him so much moved. ' Have you read the latter part of Lord J. Russell's speech ? ' he said to me. I nodded assent. ' For myself,' he added, ' if the anticipations therein expressed prove to be well founded, my interest in public affairs is gone for ever. But is it not hard upon us while we are labouring, through good and evil report, to thwart the designs of those who would dismember the empire, that our adversaries should be informed that the difference between them and the Prime Minister of England is only one of time ? If the British Government has really come to the conclusion that we are a burden, to be cast off whenever a favourable opportunity offers, surely we ought to be warned.'

" I replied that while I regretted as much as he could do the paragraph to which he referred, I thought he somewhat mistook its import : that I believed no man living was more opposed to the dismemberment of the empire than Lord J. Russell : that I did not conceive that he had any intention of deserting the colonies, or of inviting them to separate from England ; but that he had in the sentence in question given utterance to a purely speculative, and in my judgment most fallacious opinion, which was shared, I feared, by very many persons both in England and the colonies : that I held it to be a perfectly unsound and most dangerous theory, that British colonies could not attain maturity without separation, and that my interest in labouring with them to bring into full play the principles of Constitutional Government in Canada would entirely cease if I could be persuaded to adopt it. I said all this, I must confess, however, not without misgiving, for I could not but be sensible that, in spite of all my allegations to the contrary, my audience was disposed to regard a prediction of this nature, proceeding from a Prime Minister, less as a speculative abstraction than as one of that class of prophecies which work their own fulfilment.

" I left the Council Chamber disheartened, with the feeling that Lord J. Russell's reference to the manhood of colonies was more likely to be followed by practical consequences than Lamartine's famous ' quand l'heure aura sonne ' invocation to oppressed nationalities. It is possible, indeed, that I exaggerate to myself the probable effects of this declaration. Politicians of the Baldwin stamp, with distinct views and aims, who having struggled to obtain a Government on British principles, desire to preserve it, are not, I fear, very numerous in Canada; the great mass move on with very indefinite purposes, and not much inquiring whither they are going. Of one thing, however, I am confident : there cannot be any peace, contentment, progress, or credit in this colony while the idea obtains that the connection with England is a millstone about its neck which should be cast off as soon as it can be conveniently managed. What man in his senses would invest his money in the public securities of a country where questions affecting the very foundations on which public credit rests are in perpetual agitation ; or would settle in it at all if he could find for his foot a more stable resting-place elsewhere ? I may, perhaps, be expressing myself too unreservedly with reference to opinions emanating from a source which I am no less disposed than bound to respect. As I have the means, however, of feeling the pulse of the colonists in this most feverish region, I consider it to be always my duty to furnish you with as faithful a record as possible of our diagnostics.

" And, after all, may I not with all submission ask, is not the question at issue a most momentous one ? What is it indeed but this : Is the Queen of England to be the Sovereign of an Empire, growing, expanding, strengthening itself from age to age, striking its roots deep into fresh earth and drawing new supplies of vitality from virgin soils ? Or is she to be, for all essential purposes of might and power, Monarch of Great Britain and Ireland merely—her place and that of her line in the world's history determined by the productiveness of 12,000 square miles of a coal formation, which is being rapidly exhausted, and the duration of the social and political organization over which she presides dependent on the annual expatriation, with a view to its eventual alienization, of the surplus swarms of her born subjects ?

" If Lord J. Russell, instead of concluding his excellent speech with a declaration of opinion which, as I read it, and as I fear others read it, seems to make it a point of honour with the colonists to prepare for separation, had contented himself with resuming the statements already made in its course, with showing that neither the Government nor Parliament could have any object in view in their colonial policy but the good of the colonies, and the establishment of the relation between them and the mother country on the basis of mutual affection ; that, as the idea of maintaining a Colonial Empire for the purpose of exercising dominion or dispensing patronage had been for some time abandoned, and that of regarding it as a hot-bed for forcing commerce and manufactures more recently renounced, a greater amount of free action and self-government might be conceded to British colonies without any breach of Imperial Unity, or the violation of any principle of Imperial Policy, than had under any scheme yet devised fallen to the lot of the component parts of any federal or imperial system ; if he had left these great truths to work their effect without hazarding a conjecture which will, I fear, be received as a suggestion with respect to the course which certain wayward members of the imperial family may be expected to take in a contingency still confessedly remote, it would, I venture with great deference to submit, in so far at least as public feeling in the colonies is concerned, have been safer and better.

" You draw, I know, a distinction between separation with a view to annexation and separation with a view to independence. You say the former is an act of treason, the latter a natural and legitimate step in progress. There is much plausibility doubtless in this position, but independently of the fact that no one advocates independence in these colonies except as a means to the end, annexation, is it really tenable? If you take your stand on the hypothesis that the colonial existence is one with which the colonists ought to rest satisfied, then, I think, you are entitled to denounce, without reserve or measure, those who propose for some secondary object to substitute the Stars and Stripes for the Union Jack. But if, on the contrary, you assume that it is a provisional state, which admits of but a stunted and partial growth, and out of which all communities ought in the course of nature to strive to pass, how can you refuse to permit your colonies here, when they have arrived at the proper stage in their existence, to place themselves in a condition which is at once most favourable to their security and to their perfect natural development? What reasons can you assign for the refusal, except such as are founded on selfishness, and are, therefore, morally worthless? If you say that your great lubberly boy is too big for the nursery, and that you have no other room for him in your house, how can you decline to allow him to lodge with his elder brethren over the way, when the attempt to keep up an establishment for himself would seriously embarrass him? "

In pursuance of their policy of carrying on an active propaganda, the Annexationists interjected that issue into the municipal elections at Montreal. In the West

and St. Antoine wards, Messrs. Holmes and Atwater
were nominated as straight annexation candidates,
while in some of the other wards individuals were
placed in nomination who, although not avowedly
Annexationists or committed to that policy, were
known or supposed to be friendly to annexation. The
Annexationists, it was evident, were desirous of capturing the Council, and choosing the chief magistrate for
the city. The raising of the annexation issue in
municipal affairs was much resented by the loyalists.
The Gazette and *The Pilot* agreed in condemning the
folly of such a policy ; but, as the issue was forced upon
them, they resolved to fight to the bitter end the efforts
of the Annexationists to capture the city. In both the
West and St. Antoine wards, the British connectionists
placed loyalist candidates in the field.

For a time the old party lines of Tories and Reformers were superseded by the new alignment of
Annexationists and Loyalists.[1] After an exceedingly
close contest, marked by riotous scenes on the part of
some Irish Annexationists, Mr. Holmes was elected by
the narrow majority of ten, over Colonel Gugy, the
former Councillor.[2] In St. Antoine ward, Mr. Fisher,
the Loyalist candidate, withdrew, when it became
evident that Mr. Atwater would be returned by a large
majority. The personal popularity of the two annexation candidates contributed largely to their success at
the polls. This was particularly the case in St. Antoine
ward, where Mr. Atwater received the large proportion
of the French-Canadian votes. His views on the subject of annexation, according to *La Minerve*, which
supported his candidature, had nothing to do with
municipal affairs, and accordingly could be safely disregarded by the French electorate. In St. Ann's ward
(Griffith Town), the home of the Irish population, Mr.
McGrath received the support of the Annexationists,
and was duly elected. In the remaining wards of the

[1] *The Gazette*, January 10, 1850.
[2] The electors of the west ward were almost all English-speaking.

city, the annexation candidates, including the editor of *The Herald*, retired before the opening of the polls.[1] In the Centre ward, Mr. Hull, a strong pro-Britisher, was elected. In brief, in three wards of the city Annexationists were returned, but in the remaining six, annexation was not made an issue.

The result of the elections was heralded as a great triumph by the annexationist press, which boasted that the party was successful in every ward of the city in which it had made a fight. The Annexationists, however, were far from controlling the city Council. In the choice of the mayor a few days later, their candidate, Mr. Holmes, was beaten by eleven votes to five.[2] With this defeat, the question of annexation was quietly dropped out of municipal politics.

The partial success of the Annexationists in the municipal election did not succeed, as was expected, in infusing new life into the party in Montreal. The movement in fact was slowly dying out. The opposition of the Provincial and Imperial Governments, the unresponsive attitude of the United States, and the improvement in trade, all contributed to dampen the ardour of the zealots and to quiet the unrest of the public. After having been for some months the first question in Canadian politics, the annexation issue gradually disappeared from the arena of polemical journalism, and was relegated to the category of special correspondence and abstract discussion of the future of the colony.

The direction of affairs had fallen into the hands of a small Junta, made up, according to *The Gazette*, of the extreme elements of the party. This small council of eighteen arrogated all the powers of the association, and carried on its business in secret. The more moderate members of the association quietly dropped out, when the leaders of the party resolved to continue the agitation in spite of the opposition of the British Govern-

[1] *The Gazette*, March 8, 1850.
[2] *La Minerve*, March 14, 1850.

ment. This defection ruined the prospects of the Annexationists. An occasional speech was still made, or a pamphlet issued by some private member of the party,[1] but the active campaign of the association was over. It became the fashion on the street to speak of the movement as a harmless fad to be taken up or laid down at pleasure. Many of the signers of the manifesto were now free to admit that they had taken up the agitation for the purpose of procuring the recall of Lord Elgin, or as a means of coercing England into the restoration of a preferential tariff.

The passing of *The Toronto Independent* was, *The Gazette* declared, no blow to the cause of annexation in Montreal, since but few still adhered to that political persuasion. The extreme character of the views of the Annexationists, together with the vacillating record of the chief organ of the party in Montreal, had brought discredit on the movement, and produced a popular reaction. The agitation, however, in the judgment of *The Gazette*, had served a good purpose in awakening the English and Canadian people to a sense of the evils from which the country was suffering, though it would have been much better for the province if the Annexationists had adhered to the British American League, instead of organizing an independent party.[2]

Meantime *The Courier* and *The Herald* were gradually modifying the tone of their utterances. The former now admitted that some other remedy than annexation might possibly be found for the ills of the province, while the editorials of the latter were assuming a more patriotic and even distinctly nationalist character. Though still professing to support the principle of annexation, *The Herald* tended more and more to substitute the policy of protection for that of a political union with the United States. The changing attitude

---

[1] *De l'annexation de Canada aux États-Unis. Considérations préliminaires. Lecture faite devant l'Institut par L. A. Dessaules,* April 23, 1850.

[2] *The Gazette,* April 22, 1850.

of the two leading annexation organs faithfully reflected
the shifting opinion of the mercantile community of
the city. So striking indeed was the transition, that
one is almost tempted to speak of the annexation origin
of the protective policy in Montreal. Within the short
space of four years, the fiscal views of the business men
of the city were apparently revolutionized. The commercial interests, as we have seen, set out by opposing
most vigorously any change in the fiscal policy of the
motherland ; after the loss of the imperial preference,
they ardently turned to the United States for relief.

Undoubtedly some of the members of the association
were genuine Annexationists, and many more hoped to
secure in a union with the United States the benefits of
a protective policy which were denied to them under
the Union Jack, but it is safe to say that a still larger
number of the business men were merely using the cry
of annexation as a false alarm with which to frighten
England into the restoration of protective duties.
They were not Annexationists in reality, but out-and-
out protectionists. When an entrance to the American
market was denied to them by Congress, they in-
stinctively fell back upon the policy of provincial
protection. The history of the protective policy in
Canada dates from the adoption of the free-trade policy
in England. The annexation movement was one of
the passing phases of the struggle of the business
interests for fiscal favours.

Notwithstanding the repeated appeals of the loyalist
press to the Annexationists to drop their agitation, in
view of the emphatic pronouncements of Lord John
Russell against a voluntary surrender of the colony to
the United States, the Annexationists resolved to keep
up the fight. They had survived the attacks of the
Governor-General and the Secretary of State for the
Colonies, and they were not now prepared to hoist
the white flag on the summons of the head of the Whig
administration. They had been greatly encouraged
by the success of their campaign in the Eastern Town-

ships ; and now, just at the critical moment, a splendid opportunity had arisen of demonstrating to the English Government and the people of Upper Canada the real strength of annexation sentiment in Lower Canada.

The resignation of Mr. Galt, owing to the removal of the seat of Government to Toronto, brought on a bye-election in Sherbrooke County. An effort was made by some of the members of the Montreal association to secure the nomination of Mr. Rose of that city as annexationist candidate for the Riding ; but, owing to the preference for a local representative as against a comparative stranger, Mr. Sanborn, a young American lawyer who had taken up his residence in Canada a few years previously, was chosen by the nominating convention as the standard-bearer of the party. In his election address, Mr. Sanborn, who professed to run as an independent candidate, stated : " With reference to the separation of Canada from the Government of Great Britain, and her annexation on favourable terms to the States of the American Union, if peaceably obtained, and with the consent of the British Government, it is unnecessary that I should enlarge. It is sufficient that I have the honour to have my name associated with a large proportion of yours, as appended to the requisition lately presented to A. T. Galt, Esq." Although the question of annexation was admittedly one of primary importance to the province, he did not think, however, that it would be raised as a direct issue at the coming session of Parliament.[1]

Notwithstanding the fact that there seemed at first but a small prospect of carrying the seat, the loyalists determined to put a candidate in the field, if only to call foolish the boast of their opponents, that they did not dare to contest the Riding. A satisfactory standard-bearer was found in the person of Mr. Cleveland, a prominent Tory and long-established farmer of the county. A careful canvass of the constituency showed

[1] *The Montreal Gazette*, February 6, 1850.

that there was a good fighting chance of his election, especially in view of the well-known predilection of the agriculturists for one of their own class. The old party lines were eliminated ; the struggle resolved itself into a battle royal between the loyalists and the Annexationists. There was little to choose between the two candidates. Both were men of intelligence and acknowledged probity. Mr. Sanborn had the advantage over his opponent of being first in the field, and of having a strong organization behind him ; on the other hand, he was somewhat handicapped, in the eyes of the farmers at least, by his youth, his profession, and his brief residence in the district.

The importance and critical character of the struggle were quickly realized by the whole province. The Annexationists succeeded in making the election a test of their political influence, and in focussing the attention of the public upon the contest.[1] The Montreal association threw the whole of its strength into the Riding by supplying not only speakers, but funds with which to carry on the battle. The Montreal loyalists were not to be outdone. A private meeting was called of some of the leading British connectionists to determine the best means of promoting the election of Mr. Cleveland. The majority of those present were Conservatives, but it was thoroughly understood that all party politics were to be set aside for the time being, with a view to strengthening the forces which were fighting for the imperial connection. A week before the election, it was considered advisable to send a representative to Sherbrooke to see how the election was progressing. Mr. Ferris of *The Gazette* was duly chosen to undertake the mission ; but as it was feared by some of the members that the selection of such a prominent Tory might arouse a certain amount of suspicion among the Liberals of the Riding, it was determined that Mr. Bristow of *The Pilot* should accompany him.

For the moment party and newspaper rivalries were

---

[1] *The Montreal Gazette*, February 25, 1850.

forgotten ; and, much to the amusement and scandal of the annexationist press, the two representatives travelled down to Sherbrooke together.   *The Pilot* [1] assisted in the work of harmonizing the loyalists of the two parties, by strongly urging all Reformers to support Mr. Cleveland, notwithstanding his former Conservative affiliations.   On the other hand, the annexation journals professed a righteous indignation at seeing the editor of the leading Tory paper join hands with his former political opponents, to defeat a candidate who was running in opposition to the Government. *The Herald* came out with the foolish accusation that Mr. Ferris had been bought up by the Ministry, and that the political pilgrimage to Sherbrooke was part of the terms of the unholy compact.   The charge was immediately denied by all the parties concerned, but nevertheless continued to do service along the side lines throughout the election.

The election had lost its local character, and had assumed an almost provincial aspect.   On both sides, the battle was directed from headquarters at Montreal ; loyalists and Annexationists alike threw all their energies and resources into the struggle.   The Annexationists had a decided advantage in the district by reason of their superior organization, and their control over the leading local papers.   *The Sherbrooke Gazette* was rabidly annexationist in its policy, and even refused to publish the election notices of Mr. Cleveland. *The Stanstead Journal* had also gone over to the Annexationists, and *The Missisquoi News* threw its columns open to the free discussion of the question. The loyalist party and papers of Montreal were forced to intervene in the contest to strengthen the weak hands of their friends in the Riding.   *The Pilot*, in particular, waged a fierce and merciless battle against the Annexationists, as a band of dangerous conspirators against the Reform Party.   It charged them with hypocrisy, with flagrantly violating their professions

[1] *The Pilot*, February 12, 1850.

of affectionate regard and consideration for the wishes
of the motherland, and with making desperate efforts
to convince the electorate that a slave republic was
preferable to a free monarchy, that it was better to pay
higher taxes to Washington than to spend the revenues
of the province at home, and that it was more honourable
to be an insignificant state of an overgrown confederation than a free and independent member of the world's
greatest empire. Now that the British Government
had spoken, all further agitation, it maintained, was
treasonable, and should cease. *The Gazette*, in like
manner, attacked the personal qualifications of Mr.
Sanborn, and called upon all British connectionists,
irrespective of party, to use all proper means to
accomplish his defeat.[1]

The proceedings on nomination day were marked by
unusual bitterness of feeling. In his election address,
Mr. Cleveland had omitted all reference to the question
of separation ; but, on this occasion, he emphatically
condemned the policy of annexation, as unwarranted
by the past generous conduct of the motherland, and
as likely to prove injurious to the best interests of
Canada. Mr. Sanborn declared that the primary issue
before the electorate was annexation, and he had no
doubt of the result. When the question of annexation
should be properly brought before the English people
on petition of the Colonial Legislature, he believed that
they would readily grant the demands of the colony
for separation. If, however, their decision should be
averse to the aspirations of the Canadian public, the
Annexationists would rest content with British rule ;
and, in case of danger of attack, the motherland would
find no more gallant defenders than they. With most
of the Annexationists, he confessed, it was not the love
of republican institutions which led to the demand for
separation, but rather a dominant self-interest which
resulted from their close geographical and commercial
connection with the United States. Moreover, the racial

[1] *The Montreal Gazette*, February 13, 1850.

antipathies of the English and French inhabitants of the province would never be overcome, so long as they retained their colonial status. As American citizens, they would take on a higher national existence. The policy of the Annexationists in Parliament, he concluded, would be to support liberal measures from whatever quarter they might be proposed.

An objection was entered by some of the electors to the legal qualifications of Mr. Sanborn, on the ground that he was not a British subject ; but the protest was rejected by the returning officer. Mr. Ferris of Montreal was refused a hearing by the Annexationists, but no opposition was offered to any of the other supporters of Mr. Cleveland. The loyalist speakers made the most of the decision of the English Government. They charged the Annexationists with insincerity in their peaceful professions, and with a design of stirring up a revolt among the people. The agitation, it was contended, had now passed beyond the stage of constitutional discussion into an open defiance of the Crown ; it had reached the bounds where any further opposition to the royal will would be unjustifiable and seditious.

In the United States, both Webster and Clay had declared that a Congressman could not make a motion for the dissolution of the Union without committing the crime of perjury. A similar obligation of allegiance rested upon the members of the local legislature, an obligation which Mr. Sanborn refused to recognize. It was contended by Mr. Pope that the ills from which the province was suffering could be cured by local legislation. Canada had control over her own expenditures and fiscal policy ; she could reduce the salaries of her officials, and frame a tariff so as to promote home industries. The policy of protection would, he maintained, be of the highest economic value to the producers of the country, whereas a union with the United States would expose them to a competition with their more powerful neighbours.

Mr. Tyrrel appealed to the American settlers of the district to remember their past loyalty to the Crown. He reminded them that Papineau, who was now the leader of the Annexationists, had formerly aspersed their honour by the statement that they had left the land of their fathers for personal profit, and would sell the land of their adoption for dollars. They had repudiated that base calumny in the past, but some of them apparently were now resolved to demonstrate its truth. Would the Canadian people, he asked, adopt the almighty dollar as their coat-of-arms, and exchange their birthright as British subjects for a mess of pottage? Mr. Shortt rebuked the presumptuous folly of some Americans in declaring that the British colonists could leave the province, as they had left the American colonies on a past occasion, if they did not like the Stars and Stripes in Canada. He challenged the British citizenship of Mr. Sanborn, and his qualification to sit as a member of the Legislature. It was, indeed, most fitting, he declared, that an alien candidate should be chosen to represent the Annexationists. In conclusion, he appealed to the farmers of the county not to be led astray by a revolutionary movement which, if successful, would only result in a heavier burden of taxation, the proceeds of which would be spent outside of their own country.[1]

The election was closely and bitterly contested. At the close of the polls, Mr. Sanborn was declared elected by a majority of 34.[2] Charges and counter-charges were made by both parties, as to the conduct of the election. On the part of the loyalists, it was alleged that some of the officials of the British American Land Company had unduly interfered in the contest by bringing pressure to bear upon their tenants, and that the polls were not properly conducted by certain of the annexation deputy returning officers ; the Annexa-

[1] *The Pilot*, March 2, 1850.
[2] Mr. Sanborn's victory was due to the large majority he received in Compton.

tionists replied with the charges that the loyalists had polled squatter votes, and were guilty of the liberal distribution of liquor to influence the electors. In thanking the electors for their hearty support, Mr. Cleveland declared that, if he had been earlier in the field, and if all the pro-British vote had been polled, he would have been duly elected, for the majority of the electors of the county were undoubtedly against annexation. It was later decided to contest the election on the ground of numerous irregularities on the part of the agents of Mr. Sanborn.

By the annexation press the election was heralded as a great triumph over the combined forces of the Government and the opposition ; the loyalist papers, on the other hand, endeavoured to explain the defeat as due to the peculiar social and economic conditions of the constituency, in particular to the influence of the Land Company and the large body of American settlers.[1] The great majority of the Americans and of the ultra-Tories voted for Mr. Sanborn, while the most of the English-born settlers, and the bulk of the Reformers, supported his opponent. The most of the French-Canadians, according to *La Minerve*, voted for Cleveland, and practically all would have done so, but for the deceit of some of the annexation agents in representing Sanborn as the candidate of the Government.

The result of the contest was well summed up by *The Examiner* : " It is an extraordinary fact that these ultra-loyal counties are the first in Lower Canada to elect an Annexationist. It shows a great change of feeling on their part. Whatever the French population may do, it is beyond all question that the English population generally favour the annexation movement." It was not a change in the Constitution, or the measures of the Government, that provoked this transformation, but a conviction, " whether well or ill founded, that the country would be more prosperous, if united to the States, than under its connection with England. Com-

---

[1] *The Montreal Gazette*, March 15, 1850.

mercial considerations with them override political."
The mass of the people did not prefer a republic to a
monarchy ; they had no feelings against England ;
" the question, as they insist on putting it, is between
prosperity and ruin and decay."

The official opinion of Lord Elgin was expressed in a
letter [1] to the Colonial Secretary, notifying him of the
election of Mr. Sanborn, " the first instance in which
a person avowing these sentiments has been elected to
the Canadian Parliament."

" The constituency of the County of Sherbrooke
comprises a considerable number of settlers from the
United States.   Mr. Sanborn belongs, I understand, to
this class of settlers, and has only lately established
himself in the province.   That the first individual returned to the local Parliament on annexation principles
should be himself a settler from the United States, and
that he should represent a constituency in which this
element enters so largely is, without doubt, a significant
fact, and throws light on the origin and character of
the present movement.

" Another circumstance affecting this particular constituency cannot be passed over without notice in a
review of the causes which have contributed to the
result of the recent election.   The British American
Land Company are owners of a large tract of land in
the county.   Mr. Galt, the late member, is chief agent
of the company. . . . I am not able to inform your
Lordship to what extent the direct influence of the
company, which is considerable, may have been used
in this election, as on this head contradictory statements are made by the opposing parties ; but, that the
moral of the course taken by Mr. Galt in reference to
this subject must have been great is, however, unques-
tionable.   It has been throughout the policy of the
Annexationists to pretend that the British public is
favourable to their view, and that the opposition made
to them by the local and imperial Governments is inter-

[1] March 23, 1850.

ested or affected. The emphatic and formal advocacy of annexation by the agent of a body of absentee English proprietors has given, without doubt, some colour to this representation, and could hardly fail to tell with particular force in a constituency such as that of Sherbrooke.[1]

" My opinion is that, had these anomalous influences been wanting, the issue of the election would have been different, and that no inference can, therefore, be drawn from it with respect to the real sentiments of Her Majesty's Canadian subjects."

Notwithstanding the victory of the Annexationists, the outlook of the party in the Eastern Townships was far from encouraging. The movement had attained its greatest popularity, and was now on the wane. Over 1,200 persons had signed the requisitions to Mr. Galt in favour of annexation, yet five months later the strength of the party was so diminished, that it could scarcely carry the seat. The constituency was admittedly the most favourable to annexation of all the Ridings in the district. The Annexationists had expected to win it by acclamation, yet they were all but defeated by a commonplace candidate. After the election, interest in the question of annexation rapidly diminished. The popular campaign of the Annexationists was practically discontinued. Only a few of the local associations, such as that at Durham, gave evidence of an active existence. The majority of them were quiescent ; and, with the opening up of spring, all further activities throughout the various branches were suspended. An unmistakable evidence of the gradual change in public opinion was found in the establishment of a new paper, *The St. Francis Telegraph*, of pronounced pro-British opinions.

Notwithstanding the active campaign of the Rouge Party and press, the spread of annexation sentiment among the French population was exceedingly slow.

[1] The Brooks's family influence was also thrown in favour of annexation.

The habitants lived up to their traditions as good churchmen in preferring the counsels of their priests to the harangues of the politicians.[1] The quiet but effective opposition of the clergy to the movement aroused the bitter animosity of the Papineau Party. *L'Avenir* came out with the accusation that Lord Elgin had addressed a letter to the Catholic bishops in which he promised to restore the Jesuit estates, and to remove the capital to Lower Canada, if they would stifle the annexation agitation among their fellow countrymen.[2] Although the allegation was flatly denied by the hierarchy, *L'Avenir* refused to accept the denial on the ground that the statement of the bishops was disingenuous and unsatisfactory. In the bye-election in Quebec, the clergy were again accused of exerting an undue influence over the faithful. At the opening of the contest, according to *L'Avenir*, the head of the Seminary in that city entertained at dinner the editors of the three leading French-Canadian journals, with the result that all three papers at once threw the whole of their influence against the annexation candidate. However this may be, the Government succeeded admirably in identifying, in the minds of the habitants, the annexation movement with the most dangerous doctrines of anti-clericalism.

An interesting attempt was made by the Rouge Party to connect the annexation movement with the growing agitation against the seignorial system. At several meetings which were called to discuss the latter topic, an effort was made by some of the speakers to raise the question of annexation. A few of these attempts to gain a fortuitous hearing for the annexation

---

[1] Some of the early attempts of the Annexationists to obtain a hearing resulted in failure. A meeting at St. François, Yamaska, which was regularly called by the local magistrate at the instance of the Annexationists, unanimously adopted a resolution, " that this parish deems it its duty to declare publicly its determination to aid in maintaining the connection with Great Britain " (November 25, 1849).

[2] *L'Avenir*, November 24, 1849.

cause were successful; but, in other instances, the electorate objected to the interjection of an extraneous issue. At St. Jacques d'Achigan, for example, a seignorial meeting adopted a resolution in favour of annexation, but at a similar gathering, some time later, in the parish of St. Zotigue, at which Mr. J. E. Dorion introduced the question of annexation, the audience declined to express an opinion upon the matter.[1] In truth, the question of seignorial tenure was not strictly a party issue, since many of the ministerialists, including several members of the Legislature, were as heartily in favour of the abolition of the seignorial system as the leaders of the Rouge Party.

The French Annexationists were fighting against heavy odds. They were especially handicapped by the lack of newspaper organs. *L'Indépendent Canadien*, the sole organ of the party in the Quebec District, was forced to suspend publication, after a brief existence, for the want of financial support. *L'Echo des Campagnes*, which for a time was friendly to the Annexationists, changed hands, and, at the same time, its policy in regard to annexation. In his opening announcement, the new editor stated that he had received many letters protesting against the past attitude of the paper, and that, for the future, the editorial page would be conducted in conformity with the general pro-British sentiment of the country at large. The desire for annexation, he concluded, sprang from spite, a reverse of fortune and hatred of the Reform Party. *L'Avenir* and *Le Moniteur* were left practically alone to fight the battle of the French Annexationists against the united strength of the religious and ministerial press.

In the Eastern Townships, the opposition of the clergy was more openly pronounced. The influence of the Church was unmistakably felt on behalf of Mr. Cleveland in the Sherbrooke election. In the adjoining County of Huntingdon, some of the priests preached

[1] *L'Avenir*, February 8, 1849.

against annexation, and warned their congregations to
have nothing to do with the movement, on pain of
suffering the unfortuate consequences of the revolt of
1837. The decisive stand of the clergy stopped the
spread of annexation sentiment among the French-
Canadians in the border district. In the bye-election
in Megantic shortly after, the question of annexation
was not even raised on the hustings.[1]

In the meantime, the question had been taken up by
some of the French-Canadians in the United States.
For some time past they had been closely following
the course of Canadian events, and at last the moment
seemed opportune for them to intervene on behalf of
their compatriots at home. At a meeting in New
York, in December, an association was formed to
promote a political union of Canada with the United
States. The object of the meeting was clearly set
forth in the opening remarks of the chairman, Mr. G.
Franchère, an influential member of the French-
Canadian colony. The unhappy condition of Canada,
as compared with the great Republic, was due, he
declared, to the institutions of the colonial régime.
Under these circumstances, annexation was the only
recourse of their fellow countrymen. It was their duty
to assist by all legal means to make Canada a member
of the Union. A resolution, approving of the Montreal
manifesto, was unanimously adopted. A permanent
committee was appointed, with instructions to draw up
a constitution for the local association to enter into
relations with the Montreal Annexationists, and to invite
their compatriots in the United States to form similar
associations to be affiliated with the central body at
New York. An address was accordingly prepared, to
which the names of 69 persons were appended, calling
upon their compatriots in Lower Canada to embrace
the cause of annexation. The address read as
follows:[2]

[1] *L'Avenir*, May 8, 1849.
[2] *Ibid.*, January 11, 1850.

Extrait de L'Avenir *du 11 janvier* 1850

ANNEXION [1]

Adresse des Canadiens de New-York et des environs, à leurs compatriotes du Canada

Les canadiens domicliés dans la cité de New-York et ses environs saisissent la première occasion qui se présente de délibérer sur leurs communs intérêts, pour renvoyer, de l'autre côté de la frontière, l'écho des sympathies éveillées chez eux par le manifeste annexioniste, promulgué à Montréal dans le cours du mois dernier.

Tous les organes de la publicité, dans les deux mondes, se sont plus à reconnaître l'habilité et le tact qui ont présidé à la rédaction de ce document : ce concert d'éloges nous dispense à propos, d'un panégyrique qui n'ajouterait pas un iota à la force incontrovertible des arguments développés par le manifeste, ni un trait de plus au désolant tableau des calamités que chaque ligne y énumère.

Compatriotes du Bas-Canada ! en essayant de dissiper aujourd'hui les préjugés qu'une propagande contraire s'efforce de semer à l'endroit des institutions et des ressources de l'Union américaine nous pensons remplir un devoir de reconnaissance envers le pays qui nous accueille avec tant de bienveillance et qui nous traite à l'égal de ses propres enfants.

Témoins journaliers d'un mouvement commercial hors de comparaison, spectateurs intéressés d'une organisation politique sans parallèle, nous nous flattons que nos appréciations, prises sur place au foyer le plus vaste de la civilisation américaine, auront l'effet de confirmer, en ce qui concerne les Etats-Unis, les espérances mises en avant par le manifeste, et de justifier les conclusions auxquelles les griefs du présent et l'instinct de l'avenir nous ont irrésistiblement amenés.

[1] For translation see Appendix, p. 385.

Nous allons exposer d'une manière concise les bienfaits pratiques et autres qui découleraient, selon nous, de l'alliance proposée entre les deux peuples.

Le système du gouvernement responsable dans les complications duquel se débattent les Canadas, fut taillé à l'image du gouvernement de la métropole. Misérable copie! maladroits copistes! On a voulu transposer à mille lieues de distance, sur les rives de l'Amérique, l'œuvre accumulée de plusieurs siècles de privilèges aristocratiques. Aussi ce système a-t-il déjoué les projets de ceux qui nous l'avaient bâclé, aussi est-il sorti plus informe que jamais des replâtrages tentés pour lui rendre la vitalité qui se retire incessamment de lui.

Qu'on lise l'acte de 1840 qui réunit les deux Canadas, que l'on pèse les maux que cette constitution a prévenus ou allégés et les avantages éclos sous ses auspices, l'on se convaincra facilement que la seule ancre de salut qui reste à notre pays, c'est l'annexion en perspective, avec la plénitude des bénéfices et l'éclat des splendeurs que le drapeau étoilé renferme dans ses plis.

L'acte d'Union n'a-t-il pas inventé une liste civile disproportionnée aux ressources du pays ?

Pourvu à la couteuse subvention d'une armée de fonctionnaires ?

Soumis la franchise élective et l'éligibilité à certaines conditions de propriété qui rendent inaccessible à la masse des gouvernés la plus chère de leurs prérogatives ?

Erigé le gouvernement impérial en maître absolu qui règle nos affaires à sa guise et, en vertu d'un droit qu'il ne s'était pas arrogé dans ses anciennes possessions de l'Amérique du Nord, qui nomme nos gouverneurs ballottés entre la responsabilité qu'ils doivent à l'empire et celle que le cabinet provincial exige d'eux ?

N'a-t-il pas étouffé, au milieu de ces conflits, toutes les velléités réformatrices de l'administration pro-

vinciale vivant au jour le jour de cette existence
rapetissée ?

N'a-t-il pas imposé un conseil législatif dont l'influence, s'il en a aucune, est subordonnée aux change-
ments ministériels ?

Comparez maintenant les deux systèmes, et jugez.

Aux Etats-Unis, la machine gouvernementale est
d'un jeu si simple et si régulier qu'un enfant peut en
compter les pulsations.

La mer du suffrage universel porte sur ses flots
tous les aspirants de la candidature populaire.

La représentation est basée sur le thermomètre
seul vrai et juste de l'opinion publique : sur la population.

Les états particuliers, souverains dans leurs limites
respectives, délèguent au congrès fédéral leur part
mesurée de souveraineté et d'influence.

Le sénat, renouvellé à période fixe, jouit de
certaines attributions exécutives qui ravivent son
autorité et relèvent sa valeur.

Tous les pouvoirs, le pouvoir exécutif, le pouvoir
législatif, le pouvoir judiciaire, depuis le Président
jusqu'à l'agent de police, depuis le membre du congrès
jusqu'à l'alderman, depuis le président de la cour
suprême jusqu'au juge des cours sommaires, grâce
à cette perpétuelle votation élective, montent au
peuple et en redescendent.

Tous les mandats que produit la boîte électorale
sont de courte durée, afin de se retremper, par
ce baptême démocratique, l'ardeur qui pourrait se
relentir, afin de ravir aux gouvernements surtout
le tems (*sic*), s'ils en avaient l'envie, de se laisser
corrompre ou de se faire corrupteurs !

Le citoyen américain, sur la foi de sa conscience,
marche à son vote paisiblement, le secret du scrutin
pour toute nationalité, sans redouter l'or, les intrigues
et les vengeances ministériels, aussi bien que l'ire
collective de partis l'un pour l'autre animés de
sentiments hostiles invétérés.

De là contentement chez tout le monde,—de là stabilité au dedans,—de là sécurité au dehors.

Si nous passons de l'organization politique aux considérations purement matérielles qui se rattachent au commerce, à l'industrie, à tout ce qui compose enfin le tissu de la prospérité nationale, nous trouvont la différence encore plus tranchée sans doute parce-qu'elle est plus ostensible et plus palpable.

En Canada, les intérêts du gouvernement et des particuliers éprouvent une égale souffrance ; le St.-Laurent est désert ; nos canaux d'une magnificence impériale, loin de plier sous le poid des vaisseaux, attendent pour se rouvrir les bras de la navigation libre ; nos cours d'eau et nos chûtes coulent dans leur pittoresque inutilité ; à peine avons-nous quelques milles de chemin de fer ; un simple réseau télégraphique suffit à l'activité peu électrique de nos affaires ; nous hébergeons l'émigration la plus dénuée de moyens ultérieurs de subsister, qui délaisse les rivages de la malheureuse Irlande.

Voilà, en résumé, les progrès que nous avons faits depuis un demi-siècle sous l'empire du régime colonial.

Eh bien ! les Etats-Unis, durant la même période ont marché comme un géant d'un bout du continent à l'autre. Le soleil échauffe les climats les plus opposés et vivifie toutes les variétés de productions. Une émigration entreprenante s'est dirigée vers les nouveaux Etats. La finance, effrayée par le dernier tremblement de trônes européens, accourt chercher ici un terrain plus solide pour y établir ses opérations. Les communications intérieures par eau sont encombrées. Les télégraphes multipliés sur tous les points. Les chemins de fer sillonnent le pays de leurs veines d'acier. On sera bientôt en train de relier, par l'acoustique de Morse, San-Francisco et New-York, comme un chemin de fer gigantesque mettra les océans porte à porte.

L'américain, tout en demeurant chez lui, peut se nourrir, s'habiller, produire, vendre, à l'abri des tiraillements extérieurs, tandis que, faute de ressources, le jeune canadien abandonne son pays, trop incertain s'il ira coucher, au retour de l'exil, ses restes éternels près des os bénis de ses aïeux—et que sommes-nous, en effet, sinon de pauvres exilés que la patrie renvoie en pleurant à la grâce de Dieu ?

Ces antithèses historiques et statistiques à la main, nous vous le demandons : Un pays pauvre, vivotant sous la tutelle coloniale, a-t-il à perdre ou à gagner à l'union intime que nous lui proposons de consommer avec une contrée à la fois riche, contente et libre ?

Les considérations que nous avons fait valoir jusqu'ici forment les éléments vitaux de l'existence des peuples, mais elles n'en sont pas l'âme.

Quand le pont-lévis des frontières s'abaissera devant les marchandises comme devant les idées américaines, nous secouerons deux siècles de servitude pour entrer, grâce à l'annexion, dans la famille des peuples ; nous reparaîtrons au firmament de la liberté universelle où la domination prolongée de la France et de l'Angleterre nous avait éclipsés.

Elargissons donc, sans rien abjurer de ce que le patriotisme a de plus cher, et les convictions de plus sacré, ô canadiens, agrandissons la patrie aux proportions de l'hémisphère tout entier, rattachons nous à la vie sociale par ce glorieux lien ; rendons une patrie aux exilés qui seront fiers d'un pareil acte de naturalisation : et nous verrons l'aigle américain dont les ailes trempent déjà dans les deux océans, embrasser le continent jusqu'au pôle, et emporter au plus haut des cieux la charte de l'Amérique du Nord émancipée !

Habitants du Bas-Canada (nous nous adressons à vous de préférence, car nous vous connaissons mieux), croyez-en ceux de vos frères qui, du milieu de leurs peines commes au sein de leurs jouissances, ne vous perdent pas de vue un moment ; on a défiguré, pour vous les tenir en horreur, les grandes qualités qui ont élevé au premier rang des nations ce peuple grandi si vite à vos côtés.

Non ! il n'y a rien à craindre pour votre religion protégée par la liberté des cultes, inscrite au frontispice de la constitution, et incrustés plus avant encore au for de toutes les intelligences.

Non ! il n'y a pas de danger pour votre langue sauvegardée par l'omnipotence du suffrage universel et invoquant, en cas d'exclusion, les sympathies et le respect traditionnel que tout descendant de Washington entretient pour ceux qui balbutient la langue de Rochambeau et de Lafayette !

Vous puiserez à cette alliance, nous vous le promettons, cet esprit d'ordre et de sagesse qui fait jaillir, des poudres d'or de la Califournie, un état là même où d'autres peuples ne surent fonder que des mines.

Vous vous remettrez en communion nationale avec ceux de vos frères qui gagnent à pleins railroads les prairies du Far Ouest. En croirez-vous ces pionniers, monuments vivants et irréfragables de l'appauvrissement graduel du pays ?

Annexionistes du Bas- et du Haut-Canada réunis, nous vous disons : Du courage, du courage, encore du courage ; les grandes causes ne triomphent qu'à cette condition. La persécution, qu'elle vienne du gouvernement ou de ses affidés, est le premier symptôme du succès définitif qui doit couronner les révolutions sociales.

VIVE L'ANNEXION !

Vive l'Amérique, une par sa grandeur nationale, indivisible dans sa foi républicaine !

The movement spread to other American cities in which there was a considerable French population. At a public meeting at Troy, New York, resolutions were adopted declaring : (1) that the colonial status of Canada was responsible for the economic stagnation of the province, and the involuntary exile of so many of her citizens, (2) that it was the duty of all Canadians to join in the Montreal manifesto, (3) that they should do all in their power to induce England to agree to annexation, (4) that a political union with the United States would restore the prosperity of the province, and (5) that a manifesto in favour of annexation should be issued to the Canadian people. The thanks of the gathering were extended to *L'Avenir, Le Moniteur, The Herald,* and *The Courier* of Montreal, for their splendid services on behalf of democracy and annexation. An address to the Canadian people, signed by over 400 of the French-Canadian residents of Troy and the surrounding district, was duly prepared, and forwarded to Montreal for publication.[1] So far as the subject-matter was concerned, the address was a practical reproduction of the resolutions of the meeting. Shortly afterwards, another assembly was held at Cahoes, in the same state, at which resolutions of similar import were adopted. To these resolutions, there were appended the signatures of over two hundred persons.[2]

At a meeting of the New York association in April 1850, the permanent committee presented an interesting report, reviewing at length the course of the annexation movement and the existing conditions of affairs. The recent despatch of Earl Grey, in the opinion of the committee, closed the first stage of the annexation movement. The refusal of the English Government to agree to separation brought them face to face with unexpected difficulties which must needs be overcome before any substantial progress could be made towards annexation. The report strongly urged that the press and young men of the party should put forth still more vigorous efforts to convert their compatriots to the new political faith.[3] At a subsequent meeting of the association, Mr. J. E. Dorion of Montreal addressed the members, and was accorded a splendid reception.[4]

---

[1] *L'Avenir*, January 8, 1850.   [2] *Ibid.*, May 25, 1850.
[3] *Ibid.*, January 4, 1850.   [4] May 9, 1850.

Somewhat later another branch association was formed at Cooperville, New York, thanks to the zeal of Dr. Dorion of Rouse's Point. On the Fourth of July a grand celebration took place at which Mr. Dorion of Montreal was the principal speaker, and resolutions of the usual order were adopted in favour of annexation.[1]

These demonstrations in the United States were welcomed most heartily by the annexation press of Canada. The manifesto of the New York Association was accepted as the most convincing evidence of the social and economic advantages of annexation.[2] The appeal of the exiles would, it was hoped, awaken a responsive chord in French-Canadian hearts, and arouse a more independent and democratic spirit among the habitants. The addresses of the American associations were most freely used by the annexation speakers in their campaign in the Eastern Townships. But, apparently, the efforts of the American societies counted for little in Canadian politics. The counsel of the local priest was much more authoritative than the distant voice of a few Americanized compatriots. The habitants were entirely out of touch with the democratic thought and life of the American people ; and, in truth, were inclined to look upon all forms of social and intellectual progress with a certain amount of suspicion.

The advent of the New Year brought little change in the political situation in Upper Canada. On account of a change in his political opinions, Mr. John Wilson, the member for London, severed his connection with the Conservative Party. In justice to his constituents he resigned his seat, and stood for re-election in the Reform interests. In his election address, he strongly censured the Tory Party for espousing the cause of peaceful annexation. The proposal, he declared, was altogether too specious to extend far beyond the region

---

[1] *L'Avenir*, July 12, 1850.
[2] *Ibid.*, January 22, 1850.

of the originators.[1] But the question of annexation was in no way at stake in the election, for the Conservative candidate, Mr. Dixon, was a staunch supporter of the British connection. The subject was only incidentally raised by the Reform speakers in the hope of discrediting the Tory Party. The tactics of the Liberals in this regard justly met with the severest condemnation of the local Tory organ. After a bitter struggle, Mr. Wilson was again returned by a small majority.

In a speech to his constituents at Woodstock, the Hon. F. Hincks made a bitter attack upon the loyalty of the opposition. "Politics," he declared, "are in a most extraordinary state in Canada." The Conservative Party was completely disorganized. "There is, however, a political organization in the country known as the British American League, which is in fact a political society, and which, if established ten or twelve years ago, would have subjected its members to trial for high treason. . . . Its members are divided amongst themselves, and differ from each other in their opinions. One portion goes for annexation to the United States as the great remedy for existing evils. These cannot be considered as Conservatives, yet they are men who formerly belonged to the old Tory Party in Upper Canada. They are men who were disappointed in their expectations, and who, when they see no prospects of the revival of Toryism, are ready to support any party which may spring up for the purpose of embarrassing the Government. Another section of the League go for elective institutions."[2]

To this partisan attack, *The Patriot* made the spirited reply that, although in Montreal the senseless cry for annexation had been raised by a group of sordid men, some of whom were formerly allied with the Conservative Party, nevertheless the fact was notorious

[1] *The Globe*, December 15, 1849.
[2] *The Examiner*, January 9, 1850.

that, " in the country parts of Lower Canada, and through the greater part of Upper Canada, the Tory Party were thoroughly loyal, and that the strength of the Annexation Party consisted of disappointed Radicals." [1]

Speaking at Woodstock a few days later, Mr. Van Sittart, a prominent member of the League, distinctly repudiated on behalf of that body the charge of annexation tendencies, and advocated a confederation of the provinces as a strong barrier against a political union with the United States. [2]

At the opening of the York assizes at Toronto, Judge Draper took occasion to address the Grand Jury on the dangerous nature of the annexation movement. [3] He severely arraigned the specious arguments of the Annexationists in favour of a legal right to advocate annexation. " But the liberty of discussion, as of action, ought to have, in every society enjoying a constitution and governed by law, some limits which it would be criminal to exceed. To plead in favour of an object towards which one cannot take a single step without a crime, ought to be in itself something criminal ; and to speak of attaining such an object by some indefinite way by which one would adroitly avoid the danger to which one would expose himself by open acts of treason or sedition, is a sophism which ought not to deceive either those who make use of it, or those to whom it is addressed."

In their reply, the Grand Jury dealt with the delicate situation with tact and sound judgment. Although they disapproved of the propaganda of the Annexationists, they hesitated to recommend any action which might restrict the full liberty of speech. " And they do confidently believe that the good sense of the people, the surest safeguard in extremity, will operate as a sufficient restraint upon the exuberance of visionary

[1] *The Patriot*, January 12, 1850.
[2] *Ibid.*, January 16, 1850.
[3] January 7, 1850.

theorists, and resist all vague attempts of selfish political speculators." [1]

The despatch of the Colonial Secretary to Lord Elgin was heartily welcomed by the loyalist press of Upper Canada. Its views were well expressed in an editorial of *The Kingston Herald.* "We hope Annexationists will acquiesce in that decision, and that we shall see no more addresses to the country. Annexation is morally, politically and physically too, condemned by the great majority of this country, and distinctly negatived by the Imperial Government. Why, then, will men be so insane as to further protract excitement, and hold out hopes which they must be persuaded cannot be realized?" [2] Of a similar tenor was the declaration of *The Dundas Warder.* "For our part we have ever regarded the peaceful separation hobby as a humbug." The despatch of Earl Grey, it continued, was well timed, and likely to prove beneficial by convincing the public that England would not consent to separation. Under these circumstances, it was the duty of every citizen to stop agitating, and to devote himself to such practical measures as would promote the well-being of the country. [3]

In some quarters, however, the despatch of Earl Grey was ungraciously received, while in others it was misunderstood or treated with suspicion. According to *The Colonist*, it was really surprising, in view of the fatuous policy of the Colonial Secretary, that annexation sentiment was not more prevalent throughout the country. [4] *The Examiner* sarcastically remarked that his lordship had made a great discovery in regard to the loyalty of the Canadian people, in believing that their patriotism would stand the buffeting of the United States tariff. The Annexationists, it contended, had stopped short of any treasonable acts ; and so long as

[1] *The Pilot,* January 24, 1850.
[2] *The Kingston Herald,* March 13, 1850.
[3] Quoted from *The Mirror,* February 15, 1850.
[4] *The Colonist,* February 5, 1850.

they limited themselves to strictly peaceful agitation, they were entitled freely to discuss the question of annexation with their fellow countrymen, and the despatch of the Colonial Secretary would not prevent it. The only way to annexation, it concluded, lay through independence.[1]

The beginning of the New Year witnessed the organization of an annexation association in Toronto. Although regular meetings were held, little was known by the outside public in regard to the membership or proceedings of that body. It was presently learned, however, that the association was preparing an address to the people of Upper Canada. The wisdom of this action was severely assailed by *The Mirror* in an editorial entitled, "More Gizards than Brains." Annexation, it maintained, was a thing of time, and it was by no means desirable that it should be born before its time. The majority of the people were not yet qualified to enjoy the advantages of political union, for the vassalage of colonization was still upon them. The issuance of a manifesto was not calculated to promote the object in view, but rather to snuff it out.

The manifesto, which soon after made its appearance, was moderate and dignified in expression; it consisted mainly of a restatement of the arguments of the editorial pages of *The Independent*. Strange to say, the address omitted any reference to the recent despatch of Earl Grey. The document read as follows:

ADDRESS OF THE TORONTO ANNEXATION SOCIETY
TO THE PEOPLE OF CANADA

FELLOW COUNTRYMEN:
The natural advancement of this province towards a state of national maturity, accelerated by the occurrence of unforeseen events, having brought us to that critical period in our history when in our opinion the mutual benefits of our connection with

[1] *The Examiner*, February 6, 1850.

England no longer exist, it becomes our duty as a people to exercise a prudential forecast in providing for the exigencies of our altered condition, and the necessities of the future.   In no spirit of hostility to the parent state, nor with any contemplated defiance of existing authority, municipal or metropolitan, do we address you.   A candid statement of the actual condition of the country will sufficiently show the necessity of providing for its pressing and paramount want.

The geographical position of Canada—its extent—its elements of future greatness—its distance from the parent state—the impatience of external restraint, which grows up as an instinct with the progress of young communities—all forbid the hope that any commutual interests can for ever bind up our fortunes with those of the mother country.   That the separation, when it does come, as come it must eventually, may be the voluntary exercise of the free will of parent and offspring, must be the desire of every true patriot and sincere friend of humanity.   It would argue a false delicacy, and discover a mistaken prudence, were we to look on in silence while political society is outgrowing its institutions, in the vain hope that they can long survive not only the necessities, the conditions, and the wants which called them into being, but also the affections which supported their existence.

The pressing necessities of the manufacturing population of England, which operated as the motive for effecting a change in her commercial policy, subjecting the Canadian farmer to the disadvantages of independence, without its countervailing benefits, may also be a justification of the measure.   If the people of the United Kingdom, having in view the general interest of the empire and without giving undue weight to the claims of any locality, near or distant, deliberately resolved upon a commercial policy, which, upon the whole, they believed would prove most conducive to the general interests, the Canadian people cannot urge their just complaints of the sacrifice of their special interests as an adequate reason for condemning the national policy, and seeking its reversal. Were the question of free trade in England not yet decided, Canada might claim, as a right, to have her voice heard in the decision.

The acquiescence of all interests, colonial and metropolitan, should have been secured by every reasonable concession in the adjustment of such a question. But the decision of the Imperial Legislature, a decision in which we had no voice, and which, if we had, the suffrage of Canada could not have affected, may be looked upon as beyond the hope of reversal. But even though the reactionary agitation of English agriculturists should, for the moment, cause the opinions of that class to prevail in the national Councils, a counter agitation would in turn bring matters back to their present position ; while Canada, tantalized by false hopes and dreamy illusions, would realize nothing but constant buffetings amid the violent oscillations from a free trade to a protection policy. Already has the unfixedness in the commercial policy of the mother country seriously augmented the difficulties of this province, and extinguished the hope of any permanent relief from Imperial Legislation to our depressed agricultural and commercial interests.

Compelled to encounter all the difficulties of foreign competition in the English market, and deprived of that complete control over foreign commerce which independent states enjoy, we have to sustain the burdens without enjoying the advantages of independence. It is of this we conceive we have a right to complain ; and not of the national policy, which the suffrage of Canada, if permitted to be exercised, would be insufficient to change.

Thus circumstanced with regard to the mother country, our commercial relations with the only foreign nation with whom our trade is considerable are not on a more satisfactory footing. For several years we have sought in vain the establishment of a treaty of commerce based upon principles of a mutual exchange of the products of the soil. At this moment, there are in progress to secure this object the same movements which have previously, on several successive occasions, raised the hopes of the province only to add the poignancy of disappointment to the disadvantages of our position. Without speculating on the present chances of success in the pursuit of an object, which has hitherto eluded our grasp, we cannot affect to be insensible that, were there no barrier to the immediate success of this measure, it would not place our commerce with the United States upon the best and most desirable footing. In its present shape, the measure now before the American Congress would cover but a limited portion of those articles of commerce which are daily exchanged by the two countries.

In a province thus circumstanced, it would be little short of a miracle, if the great interests of industry could be buoyed up above the accumulated weight of depression. General languor, and the absence of that bold spirit of enterprise which so pre-eminently characterizes our American neighbours, are the natural consequence. Emigration and capital shun our shores. With rivers that supply the finest hydraulic power in the world, manufacturers have not taken root amongst us. A chain of almost uninterrupted water communication, in the very heart of the country, lies surrounded by forests, and but partially explored, for want of capital and enterprise to turn it to account.

The almost illimitable sources of wealth, in soil, timber, water, and ores of various metals, in which the provinces abound, place in striking contrast the rich profusion of the Creator with the inactivity of man ; and this inertness, which chills and freezes every industrial interest, stands in still more striking and humiliating contrast with the general activity and uniform progress of American states, whose settlement dates much later than the settlement of Canada.

Of the numerous colonies of England, Canada is

perhaps the one whose political institutions European capitalists regard as the most unstable. Among the many causes that have contributed to produce this impression are : the vicissitudes that have marked our political history ; our proximity to a country whose maxims of government are supposed to possess a peculiarly contagious influence ; the popular belief that we have reached that state of national manhood when colonial dependence is morally, and must soon be practically, superseded ; the apprehension that we are on the verge of a revolution in which popular violence may seek to cancel the public engagements ; the unsettled state of our political institutions. Vague ideas of this nature, floating in the popular mind of England, deter the capitalist from risking a farthing upon the. most feasible projects for constructing railways or other works of provincial utility. Thus, by a natural and necessary process, is the state of political transition made also one of commercial stagnation and industrial inactivity.

Could we even secure abroad that general confidence in the stability of our political institutions, for which it were vain and delusive to hope, there would still remain the numerous disadvantages of a mere political connection, which on the one hand implies the right of restraint, and, on the other, the necessity of submission. In the appointment of the person administering the Government, the province has no voice ; and, however the received theory of our scheme of government may define the limits of his authority, repeated facts in our history show how fallacious is the assumption that there exists any adequate safeguard against the stretching of his power beyond the range of its theoretical limits. Armed with secret instructions from England and the potent prerogative of dissolving the Provincial Parliament, a skilful or unscrupulous exercise of the functions with which he is invested, and the influence he can wield, enables the Governor of the day to change at pleasure the entire aspect and tendency of our politics. The discretionary power in the Governor to reserve, for Imperial assent or abrogation, measures which have received the sanction of the Canadian Legislature, gives rise to the most inconvenient delays, and places our interests in constant danger of being made subservient to the exigencies of Imperial Legislation.

Denied that complete freedom of action over our political and commercial interests which is the attribute and prerogative of independent states, when the countervailing benefits of the parental connection have been withdrawn, we are naturally led to seek a change in our external relations that will relieve us from the burdens of a condition prolific of evils and sterile of benefits.

From a dispassionate and candid consideration of the case, we have deliberately formed the opinion that the only remedy that can relieve us from the commercial and political disadvantages imposed upon us by the nature and circumstances of our present position, is to be found in a friendly separation of this province from England, and its annexation to the United States. Our sole object in thus appealing to the intelligence of the Canadian people is to counsel them to take preliminary steps for obtaining the assent of the executive and legislative authorities of England to this proposed measure.

Various alternatives to avert this inevitable result have been suggested, discussed, and abandoned. Of these the most prominent are : colonial representation in the Imperial Parliament, and an independent federal union of the British-American Provinces.

The first of these schemes, often broached, but never cordially supported by the public voice of either the province or the mother country, has ceased to have advocates in any section of our community whose numbers and intelligence entitle them to consideration. Besides that the right of representation in the Imperial Parliament would bring with it an additional burthen of taxation, from which we have hitherto been exempt, the practical benefits of the arrangement would be of a questionable character. The presence of our representatives might indeed serve constantly to remind the British Parliament of the political existence of Canada ; but the delegated suffrage of the province would not be felt in the scales of national legislation.

The scheme of an independent federal union of the provinces would impose upon the federation all the burthens of a national existence ; while our weakness would render us a prey to the cupidity or ambition of any powerful maritime or neighbouring nation. The means of naval protection from foreign aggression would be a necessary condition of national independence ; but the cost of creating a navy, and the burthen of its support, would far exceed our available resources. To this would be added the cost of a consular system, internal fortifications, and a standing army.

Annexation to the United States would secure to Canada all the advantages of unrestricted free trade with the other members of the confederacy. Our interests and sympathies would necessarily be fused together ; and the enterprise, so conspicuous everywhere throughout the Union, could not fail to find its way and extend itself very soon over the whole face of the province. To our statesmen and great men it would open a wide field of honourable ambition. It would raise our credit abroad, and cause foreign capital to flow into the country. Manufacturers—for which the country is so admirably adapted from its geographical position, climate, cheapness of motive power and labour, and from the abundant supply of raw material in which it abounds—would flourish to an extent unsurpassed in many of the older states. An extended system of railways would soon be carried into practical operation. These and other inducements would divert to our shores a portion of the better description of immigration, which at present sets in, in an almost uninterrupted stream, to the Western States.

A patriotic spirit of common nationality would displace the jealousies and the feuds which have so long embittered social intercourse, and a noble feeling of self-reliance would produce a general social elevation amongst all classes of our community.

In thus stating the broad grounds on which we conceive the cause of annexation should be prosecuted, it is of importance to observe that no steps should be recommended which shall not be in accordance with a friendly separation, in the first instance, from Great Britain. All constitutional means must, however, be employed to obtain the sense of the people, and through them to influence the Legislature. An extensive organization, through local societies to be linked together by a chain of correspondence, is recommended. The necessity for the adoption of this course is perhaps greater in Upper Canada than in the other section of the province—in many parts of which public sentiment has become so united on this subject as not to require the formation of societies. In Western Canada, however, where the most extraordinary efforts have been made by interested politicians to mislead and intimidate the people, organization has become indispensable as a means for the dissemination of truth, as well as for securing combined action. Already such information has been received of the state of public feeling on this great question throughout Western Canada, as to warrant the belief that there are but few localities where societies may not be immediately formed. When we see whole counties in Lower Canada coming boldly forward, and avowing their sentiments in favour of annexation, it is time that those who entertain similar views in this part of the province should at once cast their weight into the scale in favour of the movement.

The endeavours of those whose individual interests are not identified with the community at large, to retard the early consummation of this great and glorious object, must be firmly met by a manly determination to overcome every obstacle. Let it be borne in mind, on all occasions, that the connection of these colonies with the mother country is no longer regarded by any class of politicians, either in England or Canada, as a thing of permanence. The course of action recommended is merely to accelerate inevitable events, and shorten a state of transition which, whilst it lasts, must retard that rapid advance to prosperity and happiness that will speedily follow the attainment of a position amongst the independent nations of the earth.

Fellow Countrymen :—Having thus in general terms expressed our views on this momentous question, we commend the cause to the good sense and zeal of our friends in every part of Canada ; and trust that every true Canadian, every lover of really responsible and free government, who entertains a noble ambition to see his country advance in prosperity and wealth, will on this occasion manfully perform his duty.

By order of the Association,

RICHARD KNEESHAW,

Recording Secretary.

H. B. WILLSON,

Corresponding Secretary.

The manifesto, which was doubtless the work of Mr. Willson, was sarcastically likened by *The Montreal Gazette* to the famous address of the three tailors of Tooley Street. It was indeed a significant circumstance that the officers and members of the association did not follow the example of their fellow Annexationists in Montreal in appending their names to the address. The manifesto fell flat ; its appearance awakened scarcely any interest among the general body of citizens. This indifference was due, according to *The Examiner*, to the lack of novelty of the subject. One year ago, a large proportion of the people " would have been petrified by such a document," but now it did not shock the nerves of even the most sensitive. It was difficult, in fact, to gauge what was the real state of

public opinion on annexation. Public sentiment had
been materially altered, in the opinion of *The Examiner*,
by the removal of the seat of Government to Toronto.
Both pro- and anti-Annexationists were alike influenced
by selfish considerations. The choice of Toronto as
the temporary capital had made many converts to the
British connection in the city, and the removal of the
seat of Government might occasion a similar reaction
of feeling. The natural decadence of loyalty, it concluded, had been accelerated by the course of English
legislation and by the apparent antagonism of interest
between the colony and the parent state.[1]

The spirits of the Annexationists were somewhat
raised by several favourable editorials in *The Oshawa
Reformer*, and by the appearance of a new paper, *The
Whitby Freeman*—a half Tory, half Annexationist sheet.
It was hoped that the seed which had been sown in
the Perry election was about to bring forth its first
fruits. But the hopes of the Annexationists were
quickly extinguished, for the paper soon after fell into
the hands of the Reformers, and changed its political
principles. Throughout the Midland District, the annexation movement was distinctly losing ground. In
speaking of the Sherbrooke election, *The Peterborough
Dispatch* declared : " We believe that the people here
have no wish for a change . . . and that an earnest
and timely effort on the part of the imperial power to
remove from among us any cause for complaint would
go far to re-establish confidence and good feeling."
As a means to the betterment of conditions, it advocated
a retrenchment in public expenditure, the popular
election of officials, and an extension of the franchise.[2]

The views of *The Kingston Whig* were even more
outspoken. " However much the annexation movement may expand itself and its principles in the midst
of populous cities and large towns, it certainly is not
progressing in country places. The rural population

---

[1] *The Examiner*, February 20, 1850.
[2] Quoted from *The Mirror*, March 22, 1850.

of the Midland and Victoria Districts to a man seems to be dead against annexation, or any intimate connection with the adjoining Republic. A good deal of this repulsion is probably spurious, the combined effect of the Liberal Party's being in power, and the dread of want of sincerity in the profession of those Annexationists who belong to the defunct Conservative Party."

Nevertheless the various local correspondents of *The Independent* regularly informed its readers of the growth of annexation sentiment in their respective parts of the province. In the County of Norfolk, it was alleged that two-thirds of the inhabitants were Annexationists at heart. Encouraged by these reports, Mr. Willson resolved to make a tour of the Western peninsula in the interest of his paper and of the annexation cause. But on attempting to hold a meeting at Port Rowan, he was treated with such indignity that he thought it advisable to leave the district, and discontinue his campaign.

A more encouraging prospect for the Annexationists was presented in the counties along the Detroit and St. Clair rivers, where the growing spirit of discontent at last found expression. The proximity of the district to the American border brought home most forcibly to the Canadian farmers and traders the striking contrast between their condition and that of their neighbours across the river. The proof of their economic inferiority lay before their eyes, and they could not fail to see it. They were as moral, industrious, and intelligent as their American cousins, yet they did not reap the same reward for their labours. The conviction was forced upon them that the colonial status was responsible for their ills.

The rising feeling of disaffection was voiced in an open letter of Colonel Prince, the local Tory member and one of the Vice-Presidents of the League, in which he came out boldly for Canadian independence. As the policy of annexation was by no means popular, he endeavoured to give a new direction to the spirit of unrest, by advocating a union of the British-American provinces and their erection into an independent state. Personally, he declared, he was opposed to annexation. " The people would degrade themselves, if they did not make independence, not annexation, the test at the next general election." They should approach the Queen by petition to grant them independence. The voluntary grant of this boon would not compromise the honour of England, nor tarnish the reputation of Canada. The dominion of Great Britain, he concluded, was baneful to Canada ; the colonial status was commercially ruinous, and politically injurious and humiliating.[1] The opinion of the gallant colonel was based on his own business experience, to which he appealed with convincing force. He had invested a large proportion of his capital in a local brewery which, owing to the closing of the American market, had turned out to be a dead loss.

The suggestion was promptly taken up by some of the local inhabitants. A petition to the Legislature was drawn up by Colonel Prince, and signed by many of the " most respected citizens " of the united counties of Essex, Kent, and Lambton, praying for an address to the Queen in favour of independence. The petitioners alleged that they were driven to make this request by the unfortunate policy of England in withdrawing the colonial preference, and by other acts prejudicial to the interests of the province. Nevertheless, the petitioners concluded, they would remain loyal subjects of Great Britain until Her Majesty should see fit to release the colony from the status of a dependency.[2]

This outburst of discontent proved only a flash in the pan ; it was the last bright flare of a flickering flame. Annexation sentiment was gradually dying out throughout Upper Canada. Before the close of the month *The Toronto Independent* was forced to announce its approaching demise. The paper had been ably

---

[1] *Amherstburg Courier*, February 23, 1850
[2] *The Colonist*, April 5, 1850.

edited by Mr. Willson. In three short months it had increased its circulation from seven to fourteen hundred, but it could not command sufficient support to keep it going. Annexation sentiment in Upper Canada was not sufficiently developed to maintain an independent organ. In the dying confession of *The Independent*, the editor declared that he had been induced by the pressure of his Montreal friends to make *The Independent* an annexation paper. From the outset he had not been sanguine of success in taking such an advanced position. The turn of affairs in Upper Canada and the course of political parties had shown that his original intention of advocating independence only, leaving the question of annexation for future settlement, would have been more consonant with the sentiments of the Canadian public.

In agitating for an ultimate end, instead of a proximate step, the separationists had placed themselves in a false position in Upper Canada, where as yet no leading politician had come out in favour of annexation. In the light of these conditions, further agitation for annexation should be abandoned for a time. Annexation, he believed, could be peacefully and constitutionally obtained only through the winning of elective institutions, and it behoved the Annexationists to join hands with their fellow countrymen in the struggle for popular democracy. " It would be folly," he concluded, " for us to continue single-handed and alone in all this western section of the province to agitate a question, when the first step towards its attainment has got to be taken." In speaking of the disappearance of *The Independent*, *The Montreal Herald* sardonically remarked that an annexation paper could not hope to succeed in Toronto, where there was too much flunkeyism fomented by the presence of the Governor-General. But, it contended, the principles for which *The Independent* stood had not ceased to exist, as was evident from the recent conversion of Colonel Prince, and the progress of the movement in New Brunswick.

A survey of the state of political feeling throughout the province revealed the fact that the annexation campaign had been a complete failure. Outside of Montreal and Quebec, and the border districts in the eastern and western extremes of the province, the movement had not obtained a firm hold upon any considerable portion of the population. The number of signatures to the various manifestos did not amount to 5,000, an insignificant fraction of the total population. The bulk of the English inhabitants of Upper Canada, and of the French in Lower, were avowedly hostile to annexation. "As a popular movement," declared *The Globe* in language somewhat overdrawn, " the whole thing has been an entire failure ; it has not found a resting-place in any section of the country, nor with any political party." [1]

[1] *The Globe*, March 5, 1850.

CHAPTER VII

THE COLLAPSE OF THE MOVEMENT

IN the meantime, the Government was making
another serious effort to secure an entrance into
the American market for Canadian products.
Although Lord Elgin was greatly disappointed
at the failure of the Dix Bill, he had not given up hope
of securing a reciprocity agreement from the President
or Congress. The seriousness of the local situation
convinced the Ministry of the necessity of immediate
action, if the colony was not to be lost to the empire.
Mr. Hamilton Merritt was sent on a special mission to
Washington, with a view to winning over the American
Government to a more favourable attitude towards

reciprocity. Negociations for an international agreement were set on foot by Mr. Crampton, the British Ambassador, but broke down owing to the opposition of the President, who maintained that the proper mode of procedure was by legislation, and not by executive action.[1]

Although the mission was a failure, Mr. Merritt returned with the conviction that a favourable reciprocity arrangement might yet be wrung from the United States. But he was as strongly opposed to annexation as ever. In a speech to his constituents a few months later, he declared that on general principles he was in favour of free trade between England and Canada, with discriminating duties against the United States. But, since England had reversed her former policy to the disadvantage of the colonies, Canada must needs seek admission for her products into the American market. He did not believe that the policy of reciprocity would estrange the province from Great Britain, but that, on the contrary, the continued closure of the United States market would inevitably produce an ever-increasing demand for separation. He was convinced that they would soon gain reciprocity either by coercion or without, possibly within a few months, but at any rate ultimately. Annexation was a question to be seriously considered and not laughed at, as was the vogue in some of the newspapers.

He did not think that if Canada were annexed to the United States, it would receive any benefits whatever. It would have to assume a heavy federal tax, and to levy duties on all but American goods. Free trade would certainly be secured on this continent, but it would be lost with the rest of the world. He was convinced, however, that the only thing to stop annexation was to remove the high custom duties which tended to drive men into seeking it and desiring it.

A portion of the commercial community heartily

[1] *U.S. Ex. Doc.* No. 64, 1st Sess. 31st Cong.

supported the efforts of the Government to secure reciprocity. A group of public-spirited business men united to send a petition tó the British Government by the hands of Mr. Henry Moyle, requesting it to use its influence and good offices with the American Executive, to secure on mutual conditions the free access of Canadian grains to the United States market, and, failing in this, to retaliate upon the Americans by imposing on their produce a duty equal to that which the United States tariff levied on the products of Canada. Through the columns of *The St. Catherine's Journal*, Mr. Merritt kept up an active agitation for reciprocity. One of the advantages of that policy would be, *The Journal* declared, " to remove the uncertainty " which now existed in the minds of men as to the future relations of the colony to the mother country and the United States. " Make Canada prosperous, and nothing more would be heard about annexation." But prosperity, it concluded, could only be attained by a bold comprehensive scheme of reciprocity.[1]

The cry was heartily taken up by the majority of the Reform papers, as the best antidote to the clamour of annexation. *The Examiner* voiced the feelings of many of the party in declaring that, if reciprocity were refused, Canadians would be driven to some other remedy to extricate themselves from the disadvantageous position in which they were placed.[2] It expressed grave doubts as to the wisdom of resorting to retaliatory measures against the United States, even though England should consent to adopt such tactics, which, however, was most improbable. Reciprocity as an antidote for annexation was, under existing circumstances, not a very hopeful policy. It was ready to admit, however, that the passage of a Reciprocity Bill in Congress would put the question of annexation in abeyance for the time being, though it was extremely doubtful if such a measure would extinguish all future

---

[1] *The Journal and Express*, November 1, 1849
[2] *The Examiner*, September 5, 1849.

agitation.[1] In their exasperation against the selfish
policy of the United States, some of the Reformers
went so far as to join with the Conservative Party in
advocating the imposition of retaliatory protective
duties on American products, in case the United
States would not agree to reciprocity.[2]

The Governor-General continued to urge upon the
Secretary for the Colonies the imperative necessity of
securing a market for Canadian products in the United
States. The prices of all natural products were, he
pointed out, considerably lower in Canada than across
the border. " So long as this state of things continues,
there will be discontent in this country ; deep growing
discontent. You will not, I trust, accuse me of having
deceived you on this point. I have always said that
I am prepared to assume the responsibility of keeping
Canada quiet with a much smaller garrison than we
have now, and without any tax on the British consumer in the shape of protection to Canadian products,
if you put our trade on as good a footing as that of our
American neighbours ; but, if things remain on their
present footing in this respect, there is nothing before
us but violent agitation, ending in convulsion or annexation. It is better that I should worry you with
my importunity, than that I should be chargeable with
having neglected to give you due warning. You have
a great opportunity before you—obtain reciprocity for
us, and I venture to predict that you will be able
shortly to point to this hitherto turbulent colony with
satisfaction, in illustration of the tendency of self-
government and freedom of trade to beget contentment
and material progress. Canada will remain attached
to England, though tied to her neither by the golden
links of protection, nor by the meshes of old-fashioned
Colonial Office jobbing and chicane. But, if you allow
the Americans to withhold the boon, which you have

[1] *The Examiner*, February 20, 1850.
[2] See resolution of the Reformers in Lough, *The Examiner*,
February 13, 1850.

the means of extorting, if you will, I much fear that
the closing period of the connection between Great
Britain and Canada will be marked by incidents which
will damp the ardour of those who desire to promote
human happiness by striking shackles either off commerce or off men." [1]

The introduction of two Reciprocity Bills into Congress revived the hopes of the Canadian people. A
group of Toronto business men resolved to send the
Hon. M. Cameron to Washington to cultivate the acquaintance of Congressmen, and to promote as far as
possible the passage of a satisfactory Bill. Although
of a private nature, this mission was undertaken with
the approval and sanction of the local Government.
A treacherous attempt was made by some of the
Annexationists to defeat the object of the mission. In
Toronto, an effort was made to persuade the mercantile
community that the real purpose of Cameron was " to
frustrate reciprocity and promote annexation." [2] The
two annexation organs in Montreal did not hesitate to
call upon Congress to defeat any reciprocity measures,
for fear that the enactment of such a Bill might stifle
the demand for annexation in Canada.[3] So far did
they carry their opposition, that they endeavoured to
prejudice the Southern Congressmen against Cameron
by pointing out that he was a strong opponent of
slavery. They preferred, according to *The Kingston
News,* " to see reciprocity in human chattels rather
than in trade." [4]

After the failure of the Dix Bill, the agents of the
British Government at Washington resolved to adopt
somewhat different tactics in order to overcome the

---

[1] November 8, 1849 (*Letters and Journals of Lord Elgin,* p. 102).
[2] *The Examiner,* February 13, 1850.
[3] *The New York Herald* maintained, on the contrary, that the
closer the commercial relations of the two countries, the nearer they
would be drawn together politically. It disapproved of both the
tactics and the arguments of *The Montreal Courier* upon this phase
of the question.
[4] Quoted from *The Colonist,* March 5, 1850.

opposition of the Congressmen from the South. The latter, as we have seen, were inclined to look upon reciprocity as a disguised scheme of annexation, to which they were resolutely opposed. A strong effort was made to remove this erroneous impression, and to present the question of reciprocity in relation to annexation in its true light. Representations were accordingly made to the Southern members to the effect that the heart of the Canadian demand for annexation was not the desire to become Americans, but rather the desire, amounting almost to a necessity, of securing an entrance into the United States market. It followed, as a natural consequence, that the best and simplest way of defeating all projects for a political union would be to satisfy the Canadian demand for reciprocity.[1] Mr. Cameron was likewise advised, prior to his departure, to make similar representations to the Southern Congressmen.[2]

But the combined efforts of the English and Canadian Governments again failed to move Congress. At first the prospects seemed favourable. On January 29, a Reciprocity Bill was reported in the House of Representatives by Mr. McLean, from the Committee of Commerce, and after the first and second readings was referred to the Committee of the Whole.[3] A few days later Senator Douglas presented a Bill in the Upper House providing for the free navigation of the St. Lawrence and the reciprocal free exchange of certain products of the respective countries. But both measures were subsequently lost in committee. The hostility of the Southern members and the opposition of the Northern protectionists again proved too strong for the supporters of reciprocity. *The New York Tribune,*[4] the leading protectionist organ of the country, came out flatly against any commercial arrangement

---

[1] *The New York Herald*, quoted in *The Colonist*, October 9, 1849.
[2] *The Mirror*, February 15, 1850.
[3] *J. H. R.*, 1849–50, p. 428.
[4] February 11, 1850.

with Canada, unless accompanied by annexation.   In the face of all these hostile influences, the diplomacy of the Canadian authorities was of little avail.   Congress was not yet ready to consider the question of reciprocity upon its merits.   Reciprocity was not a subject " about which any national or even party feeling could be aroused.   It was one which required much study to understand its bearings, and which would affect different interests in the country in different ways.   It stood, therefore, especially in need of the aid of professional organizers ; a kind of aid of which it was of course impossible that either the British or the Canadian Government should avail itself." [1]

The approaching session of Parliament promised to be unusually interesting, owing to the peculiar position and uncertain relationships of the various party groups in the Assembly.   Nominally the Ministry had a large majority in the House, but in fact the Reform Party was rent in twain.   The possible organization of a separate annexationist group further complicated the situation.   The standing of the several parties was approximately : Reformers 34 ; Clear Grits 22 ; Conservatives 20 ; Annexationists 7.   In the last-mentioned group were reckoned DeWitt, Holmes, McConnell, Egan, Papineau, Sanborn, and Prince.   The keenest speculation was rife as to the attitude of the Clear Grits towards the Government, and as to the policy of the Annexationists.

The question as to whether the annexation members should form a separate party or not had already been discussed at length by some of the annexation journals. *The Toronto Independent* did not think that the group was strong enough as yet to organize an independent party ; nor did it approve of the several members of the group retaining their former political affiliations for general party purposes ; it recommended, on the contrary, an opportunist policy of friendly co-operation with the Clear Grit members.   It laid down the

[1] *Letters and Journals of Lord Elgin*, p. 107.

dictum that every measure should be considered in reference to its effect upon annexation. " As elective institutions from the Governor downwards would be one of the most striking changes which would accompany the admission of Canada as a sovereign state into the American Union," the annexation members would be expected " to take every opportunity of urging the adoption of elective institutions, not as an end, but as an instalment of the reforms they seek, and as a preparation for it." [1] For similar reasons, added *The Montreal Herald*, the annexation group would naturally support the principle of religious equality, the curtailment of the civil list, and all such measures and reforms as were calculated to prepare the way for union with the United States.[2]

At the opening of the session, a clever appeal was made by *The Montreal Courier* to the Clear Grit Party to assume the leadership of the progressive forces in opposition to the Government. " With such pilots at the helm, we shall have some hope for the advancement and prosperity of our common country, besides the assurance that we shall then have made one capital move in the right direction for independence." [3] But the Clear Grit Party was not in a position to lead, even had it so desired ; it was sadly in want of responsible leaders, and by no means certain of its own policy and political principles.

The speech of the Governor-General, in opening Parliament, referred to the annexation movement in the following terms :

" I have deemed it my duty in the exercise of the prerogative . . . to mark Her Majesty's disapprobation of the course taken by persons holding commissions at the pleasure of the Crown, who have formally avowed the desire to bring about the separation of this province from the empire. . . .

---

[1] Quoted from *The Hamilton Spectator*, January 5, 1850.
[2] Quoted from *The Toronto Mirror*, January 18, 1850.
[3] Quoted from *The Globe*, May 14, 1850.

" The views put forward by these persons, and by those who act with them, .do not, I have reason to believe, find favour with any considerable portion of Her Majesty's subjects.

" The great majority of the people of the province have given at this juncture proofs not to be mistaken of loyalty to the Queen and attachment to the connection with Great Britain.

" They look to their own Parliament for the redress of grievances which may be proved to exist, and for the adoption of such measures of improvement as may be calculated to promote their happiness and prosperity."

In the Legislative Council, the Hon. P. B. De Blaquière moved an ultra-patriotic address to the Queen expressive of the devoted loyalty of the Upper Chamber to the mother country. It was highly important, in his judgment, that the Council should pronounce its opinion on the subject of annexation, since the views of various irresponsible bodies had been freely expressed throughout the province, and had created a false impression in England as to the state of Canadian feeling. The motion was supported by the Hon. A. Ferguson, on the ground that " it would have the effect of attracting a large number of immigrants to Canada." On both sides of the House there was general condemnation of annexation. The motion was carried unanimously.

In the Legislative Assembly, the question of separation was raised at the very outset by Colonel Prince in presenting the petition of his constituents for independence. He took occasion to deny the allegation that the petition was signed by Americans ; it was, in truth, a Canadian document, to which were appended the names of many of the most respected residents of the district. He was proud to introduce " the first petition ever presented to a British Parliament for separation from the British nation." At this point the Speaker intervened to call the attention of the House to the singular character of the subject-matter of the petition ;

whereupon Mr. Baldwin moved that the petition be not received.

The motion of the Attorney-General brought on a brief but animated discussion. It was contended by Colonel Prince that all British subjects had a constitutional right to present their petitions to Parliament, and that it was a tyrannical exercise of authority to dispose of the matter in so cursory a fashion. Other petitions of a similar character would soon be forthcoming. There was a time, he claimed, when Baldwin would have signed the petition ; but the truth of the statement was immediately challenged by the Attorney-General. Mr. Papineau came to the support of his colleague. The House, he maintained, had no constitutional right to stand between the petitioners and the Throne. He charged the Government with pursuing a deliberate policy of endeavouring to suppress freedom of thought and speech, outside the House as well as within. There was not, he concluded, an English statesman who did not admit the incapacity of England to administer the colonies.

Colonel Gugy stirred up the feelings of the members by making a slashing attack on the principle of independence. Canada, he asserted, was incapable of sustaining at present an independent status. Under such a régime " the country would be overrun and destroyed by loafers." Malcolm Cameron calmed the rising temper of the House by a dispassionate discussion of the legal aspects of the question. He was afraid that his conduct in supporting the member for Kent might be misunderstood ; for, although he did not share the opinions of the petitioners, he was compelled on constitutional grounds to vindicate their right of petition. He did not think that there were more than thirty persons in favour of independence in all the Western District. Canada, he believed, was much better off as a colony than she would be if annexed to the United States. He urged that the petition be referred to a committee where it could be more effectually repudiated, than by summarily refusing to accept it. Notwithstanding this able plea for due consideration of the petition, the motion of the Attorney-General was adopted by the overwhelming vote of 57 Ayes to 7 Nays, the latter consisting of Messrs. Cameron, De Witt, Holmes, McConnell, Papineau, Prince, and Sanborn.

The summary action of the Assembly in throwing out the petition was intended to show to the country at large that the popular chamber had no sympathy whatever with any schemes of disloyalty, and would refuse to entertain any such proposals. The decisive action of the Ministry in moving the rejection of the petition won the general commendation of the Reformers throughout the province, but was severely criticized by the annexation organs and by a few of the Tory papers, in particular by *The Montreal Gazette.*[1]

In the debate on the address but little attention was paid to the question of annexation. The mover of the address merely referred to the general satisfaction of the public at the dismissal of the objectionable officials, while the seconder failed to notice the topic. Several members of the opposition, however, took occasion to censure the Government for arbitrarily interfering with the liberty of its servants, and for misrepresenting the condition of the country in the speech of the Governor-General. In reply to these criticisms, the Inspector-General, the Hon. Francis Hincks, briefly stated that there was the greater reason in this case for prompt and decisive action on the part of the Ministry in making the dismissals in question, since some of the members of the Government had been wrongfully suspected of disloyalty. Under these circumstances, a mere passive attitude, or a failure to act, would almost certainly have been construed by the country at large as a tacit approval of the treasonable activities of some of the servants of the State. The Government was in honour bound to vindicate its own loyalty, as well as to maintain the supremacy of the Crown.

[1] *The Gazette*, May 21, 1850.

The question of annexation came up for a lively discussion, upon an amendment to the address in favour of household suffrage and an elective Legislative Council, which was introduced by Mr. Boulton of Norfolk, at the instance of the Radical section of the Clear Grit Party. The Ministers found themselves attacked on all sides by the different party groups. The annexation members joined with the Tories in making a vigorous assault upon the general policy of the Government, while the Clear Grits added their quota of criticism in respect to certain features of the administration. But little attempt was made to confine the discussion to the specific amendment before the House.

On the Tory side, the principal speakers were Sir Allan MacNab, Colonel Gugy, and Mr. Badgley. The disorganization of the party was revealed most clearly in the divergent opinions of the party leaders upon the question. Some of the members of the party condemned the action of the Executive on general party principles, while others supported the Government on patriotic grounds. To the first of these classes belonged Sir Allan MacNab, who made an ill-advised effort to justify the Tory Annexationists of Montreal. The annexation movement was occasioned, in his judgment, by the Rebellion Losses Bill. " He believed that there was not a more loyal body of men in the world " than the self-same Montreal Annexationists.

But the attitude of the Conservative leader did not commend itself to some of his colleagues, who were not yet ready to justify, let alone commend, the treasonable conduct of their fellow partisans. The gallant knight was severely taken to task by Colonel Gugy for his cordial tone towards the Annexationists. On this question, the latter declared, he was forced to part company with his political friends, and impelled to support the policy of the Government. He warned the leaders of the party, that, even though an alliance were made with the republican members of the House, for the overthrow of the Government, it would still be impossible to form a Coalition Ministry out of such discordant elements. The result of the annexation movement " had been the complete disruption of the Conservative Party. They had now no party to fall back on." The Annexationists had appealed to the selfish interests of the public, and had sought to deceive the people by glowing prospects of prosperity. But the effect of the investment of American capital would not, as represented, redound to the advantage of Canada ; on the contrary, it would serve to " create a moneyed aristocracy of foreigners," and reduce the native population to the European level of dependents upon their wealthier neighbours.

In the heat of his temper, the gallant Colonel allowed his tongue to run away with his judgment, and most brutally assailed the character of the Annexationists in coarse and vulgar language, unbecoming a gentleman, and unworthy of a member of the Chamber. Some of the leaders of that party were accused of speculating in flour ; " and the vice of avarice was common to them all." Mr. Redpath was aptly described as an ambitious tradesman who had amassed a fortune, and wished to heap up more. In conclusion, the honourable member most heartily commended the course of the Government in dismissing those officials who were basely using an influence derived from the Crown for the overthrow of the institutions they had sworn to maintain.

A much more liberal view of the conduct of the Annexationists was taken by Mr. Badgley, who contended that, if the manifesto was treasonable, there was an excellent precedent for it in the memorial of the Montreal Board of Trade. Moreover, the question of separation had been freely discussed in England without public criticism or suspicion of seditious proceedings. Twenty years before, Canning had stated that he was bringing up the Canadas with a view to handing them over to the United States. The fact that annexation was not making progress throughout the province afforded the best of reasons for declining to dismiss the Annexationists. As it was, the arbitrary action of the Government had occasioned much bitterness of feeling, whereas an effort should have been made to win the wayward officials back to a sense of their duty to the Crown and country.

The annexation members, as was to be expected, took a prominent part in the discussion. The slanderous attack of Colonel Gugy upon the morality of the members of the party naturally aroused the ire of the annexation group, and fortunately afforded them a distinct point of advantage in the ensuing debate, of which they made good use. They did not fail to point out that this sweeping indictment would include a majority of the Colonel's fellow partisans of Montreal, and a large proportion of estimable citizens throughout the province. The members of the group carefully avoided, throughout their speeches, any political appeal to either of the old-line parties. The purity of their motives, the evils of the colonial régime, the natural advantages of separation, and the commercial benefits of annexation were the recurrent themes of all their arguments.

Mr. Sanborn, against whom the brunt of the loyalist attack was directed, acquitted himself well under the circumstances. He professed to enjoy a privileged position in the House, as an independent member free from all party restrictions and control. He took exception to the assertion of the leader of the Opposition that the Rebellion Losses Bill was the occasion of the annexation movement. There was, in his opinion, far more sympathy in the Legislature with the cause of annexation than appeared on the surface, since many of the members did not think the moment as yet opportune to express their true feelings upon the question. The Executive, he asserted, had exercised the power of dismissal in an arbitrary manner. Some of the victims of the Government's displeasure were "notoriously the best men in the country."

Upon Mr. Holmes devolved the task of developing the chief constructive argument for the Annexationists. His speech on this occasion was delivered with more than ordinary force and persuasiveness. He prefaced his argument by a roseate picture of the progress of annexation sentiment throughout the province, and by a tribute to the respectability of the adherents of that faith. "In Lower Canada, and especially in the district of Montreal, a large proportion of the people were in favour of annexation." They might be slightly in advance of the time, "but the day was not far distant when the farmers, merchants, and people of Upper Canada would also see that their best interests would be promoted by annexation."

Turning then to the consideration of Canada's relation to the mother country, he maintained that the public had a right freely to discuss the subject of annexation, provided they did so peaceably, and with due respect to the wishes of Great Britain in the matter. He did not think that the despatch of Earl Grey had had the anticipated effect of checking the annexation movement. The Colonial Secretary, he averred, would never have dared to address such minatory language to the people of England, though many of the latter had publicly expressed more decided opinions on the advantages of colonial independence than were to be found in the Montreal manifesto. The despatch of his lordship was, in fact, characteristic of the ignorance and superciliousness of Downing Street officials, which rendered a further continuance of the imperial régime injurious to the interests of Canada, if not politically impossible. Strikingly different, however, was the situation of the United States. "He believed that the United States possessed more freedom than any other nation, that they had more energy and less poverty, and that education and the elements of happiness were more generally diffused than among any other people, and he hoped that Canada would one day be joined to that nation, and he was not ashamed nor afraid to express that opinion. He was ready, as he had been before, to sacrifice his life in defence of Britain, so long as we remained connected with her, both for the interests of Canada and the mother country ; but, for the interests of himself and his family, he desired to see annexation effected with the consent of both parties."

The speech of the member for Kent was much more defiant in tone, but proportionally less substantial in subject matter, than that of his colleague. Notwithstanding his professed opposition to annexation, Colonel Prince was always found co-operating most heartily with the annexation members, and was regarded by the House at large as a regular member of that group. With him, in truth, independence was only a means to an end, and that end was annexation. He boldly defied the Colonial Secretary to prosecute him for advocating independence, or to punish the Annexationists for their political acts. The annexation movement, he averred, had taken a firm hold on all sections of the community, as was evinced by the representative character of the annexation members of the House : Mr. Holmes was a representative of the commercial, De Witt of the banking, and Sanborn of the agricultural interests of the country. In reply to an inquiry of some of his constituents, he had offered to resign if 150 of the electors should express their dissatisfaction with his advocacy of independence ; but in the face of that offer, no steps whatever had been taken to unseat him. The people along the frontier, he claimed, were intimidated at present by the tyrannical action of the Government, but the result of the next election would unmistakably prove that the country was ripe for separation. He did not favour a revolt; nor would he raise an arm against the Queen, but he did demand the right to petition Parliament for the redress of grievances. He denied the accusation of *The Montreal*

Pilot that he had induced one of his French-Canadian constituents to canvass the French members of the House in favour of annexation.

Mr. McConnell declared that he was an out-and-out Annexationist. He did not believe that the sentiment of the Eastern Townships was more pronouncedly for annexation than that of other parts of the country. The withdrawal of the English preference had been ruinous to the business interests of Lower Canada. Grass was growing in the streets of Montreal ; their sons were leaving for the United States, and their daughters were following after. There was no local market in Lower Canada, and but a limited one in Canada West ; and at the American border their products were met by a 20-per-cent. duty. Under such circumstances, he concluded, annexation was imperative.

Papineau was the only French-Canadian speaker to support the amendment. Taking his cue from his fellow Annexationists, he wisely avoided all reference to recent racial issues, and confined his remarks to the consideration of the commercial advantages of a political union with the Republic. " Prosperity," he declared, " would coincide with their annexation to the United States."

On the ministerial side of the House, participation in the debate was confined to the back benchers. It was very interesting to see Dr. Wolfred Nelson, the former lieutenant of Papineau, now fighting on the pro-British side against his old leader. Into the political arena he carried the same courage and high-mindedness he had previously shown on the battlefield. He was quick to resent the taunts of some of the Tory members that the Reformers of 1837 were rebels, and that the object of that revolt was to throw off the British yoke. The so-called rebels of that day had been the truer patriots, for they had struggled to secure for their fellow citizens those liberal principles of the British Constitution which they were now enjoying.

Very different, he contended, in origin and character was the present annexation cry, which had been worked up by a few disappointed Tory politicians who found they could no longer rule the Colonial Office by backstairs influence.

Mr. Ross, the newly elected member for Megantic, severely rebuked the member for Sherbrooke for venturing to advocate annexation in the House, after having so recently sworn allegiance to the Sovereign on taking his seat in the Chamber. Mr. Couchon voiced the sentiments of the French-Canadian supporters of the Government in condemning the agitation of Papineau in favour of annexation. The latter, he claimed, had not only signally failed in his propaganda among his fellow countrymen, but could no longer be considered as truly representing the views of his own constituency.

Upon division, the amendment was defeated by 51 to 13. The majority of the Government was unexpectedly large, owing to the defection of a number of Clear Grits, who, notwithstanding their approval of the amendment, refused to assist the Opposition in an adroit attempt to turn out the Government on a specious issue. In accordance with their political programme, the annexation members supported the amendment in a body.

The annexation issue was fought over again on an amendment of Colonel Prince condemning the Government for the annexation dismissals : " That this House regrets that the policy of Great Britain towards this colony, and the conduct of the Government here, should have been such as to give cause to many of the most loyal and upright men in the country to seek for a remedy to the evils they complain of, in a change of our institutions ; and this House cannot admit that the declaration of political sentiments, not coupled with any hostile intent against the Crown and Sovereignty of Great Britain, is sufficient to warrant the Executive in dismissing persons from offices of honour, and that such a proceeding is, in the opinion of this House, calculated to increase the prevailing discontent."

The speech of the member for Kent, in support of the motion, was largely a repetition of his former utterances. He triumphantly referred to the fact that no petition against annexation had been presented to the House, as an evidence of widespread sympathy with that cause. It was useless for the public, he contended, to look to Parliament for relief, since the local Legislature was powerless to obtain reciprocity or independence, the two chief boons which the country desired. Mr. Holmes was again the chief spokesman of the Annexationists. He developed at length his previous argument as to the respective advantages and disadvantages of the imperial connection and of a union with the United States. A peaceful separation with the consent of Great Britain would, he maintained, be mutually beneficial to the motherland and Canada ; but, without such consent, the Annexationists would consider it " neither practicable nor desirable." As a part of the United States, Canada would share in the large investments of English capital which now went to the United States in preference to the colonies. Nothing, he concluded, could stop the progress of the annexation movement. Instead of 7, there would soon be 70 members of the Legislature signing petitions to the Crown for independence.

The remaining annexationist speakers did not contribute anything new or valuable to the discussion. Mr. Sanborn, however, got in one good home-thrust at the weakness of the Ministry. The Government, he bitingly remarked, could not be as strongly supported on this question as they pretended to be, or else they would not require the valiant assistance of Colonel Gugy.

The views of the Tory speakers were again at sixes and sevens, varying all the way from an attempted justification of the propaganda of the Annexationists, to the severest condemnation of their proceedings.

Sir Allan MacNab insinuated that some of the members of the Cabinet were favourable to annexation. An alleged confession of *La Minerve* afforded evidence of the complicity of the Government in the movement. Unfortunately for the honourable member, he was unable to substantiate his charge when its truth was called in question by Mr. Hincks. With singular inconsistency, he subsequently accused the Government of making use of the columns of *La Minerve* to give currency to their opposition to annexation.

Of the other Conservative speakers, Messrs. Cayley and Robinson were principally concerned in an attempt to make political capital out of the situation. The former assumed the diplomatic position of declining on general principles to censure the dismissal of the annexation officials ; but, at the same time, he condemned in this instance "the unscrupulous exercise of the prerogative for party advantage." His colleague, Mr. Robinson, went one stage further in criticism of the Government. The Annexationists, he contended, ought not to have been dismissed, since they did not intend to take any decisive action without the previous consent of the Crown. He accused the Ministry of unjust discrimination in the infliction of penalties. Why, he demanded, had they punished the signers of the manifesto, while they permitted the publication of annexation papers to proceed untouched ? The Government were responsible for the existing spirit of discontent, which, unless soon checked, would sweep the whole population into the annexation movement.

On the other hand, a few Tory members rallied patriotically to the support of the Executive. Mr. Sherwood of Toronto expressed the strongest disapproval of the actions of the Nationalists and Annexationists alike. No Government which was worthy of the name could supinely permit its servants to attempt its own overthrow ; from its very nature, a Government was bound to suppress with all its authority all acts " of constructive treason." The extenuating pleas of Mac-

Nab and Robinson for the Annexationists again called forth a fiery protest from Colonel Gugy. The signers of the manifesto, he maintained, had forfeited their right to object to the proceedings of the Executive, as had also their defenders in the House. Some of the Annexationists, it was evident, were determined to effect their object by force if necessary, but he warned the plotters that, should such an attempt be made, two or three hundred thousand men would be ready to attest their loyalty to the Crown and country. Whatever might be the political differences of the two sides of the House on matters of general policy, both Reformers and Conservatives would unite to uphold the British Constitution. He derided the specious professions of loyalty on the part of the Annexationists. " Were he to set up his previous loyalty as giving him the right to overthrow the institutions of the country, he should expose himself to condemnation." He believed that the attention of the country should be directed to the impolicy of extending political privileges to persons of Sanborn's class, who came into the province with Yankee prejudices, and with the intent to overthrow, if possible, English institutions. In conclusion, he made an embittered attack upon the capacity and character of the member for Sherbrooke, whose defeat he regarded as certain at the next election.

Of the Clear Grit members of the House, Messrs. Cameron and Lyon heartily commended the action of the Government in making the dismissals. They likewise shared the opinion that annexation would not improve the condition of Canada. The latter further maintained that the political institutions of the colony were freer than those of the United States. By annexation, Canada would lose control over her own administration, and subject herself to the will of her more powerful neighbour. Mr. Cameron approved of the strongest repressive measures against the Annexationists. The signers of the manifesto should, in his opinion, have been immediately dismissed from office without the formality of an investigation. Notwithstanding the vain boastings of Colonel Prince, as to the strength of annexation sentiment in the west, he was prepared to certify to the loyalty of the great majority of the people of Kent.

Mr. H. J. Boulton, on the other hand, contended that it was folly to suppose that the Canadian public would remain loyal to the British connection in the face of the growing distress of the country. He was not an Annexationist, but an advocate of unrestricted reciprocity. There was nothing illegal, he maintained, in the conduct of the signers of the manifesto, many of whom, in fact, were as loyal as himself. The action of the Ministry in making the dismissals was in this case the more reprehensible, since, according to the admission of the Inspector-General, the Government was obliged to punish its servants, in order to remove suspicion from some of its own members.

On the Government side of the House, two members of the Ministry participated briefly in the debate. In reply to Mr. Robinson's criticism of the immunity from prosecution of the annexation journals, the Hon. F. Hincks pointed out that there was a fundamental difference between the status of a servant of the Crown and that of a mere private citizen, a difference which placed upon the former a distinct responsibility for his political acts, to which the ordinary member of society was not subject. He challenged the member for Sherbrooke to compare, in his own case, the freedom of parliamentary discussion in the Canadian House with that in Congress. Would the latter, he demanded, permit one of its members freely to advocate the dismemberment of the Union? He believed not. Yet Mr. Sanborn was claiming and exercising as a British subject a right which he would not enjoy as an American citizen.

Mr. Drummond, the Solicitor-General, refuted the contention of the Annexationists that the Eastern Townships were favourable to annexation. Outside the

County of Sherbrooke, he was convinced, a majority of the inhabitants were against it. He denied that *La Minerve* was the organ of the Government, or that the Ministry was in any way responsible for its utterances. True, a determined effort had been made to win *La Minerve* over to the side of the Annexationists, but the editor had nobly resisted all such pressure, and stood staunchly by the British connection.

After an all-day debate, a division was taken which resulted in a crushing defeat of the amendment by a majority of over 30.[1] The vote was a splendid vindication of the decisive policy of the Executive in dealing with the Annexationists. The division list revealed the fact that the whole body of the Reformers, together with a few Clear Grits and Tories, rallied to the support of the Government. The majority of the Clear Grit members, including Perry and Hopkins, did not vote ; only two of the party voted for the amendment. The Tory Party also was sadly divided. A small minority threw aside their party prejudices, and loyally supported the Ministry in the division lobby ; a considerable number failed to vote ; while a small group of irreconcilables joined with the Annexationists in supporting the amendment.

A second division was taken upon Mr. Boulton's amendment for the expunging of the last three paragraphs of the address, and the insertion of the following paragraphs :

" That, while this House deeply regrets that the altered policy which the parent state has felt it necessary to adopt for her own advantage, and quite irrespective of colonial interests, has led many loyal men in this province to consider whether they might not with equal right review their positions as Canadians, thus substantially changed to their detriment, yet this House is not prepared to concur with Your Excellency

---

[1] Ayes, 14; Noes, 46. Ayes, Badgley, Boulton (Norfolk), Boulton (Toronto), Christie, De Witt, Egan, Holmes, MacNab, McConnell, McLean, Papineau, Prince, Robinson, and Sanborn.

in the opinion that persons, many of whom have heretofore perilled their lives and fortunes, and sacrificed their property in defence of the unity of the empire, should, while suffering under the adverse circumstances which have since befallen them, and which they believe are the result of that change of policy which they could neither avert nor control, and without any misconduct of their own, be now dealt with as persons innately disloyal, and scarcely less than traitors, and unworthy of being longer retained in Her Majesty's service, because they ventured in calm and temperate language to discuss the cause of their misfortune, and to submit for the consideration of the parent state the unreasonableness of her placing them upon the footing of foreigners with regard to her markets, while their colonial dependence forbids them availing themselves of those advantages in foreign markets which a really national character would not prevent them from acquiring.

" That this House is firmly convinced that the great body of the people of this province will yield to no other portion of Her Majesty's subjects in loyalty to Her Majesty, and attachment to the parent state ; but they would fail in their duty to Her Majesty, were they to abstain from expressing a strong opinion to Your Excellency that it is not by distrusting some and punishing others, and stifling discussion through fear of official displeasure, that erroneous opinions either of duty or interest are to be eradicated, but by upholding and maintaining that greater guarantee of national freedom, the right of public discussion."

This amendment was likewise defeated on a similar division list, by 44 votes to 12.

The conduct of some of the Tory and Clear Grit members in supporting these amendments was undoubtedly open to question, but a considerable portion of the responsibility must be credited to the faulty tactics of Sir Allan MacNab, and to the general demoralization of parties in the House, which, for a time, weakened the sense of political responsibility. The majority of the Tory members were unquestionably loyal at heart, but some of them could not resist the chance of embarrassing the Government by a temporary mis-alliance with the Annexationists. A few of the Clear Grits, likewise, were tempted to vote against the Government by a feeling of political disappointment, rather than by any settled conviction in favour of annexation. On the other hand, it should not be for-gotten that the patriotic stand of a small minority of the Tory and Clear Grit members materially assisted the Government at a truly critical moment.

This series of rebuffs apparently convinced the Annexationists of the hopelessness of again raising the question of annexation in the House, for the subject was allowed to drop for the remainder of the session. The cause did not make any converts in either chamber. A few of the Tory and Clear Grit members were inclined to sympathize with the Annexationists, partly on economic, and partly on political, grounds, but their sympathies were not sufficiently developed to commit them to the policy of separation. They preferred to stand aside from the agitation, and await the course of events. With the gradual return of prosperity, and the raising of new political issues, the question of annexation fell completely into the background in Parliament. The speech of the Governor-General in proroguing the Legislature fittingly contained a refer-ence to the loyal addresses of the two Houses, which expressed " the sentiments of the great body of the Canadian people as truly as those of Parliament." The Government, in fact, heartily congratulated itself and the country at large upon the collapse of an agitation which was dangerous alike to the Crown and the political institutions of the province.

Thanks to a bountiful harvest in the Fall of 1849, economic conditions in Upper Canada began slowly to improve. American buyers invaded the Western District, and carried away the surplus products of the

Canadian farmers.[1] The upward tendency of trade was revealed in an increase of customs receipts, an easier money market, and a slight improvement in industrial conditions. The merchants of the country began to take heart. The Council of the Board of Trade of Toronto, in their annual report,[2] declared that it looked forward with confidence to the increasing prosperity " which the liberality of the motherland in altering the Navigation Laws could not fail of producing." This confidence was not misplaced. The commercial prospects of the country were, according to *The Globe*,[3] never more auspicious. With the opening up of navigation, the ships of all nations sought out the ports of the St. Lawrence for ocean cargoes. The business instincts of the Montreal tradesmen were again aroused. They were, after all, primarily domestic economists, and not politicians ; only the force of circumstances had turned their minds towards political agitations.

The revival of business dealt a crushing blow to the cause of annexation. The rapid spread of the agitation had been largely due, as we have seen, to the belief that the imperial connection was responsible for the depression of the colony. The gradual return of prosperity destroyed this fundamental tenet of the Annexationists. The mercantile community recognized the mistake they had made, and were glad to return to their former political allegiance. The annexation movement was in reality but a passing phase of the economic history of the colony ; it was essentially the product of adversity and resentment against the English Government, and it could not thrive during a period of returning prosperity. The history of Canada shows that, at each recurrent cycle of commercial depression, the thoughts of a section of the public as naturally turns to the United States as the

---

[1] *The Globe*, November 20, 1849.
[2] January 19, 1850.
[3] *The Globe*, March 14, 1850.

minds of the Western American farmers to fiat money. Depression and annexation on the one hand, contentment and loyalty on the other, have been, and perhaps may still be, correlative terms in the records of the country.

Among the various factors which contributed to the failure of the annexation movement should be mentioned the sound political tactics of the Governor-General and his advisers. The presence of Lord Elgin undoubtedly had an unfavourable influence on many of the members of the Tory Party, and, to some extent, justified the boast of the Annexationists that every day of such a Governor " adds to the unpopularity of the connection of a country which saddles us with such a man " ; but, at the same time, it brought even greater compensating advantages, for his far-seeing statesmanship had disarmed the hostility of the French and English Reformers, and had bound up their interests with the maintenance of the British connection. He had established the most cordial relations with Lafontaine and his friends ; and, by his liberal sympathies with the aspirations of the French, had succeeded in winning over the bulk of the French-Canadian population to the support of the policy of the administration. By the Reformers of Upper Canada he was held in the highest honour. As a strictly constitutional Governor, he was able to exercise a much greater influence than any of his Tory predecessors.

One of the most manifest weaknesses of the Annexation Party, which foredoomed it to dissolution, was the almost total absence of unity or harmony among the members. The discordant elements of the party had never been properly united. The original alliance of the ultra-Tories and French Radicals had been irksome and unnatural for both parties, and entirely lacking in the elements of cohesion and stability. The Tory members of the Bund were glad to withdraw from such an impolitic association. On the other hand, the decision of the British Ministry exercised little influence on the " Young Canada Party." They did not, like their allies, profess any attachment to the mother country, nor derive their political principles from her ; they were, on the contrary, by tradition and policy the bitter critics and foes of the administration of the Colonial Office. Save for the question of annexation, and a feeling of resentment against the Provincial and Imperial Governments, they had nothing in common with their Tory allies, while, on the other hand, they were seriously embarrassed in their democratic propaganda by their compact with their former foes. They were exposed to the merciless criticism of betraying their nationality, for which they professed most ardently to stand.

To the land speculators and mercantile community, as we have seen, the question of annexation was essentially an economic, and not a political, issue. Patriotism, with them, was a mere matter of book-keeping—a question of dollars and cents. They had little political sympathy with their partisan fellow members, whose bitter struggles had intensified the distress of the province. Least of all had they any fellowship with the French Radicals, whose political dogmas were anathema to them. With all these groups, in fact, a temporary policy of opportunism was the only bond of union. For the time being, their common commercial interests were sufficiently powerful to produce a semblance of co-operation ; but, with the revival of trade, the old underlying social and political differences among the members soon cropped out again to disintegrate the local associations.

Among the chief factors in defeating the annexation movement in Lower Canada was the loyalty of the bulk of the French population. Lord Elgin had keenly realized the importance of cultivating the friendship of the French-Canadians. In an early letter to the Colonial Secretary, he expressed the opinion that " the sentiment of French-Canadian nationality, which Papineau endeavours to pervert to purposes of faction, may yet perhaps, if properly improved, furnish the best remaining security against annexation to the United States." To this end, he deliberately set to work to cultivate the most friendly relations with the French-Canadian bishops and clergy, as the most important factor in the life of the French population. This skilful diplomacy was rewarded with success. At the time the annexation agitation was rampant in Montreal and the Eastern Townships, the mass of the French-Canadians remained calm and unconcerned. With but few exceptions, their ears were closed to the popular appeals of the revolutionaries. The spiritual and political leaders of the people were shrewd enough to see that the preservation of their special religious and political privileges was bound up in the maintenance of the British connection, and that annexation would almost necessarily involve the loss of constitutional guarantees of their distinct nationality.

At the critical moment in the struggle, the clergy and seigneurs joined hands with the Government to defeat the policy of the Annexationists. They were loyal, not so much because they preferred to remain British subjects rather than to become American citizens, but because they desired to retain unimpaired their own language, religion, and nationality. They were passive rather than active loyalists, but their loyalty was based upon the strongest sentimental considerations. Against the united forces of Church and State, the Rouge Party could make little progress. The loyalty of the Catholic clergy, and the devotion of their simple parishioners, saved the day for the British connection ; for, had the French population been swayed by the same political and commercial considerations which appealed to their English fellow citizens, the Annexationists would almost certainly have swept the lower half of the province into the arms of the United States. The racial conservatism of the French habitants, by checking the rapid speed of annexation sentiment, afforded to the English population an opportunity of more carefully reviewing the situation of affairs ; and, on sober second thought, many of the latter were inclined to regret the hastiness with which they had joined in the agitation for separation. The cautious conduct of the French-Canadians not only furnished a striking object-lesson to the English inhabitants of Lower Canada, but exercised a determinative influence upon the course of events in British North America.

The annexation movement among the Clear Grits of Upper Canada was quite distinct in origin and character from that on the Lower St. Lawrence. It was undoubtedly greatly stimulated by the agitation in Montreal ; but, in reality, the Radicals of Upper Canada had but little social or political sympathy with the leaders of the movement in Lower Canada. The restlessness of the Clear Grits was due primarily to the existence of legitimate grievances which ought, long before, to have been rectified. There was little or no prospect of the redress of these grievances by an alliance with the Annexationists of Montreal, since the aims of the latter were directed to the attainment of different objects. For this reason, no intimate relationship was ever established between the scattered Annexationists among the Clear Grits and the various associations in Lower Canada.

Matters might have been somewhat different with the Annexationists if they had succeeded in connecting the isolated movements in the various parts of the province. In Lower Canada, an effort was made to develop a provincial organization by affiliating the various local associations with the central body at Montreal. But the campaign in Upper Canada signally failed ; only two local associations were formed, and both of them were exceedingly weak. There was not even the semblance of a political organization. Under these circumstances, it was folly to think of calling a provincial convention, as had been the original intention of the Montreal association. In truth, the motley and discordant elements of which the annexation party was composed were incapable of forming a provincial association, after the model of the League ; and, without some such organization, the movement could not make headway in the outlying districts against the overwhelming strength of the loyalists.

Among the contributing causes of the failure of the movement should be included the unfavourable condition of affairs in the United States. The Canadian Annexationists were greatly disappointed at not receiving a heartier response to their overtures from their American cousins. They had expected that their movement would be supported by the full force of American public opinion, and that they might count upon their American friends for financial backing and moral support. But discouragement met them on every hand. No assistance or encouragement whatever was forthcoming from the Government at Washington ; and the public at large, except in a few neighbouring states, turned out to be indifferent or hostile. To make matters worse, the slavery issue was daily becoming more acute. The Republic was divided against itself, and already a war cloud was looming up on the horizon.

The Canadian people were not blind to these dangerous portents. From the very beginning of their constitutional history, they had been opposed to the curse of slavery, and had driven it out of the country. At the prospect of annexation, the Reform press flew to arms to defend the free soil of Canada against the threatening danger of slavery. The Annexationists found themselves in an embarrassing position. Few of them ventured in any way to defend slavery ; they preferred, on the contrary, to disregard the issue entirely ; when driven to bay, they endeavoured to argue that by a political union with the United States, the people of Canada would aid in the extinction of slavery throughout the Republic. But the Canadian public could not be deceived by any such specious claim. They refused to have any connection with the accursed thing. The bitter struggles in Congress and the angry threats of secession amply proved that all was not peace and contentment in the great Republic, and served to warn the colonists of the danger of sacrificing their autonomy at such a moment. "It would," said *The Montreal Gazette*, "be a sorry instance of our wisdom to make a present of our country to a foreigner, and buy a civil war at the same time. We would have less reluctance to annex to the disunited states than to the present United States. People who may be hanging towards annexation had better hang on, than run the great risk of doing much worse."

The enactment of the Fugitive Slave Law outraged the sensibilities of even the most ardent Annexationists. With few exceptions, they declined to commit the province to the maintenance of the slave trade, as was demanded by that infamous act. The highly sensitive conscience of *The Witness* could stand it no longer. "We have hitherto advocated annexation," it declared, "provided certain preparations were made on both sides ; but, rather than consent to the annexation of Canada to the United States, while this slave-catching law remains in force, rather than the free soil of Canada should be made a hunting-ground for the slaveholder and his infamous agents, rather than the fugitive African should be deprived of his last refuge on this continent, we would be willing not only to forgo all the advantages of annexation, but to see Canada ten times poorer and worse governed than she is ; and we have no doubt this feeling is shared by Annexationists whose objects were higher than mere pecuniary interests." [1] The slavery issue hung as a millstone around the necks of the Annexationists, and dragged them down to defeat. The moral conscience of the people could not be bribed by material considerations into consenting to an extension of the territory within which the traffic in the bodies and souls of their fellow men would be legally recognized.

[1] Quoted from *The Colonist*, October 25, 1850.

The last material factor in discrediting the annexation movement was the unexpected hostility of the English Government and nation. At the outset of their propaganda, the annexationist leaders had realized that the province was altogether too loyal at heart to think of rebellion. They had sought, accordingly, to disarm the opposition of the loyalists by expressions of the highest regard for the motherland, and by professing their readiness to accept the judgment of the British Government upon the policy of separation. In their political strategy, they had rashly counted upon the neutral attitude of the Whig Ministry, and the hearty support of the Radical Party in Parliament. But in both of these anticipations, they were sorely disappointed. They found themselves exposed to the public as false prophets, as blind leaders of the blind. From the day of the receipt of Earl Grey's despatch, the struggle went steadily against the Annexationists. The loyalists quickly rallied to the appeal of the Colonial Secretary, and carried the war into the territory of the enemy. In the face of his lordship's despatch it was no longer possible for the Tory members of the party to keep up the pretence of loyalty to Great Britain. The Annexationists found their own weapons turned against themselves. They had either to drop their agitation, or choose the pathway of revolution. To many of the party, discretion seemed the better part of valour ; and the remainder were not sufficiently strong in numbers and influence to persevere for any length of time in a hopeless struggle against the combined forces of the Government and public opinion in both England and Canada. The local associations were not formally dissolved ; but, here and there throughout the province, they quietly disappeared through lack of interest and the falling off of membership. So rapid was the process of disintegration, that, by the end of the year, all semblance of a party organization had vanished. The appeal of the Colonial Secretary to the loyalty of the Canadian people was splendidly vindicated.

CHAPTER VIII

THE MOVEMENT IN THE MARITIME PROVINCES

The struggle for responsible government—Chagrin of the Tories—
Economic distress—Annexation movement among commercial
class—Similarity of movement to that in Canada—Failure of
the agitation.

THE course of events in Canada was reproduced,
to a large extent, in the Maritime Provinces.
The question of responsible government had
been bitterly fought out between the Reform
and Tory parties in Nova Scotia and New Brunswick.
The victory of the Reformers in both provinces filled
the Tories with bitter exasperation against the English
Government which found vent in loud mutterings of
discontent, and in some cases in open declarations of
disloyalty. *The Halifax Colonist* expressed the opinion
that the connection with Great Britain was seriously
endangered by the policy of the Whig Ministry. " The
best way," it declared, " to recall us to our former
affection would be to hang Earl Grey, whose vile misconduct will be the principal cause of the loss of these
colonies."

At the same time, the cry for annexation had arisen
among a section of the mercantile community. The
repeal of the English preferential duty on lumber had
inflicted a staggering blow on the principal industry of
New Brunswick. As the economic life of the province
was almost entirely dependent upon that industry, the
outlook of the colonists for a time was exceedingly
dubious. Many of the traders and lumbermen lost
faith in the future of the province, and cried out for a

political union with the United States. In the city
of St. John and in the Northern counties, an active
movement in favour of annexation was set on foot.
The New Brunswicker [1] and *The Miramichi Gleaner*
espoused the new political tenets, primarily on commercial grounds, as a means of restoring the prosperity
of the province. A similar agitation broke out in
Nova Scotia. There was in the Maritime Provinces,
declared *The Nova Scotian*, a set of men who traced all
their political grievances to the fact that they were
colonists and not American citizens. So long as England was willing to tax herself for the corn growers and
lumbermen of this country, nothing could exceed their
loyalty to the Crown ; but, with a change in England's
fiscal policy, loyalty was at a discount at St. John, as
well as in Canada.[2]

The similarity of the annexation movement in the
Maritime Provinces to that in Canada was, indeed, most
striking. The political discontent of the Conservatives
merged into the commercial distress of the people.
Out of the fusion of these two elements there emerged
the same republican theories and annexation tendencies
as developed in Canada. The Conservative Party by
the sea took up the demand of the Radicals for a change
in the status of the Governor, and the adoption of
elective institutions. But the Reform Government in
both provinces resisted the clamours of the discontented, and stood fast by the British connection.

The satisfactory working of the principle of responsible government killed the agitation of the Conservatives. With the settlement of the constitutional issue,
" the silly fever of annexation " which had prevailed
for a time " amongst a disappointed clique, quickly
subsided, for the colonists had no liking for American
slavery." [3] The Tory recalcitrants soon realized the

1 *The New Brunswicker*, February 8, 1850.
2 Quoted from *The Toronto Globe*, October 4, 1849.
3 *The New Brunswick Reporter*, quoted from *The Toronto Globe*,
September 27, 1849.

mistake they had made ; they cast down the false idols they had set up in a moment of chagrin, and returned with renewed zeal to the first principle of the party : loyalty to the Crown and the British connection. The business interests of the provinces gradually adjusted themselves to the new economic conditions. With the return of more prosperous times, the commercial community dropped its agitation, and turned to the more congenial task of making money. The annexation movement sprang up quickly under the most favourable conditions, a fortuitous combination of economic adversity and political discontent ; but it as quickly died away because of the revival of prosperity and the prospect of office under the British flag.

CHAPTER IX

THE ATTITUDE OF GREAT BRITAIN

Interesting colonial questions—*The Times*—Attitude of the Whig press—Views of the Radical organs—Attitude of the Tory press—Imperial ideals of the parties—Subordination of imperial interests to English party politics.

IN England, the course of Canadian events had attracted a larger amount of public interest than was usually bestowed upon colonial matters. But just at this moment, colonial questions were playing a large part in English politics. The Colonial Secretary, as we have seen, had taken a deep personal interest in the annexation movement, and had intervened in Canadian affairs in his usual decisive fashion. Parliament, on the other hand, was too much immersed in the discussion of the fiscal policy of the United Kingdom, and the framework of the Australian Colonies Bill, to devote much attention to the question of annexation. But the unusual interest of the press in Canadian affairs offset, to a large extent, the indifference of Parliament. Almost without exception, the English journals recognized the seriousness of the situation in Canada, though they differed widely in their opinions as to the origin and significance of the discontent of the colony, and as to the ultimate outcome of the annexation movement. Happily, the discussions of the press did not display any coercive disposition towards the colonies. Some of the chief party papers could not refrain, however, from interjecting a certain amount of political animus into their leading articles.

The Times, the chief organ of the Government, discussed the question of separation in a calm and reasonable manner, and with a due sense of imperial responsibility. It duly acknowledged the importance of the manifesto, and the skill and moderation of the presentation of the case for annexation. " It is neither inspired by vindictiveness nor fraught with violence. It is earnest in its tone, but its earnestness partakes of the character of deliberateness ; it reasons, even though it may reason wrongly, and proceed from incorrect premises to erroneous deductions. It is on this account that the Montreal address is entitled to a patient, we were almost saying a respectful, attention at our hands. It breathes no hostility against the British Crown and people ; on the contrary, it emphatically records the kindly feelings of the Canadian people to both ; it makes no vehement protestations of affection for a republican form of government ; but simply rests its preference of republican institutions upon local and peculiar conditions ; it advises separation from England, as it suggests annexation to the United States, from the motives by which communities not less than individuals are impelled—motives of self-interest and self-advancement." *The Times* went on to declare that, although there was a time when such a manifesto would have been considered treasonable, England would not now think of going to war for " the sterile honour of maintaining a reluctant colony in galling subjection."

But, in a later editorial, it assumed a distinctly unfavourable attitude towards the separation of Canada. It expressed grave doubt as to whether the address correctly expressed the sentiments even of a majority of the inhabitants of Montreal. But, however this might be, it was convinced that the feeling in that city could not be held truly to reflect " the general state of Canadian parties and politics." Montreal for many years had been distinguished by its turbulence ; racial animosities, religious differences, and party antipathies had stirred up a spirit of unrest and discontent among the citizens. Recently the city had suffered a severe economic setback; the colonial preference had been withdrawn, and it was proposed to remove the seat of Government. It was little wonder, under the circumstances, that Montreal was disaffected. The men who were loudest for annexation would be most reluctant to realize their own menaces; for, as it sarcastically explained, with two or three exceptions, they would be less considerable persons as American citizens than they were as British subjects. Notwithstanding their roseate pictures of the economic advantages of a union with the United States, the annexation leaders would find it as impossible for a republican, as for a monarchical, Government to force prosperity upon the province; they would sink back into the unendurable position of legislators without influence, and speculators without capital. Some of the Canadian statesmen clearly saw the sorry predicament into which annexation would lead the colony, and were doing everything in their power to ward off the danger.

It was difficult to see of what elements the Annexation Party would be permanently composed. A political union with the United States would swamp the French population in the mass of Anglo-Saxon republicans; the eastern Canadians had not suffered much from the change of fiscal policy, and would not be greatly benefited by annexation; while the ultra-loyalists and Orangemen of the Western District, although irritated at the action of the English Government, could scarcely agree to accept republican institutions. "But, if under the pressure of temporary adversity, or from an undue estimate of the benefits of republican institutions, the Canadian people deliberately propose to exchange the freest policy that any colony ever enjoyed, for the ambiguous honour of forming a small part of an unwieldy confederation, then let them understand that the conduct of the people of England will be directed by motives of prudence and interest alone. If they think that they can do without Canada, then, and then only, will they give up Canada. But in surrendering Canada, they will take care not to surrender one jot of sea or land the possession of which effectively concerns the maritime and commercial importance of Great Britain. They will not cede Nova Scotia, they will not cede Cape Breton ; they will not cede the seaboard and those harbours which must ever command the mouth of the St. Lawrence and protect the trade of the Atlantic. In parting from England Canada will lose the name of a dependent province, to be brought more nearly in view of the force which might have perpetuated her dependence ; in losing her hold on Canada England will take care to lose only the responsibilities and the expense of her retention. But we apprehend that the destined future of Canada, and the disposition of her people, make all such anticipations as these wholly superfluous." [1]

Although *The Morning Chronicle* lightly dismissed the danger of a rebellion in Canada, it expressed the fear that "an inveterate and chronic disaffection, fostered by perpetual comparisons of the most damaging sort, between the rapid and prosperous development of a United States territory and the industrial and social stagnation of a British colony," might take possession of the Canadian people, and gradually estrange them from their allegiance. But notwithstanding this danger, it refused to surrender willingly the North American provinces. The Annexationists, it asserted, had worked themselves into the belief that England was favourable to the dissolution of the empire, because she had made no fuss or outcry against the Montreal manifesto. But, in truth, the English public had not as yet given serious thought to the question. "The loss of Canada would, under any circumstances, be to the last degree distasteful to

[1] *The Times*, November 2, 1849.

Great Britain ; and, under no circumstances, would this country voluntarily hand over to a rival any single port, harbour, city, or fortified place, which she deems useful, either for the protection of her commerce in peace, or for the assertion of her rights in war." [1]

The Glasgow Daily News emphatically declared that any ministerial proposal to consent to the annexation of Canada to the United States would seal the fate of the Government making it.[2] *The London Globe*, reputed to be the private property of Lord Palmerston, combated the views of the Annexationists on economic grounds ; while *The Economist*, the leading organ of the financial world, advocated the adoption of a reciprocity agreement with the United States, as likely to prove more advantageous to Canada than annexation.

There was a decided inclination on the part of some of the ministerial organs to treat the annexation movement as a purely partisan manœuvre to secure the restoration of protective duties in England. " It is not," said *The North British Mail*, " the tyranny of the Colonial Office, the partisanship of Lord Elgin, the predominance of the French race, the inconveniences of monarchy, or the superior advantages of republicanism which form the impelling force of the Canadian Annexationists, but the loss of protection previously afforded to Canadian products. The loyalty of these gentlemen begins and ends with a discriminating duty in favour of their wheat and butter. Give the merchants of Montreal a monopoly of the British markets, and they are red-hot Britons ; place them on a fair equality with the merchants of the world, and they become true-blue Americans. The abolition is the one and only grievance of which they complain ; and in order to recline once more under its darling shade, they throw off their allegiance like an old worn-out coat, renounce all their past principles, scrape up

---

[1] *The Morning Chronicle*, January 5, 1850.
[2] *The Glasgow Daily News*, November 2, 1849.

acquaintanceships with revolutionists and Yankees, and proceed, in this motley companionship, to rend asunder the very empire to which they vowed a thousand times their indissoluble attachment." It ridiculed the pretension—" the truly Jesuitic proviso "—that annexation would be brought about only with the consent of Great Britain. " By this salvo, the Annexationists expect to secure the signatures of the loyal and peaceful part of the population, till they have committed them so far to their treasonable purposes that they cannot turn back."

Some of the journals of the Manchester School were much more sympathetic towards the Canadian Annexationists. *The London Examiner* spoke of the ultimate separation of the colonies in a tone of quiet assurance. " That the colonies of any nation will continue colonies for ever is a notion that revolts common sense, and could be seriously entertained by none but idiots. The very notion of the colonial condition precludes the idea of permanency. The latent instinct of national pride never fails to develop itself, when a community possesses the capacity and the elements of individual existence." Annexation, it prophesied, might " come at last " ; but, in the meantime, no one of the parties interested in the question (England, United States, and Canada) was ripe for it. The pride and prejudice of the English nation were unquestionably against it.[1] *The Examiner* much preferred a union of the British-American colonies and their erection into a sovereign state. " Social necessities and the healthy progress of mankind require two independent states in North America." [2] Should annexation, however, be the choice of the Canadian people, it must be brought about peaceably, by means of friendly negociations between the three countries. England, it concluded, would undoubtedly be the greatest gainer by annexa-

[1] This view was strongly emphasized by the London correspondent of *The New York Tribune.*
[2] Quoted from *The Colonist*, November 2, 1849.

tion, since she would be relieved of the heavy responsibility of administering a distant territory.

The London Morning Advertiser joyfully announced that the Cabinet had concluded that the maintenance of British authority in Canada was unprofitable and burdensome to the mother country. "The result of a careful examination of the Canadian connection, in all its aspects, is that so far from England being a sufferer from the renunciation of their allegiance to the British Crown on the part of the Canadians, she would be an actual gainer. It is a well-ascertained fact that the expenses of the connection have more than counterbalanced its advantages. The maintenance of that part of our colonial possessions subjects us to a yearly expenditure of more than £800,000 in hard cash. Will any one tell us that the Canadas confer on us benefits at all equivalent to this? It may, indeed, be debated whether our exports to the Canadas would not be as great as they have been at any former period. At any rate, we speak advisedly when we say that this country will be no loser by the secession of the Canadas. That is certainly the conclusion to which the ministers have arrived, after the most able and careful deliberation."

The Liverpool Mercury had a very poor opinion of the loyalty of the Canadian Tories. The clamour for annexation, it was convinced, was a mere party manœuvre and not a national movement. Nevertheless, it confessed its inability to share the moral indignation with which some of its contemporaries regarded the speculations of the United States press on the probable incorporation of Canada with the American Union. So far as England was concerned, it concluded, it would be perfectly "fair and legitimate for Canada to annex herself to the United States according to her own free will and pleasure."

Some of the Tory protectionist papers were inclined to make party capital out of the discontent of the colonies—the existence of which was charged to the fiscal policy of the Government. " Now," said *The London Morning Post*, " that the question is thus broadly put to Her Majesty's ministers, and to the public of this United Kingdom, whether free trade is to be abandoned, or Canada is to be abandoned, there cannot be other than one choice, to revive protection ; and it must be revived at this coming session. Canadians of all parties, take from us these words of comfort : You have despaired too soon. You shall have back protection. Your position as British subjects shall not go for nothing in British markets. Your labour and capital shall be secured their due return, and the flow of wealth from England in payment for your productions shall not be stopped or transferred to your neighbour." [1] *The London Morning Herald* severely arraigned the policy of *The Times* in complacently accepting the ultimate separation of the colonies as the natural destiny of the empire. " If," it declared, " Canada should depart, she will go, leaving the brand of shame upon the cheek of Great Britain ;· she asked for justice in her commercial dealings, and we denied it ; she prayed for equal rights on Canadian ground for every subject of the Crown, and we declared in the face of the world that there are rights which the rebel in arms may claim, but in which the defender of the Throne must not hope to participate."

The attitude of the several parties towards the annexation movement was in fact truly expressive of their general political conceptions of colonial politics and imperial relationships. Both the Whig and Tory press were inclined to view Canadian affairs from the standpoint of the primary interests of the motherland. Neither the Government nor the Opposition could be justly charged with a neglect of imperial responsibilities, but they were equally prone to identify the interests of the colonies with their own political and commercial policies. Generally speaking, the Whigs were of the opinion that the interests of the empire would

[1] *The London Morning Post*, November 1, 1849.

be best promoted by devolving upon the colonies the
responsibility of their own administration ; each one
of the self-governing units of the empire, it was believed, should be left free to frame its policy in conformity with its own peculiar needs.   They claimed for
England the same rights in this respect as they granted
to the colonies.   The latter, they maintained, were not
entitled to demand sacrifices from the motherland at
the expense of her own population.   The Whig ministers were ready to lend an attentive ear to the prayers
of the colonies, they even sympathized with them in
their distress, but they refused to abandon a fiscal
policy which they were firmly convinced would prove
in the long run as advantageous to the colonists as to
the citizens of Great Britain.   For this reason, they
declined to be frightened or stampeded by the cry of
annexation, but preferred to leave the determination
of the future of the North American Provinces to time
and the good judgment of the Canadian people.

The Tories, on the contrary, believed that the unity
and permanence of the empire could only be assured
by binding the colonies to the motherland by the closest
ties of constitutional obligation and material interest.
They placed little reliance upon purely sentimental
consideration or the spiritual factors of society as a
basis of imperial relationship ; they preferred to place
their trust in an economic organization of the empire
on the basis of mutual interest and reciprocal advantage.   Upon this solid foundation, it was believed,
a strong political organization could be erected.
Throughout the Canadian crisis, the Tory Party stood
forth as the special champion of colonial and imperial
interests.   But it must be admitted that when the
interests of the colonies conflicted with the interests
of the motherland, as in the case of the repeal of
the Navigation Acts, the Tories were the smallest of
" Little Englanders."   True, they supported the claims
of the Canadian protectionists and malcontents for a
colonial preference, but they did so in the hope of

securing the restoration of protective duties in England, rather than from any high imperial motives. Imperialism was the cloak under which the principles of protection was masquerading ; the cloak was quickly discarded when the Canadian Parliament demanded the right of free navigation, which was incompatible with the monopoly of English shippers.

The Radicals, as was to be expected, were much more favourable to the development of a spirit of colonial nationalism, than either of the historic parties. But, in favouring the independence of the colonies, the Manchester Schoolmen were as deeply concerned in promoting the welfare of the colonies and the interests of the empire at large, as the most liberal Whig or the staunchest Tory imperialist. In some instances, as we have seen, they proved themselves the truest imperialists, by vindicating the rights of the colonies against the selfish pretensions of their fellow countrymen.

But, it must be confessed, Whigs, Tories, and Radicals alike subordinated the interests of the colonies to their own distinctive domestic policies. Whatever their political professions, they were all prone to look at colonial questions from an English, rather than from an imperial point of view. It was indeed but natural that they should do so.

CHAPTER X

THE ATTITUDE OF THE UNITED STATES

American expansion—Declaration of General Scott in favour of annexation—Annexation sentiment in Vermont—Resolution of the Legislature—Resolutions of New York Assembly—Attitude of Congress—Hostility of Democratic Party to annexation—Influence of the slavery issue—Views of the Whig and Free Soil Democratic press—Opinion of the West—Principle of non-intervention—Absorption in domestic questions.

IN the United States, the course of Canadian events had aroused a larger amount of interest than was usually devoted to external affairs. The country was passing through a period of rapid territorial expansion. Texas, Oregon, California, and a large slice of Mexico had been incorporated in the Union within a short space of time, yet the desire for further aggrandizement was not yet satisfied. Visions of the Stars and Stripes flying over the whole of the North American continent and the Isles of the Caribbean Sea were floating through the intoxicated minds of many of the people. In the hope of diverting attention from the approaching domestic crisis, some of the politicians at Washington were not averse to promoting a vigorous foreign policy. But the adoption of such a policy was seriously complicated by the growing antagonism of the Northern and Southern States over the question of slavery. The policy of annexation became inextricably bound up with the fundamental issue of free or slave territory. The Canadian annexation movement appeared, therefore, at a critical moment. The two great political parties in the Republic were almost equally balanced in strength. Economic and political considerations combined to foster throughout the Northern States a friendly feeling towards the Montreal Annexationists. The New York and New England merchants were especially interested in the development of Canadian trade. The abolitionists and many of the supporters of Van Buren and Seward were naturally favourable to the acquisition of more free states. But the Southern people were strongly opposed to any disturbance of the balance of power within the Union by the annexation of Canada.

For the moment, it appeared as if the Whig Party might take up the question of a northern extension of territory as a campaign issue. General Winfield Scott, a leading candidate of the party for the Presidency, came out with an open letter in favour of the annexation of the British-American Provinces. The policy of the English Government would, he believed, increase the discontent in Canada, and bring about a separation in a few years' time. The interests of both Canada and the United States would be promoted by annexation, and in all probability the people of Canada would prefer a union with the States to national independence. Annexation would be especially beneficial in doing away with border customs duties. Fully two-thirds of the American nation would rejoice in the consummation of such a union, and the remaining third would soon see the great benefits of it. But, he concluded, no underhand measures should be taken against Great Britain, since the retention of her goodwill was second only in importance to that of winning the favour of the colonists themselves.[1] The views of General Scott appeared to find a certain amount of support in Washington. A rumour was abroad that,

---

[1] This letter first appeared in *The Saratoga Whig*. *The Examiner*, July 18, 1849. *L'Avenir*, July 24, 1849, warmly welcomed the letter of General Scott. The General, it asserted, was especially friendly towards Canadians, and in 1837 had supported the proposed intervention of the United States Government on behalf of the Canadian insurgents.

for some months past, the Cabinet of President Taylor had been considering the advisability of taking up the question of annexation of Canada and Cuba as a popular campaign issue for the coming election. It was believed in some quarters that the early declaration of General Scott was designed to anticipate any such action on the part of the President.

Some of the Northern Democrat papers were afraid that the Whig Party might gain credit for the policy of annexation. That policy, it was claimed, was the distinctive property of the Democrats. " Both Cuba and the British colonies," said *The Washington Union*, " at the proper time and in the proper manner will ultimately be annexed to the American Union. But these great measures will be effected by the Democratic Party and a Democratic administration, and not by the Whigs. It will, however, be done at the proper time, when it can be accomplished with honour and without violating either the rights of Great Britain or Spain. When Canada and her sister colonies shall have secured their independence, and when Cuba shall have done the same, then will it be time enough for us to seriously discuss and finally decide on these questions." Although many of the Northern Democrats were favourable to the annexation of Canada, the implacable hostility of the Southern Democrats, who controlled the policy of the party, effectually prevented any steps being taken in that direction.

Along the northern boundary, especially in Vermont, there was a general feeling of sympathy with the annexation movement. For some time past, an effort had been made to develop a closer commercial connection between the St. Lawrence and Lake George. The merchants of Montreal had met in conference with their confrères of Burlington for the promotion of improved means of communication. An imaginary boundary line divided the allegiance, but did not sunder the social and commercial relationships of the citizens of Vermont and their neighbours in the Eastern

Townships. The appearance of the Montreal manifesto furnished a sufficient occasion for intervening in Canadian affairs.

At the Democratic State Convention at Montpelier, a grandiloquent resolution was adopted : " That, in the true spirit of democracy, deeply sympathizing with the downtrodden, oppressed, and over-restricted of every clime and country, we hail with joy the rising spirit of liberty in the provinces of Canada, as expressed recently in the published opinions of its citizens upon the subject of annexation ; that we appreciate the efforts and emulate the movements of the friends of republicanism in Canada, and that we cordially extend to them the hand of friendship, fellowship, and brotherly love ; that we will use all peaceable means in our power to further their object in becoming members of this our glorious union of free, independent, and sovereign states." [1] The Whig State Convention likewise adopted a resolution of somewhat similar import in favour of annexation.[2] No reference was made to the question at the convention of the Free Democratic Party, an omission, however, which, according to *The Burlington Courier*, was purely accidental.

The leading organs of all three parties were enthusiastically in favour of annexation. *The Brattleborough Whig* announced that the Whig Party proposed to try its hand at annexation, but was going to make the attempt by peaceful means, without a thought of resorting to war. *The Burlington Sentinel*, the most influential Democratic paper of the state, declared : " Woe be to that party which in Vermont shall in any manner oppose the accomplishment of this popular and desirable event. . . . To those living along the lines, it is the dictate of patriotism, as well as of interest, to hasten the day of annexation by every means in their power. If it be unnecessary, or impolitic, to bring physical means to bear, we have moral means

[1] *The Burlington Daily Sentinel*, October 22, 1849.
[2] *Ibid.*, October 31, 1849.

against the use of which there is no law and no rules of propriety. By expressions of sympathy in our conventions, legislatures, and presses, by private and public means, we may encourage those enlisted in the cause beyond the lines, and lend an important aid in securing the final success of the magnificent enterprise, which promises so splendid an acquisition to our commercial wealth and national glory." [1] It was even ready to resort to force, if the liberation of the colonies from the Crown could not be secured by any other means " after a fair trial." [2] *The Burlington Courier*, the principal organ of the Free Democrats, urged upon the members of the party in the Legislature to take an early occasion to show " that the free democracy of Vermont will be among the first to welcome to the blessings of the Union a neighbouring nation, whose accession, instead of adding to the slavery side of the balance, will permanently strengthen the interests of freedom."

At the meeting of the Legislature shortly after, a resolution was introduced in the Senate by Mr. Weston sympathizing with the people of Canada in their desire for freedom, and favouring the annexation of the province to the United States. An amendment was moved by Mr. Thomas, to instruct the Senators and Representatives of the State in Congress to use a proper means to bring about peaceful annexation. Mr. Thomas subsequently withdrew his amendment, upon the motion of Mr. Weston to amend his resolution by the omission of all invidious references to the state of Canada. The resolutions as amended were unanimously adopted by the Senate, with the concurrence of the House. [3]

Similar action was taken by the Legislative Assembly of New York early in 1850. A series of resolutions was

---

[1] *The Burlington Daily Sentinel*, October 31, 1849.
[2] *Ibid.*, November 6, 1849.
[3] The text of these resolutions will be found in the second Montreal manifesto, pp. 170, 171.

introduced by Mr. Wheeler, expressing the pleasure of
the Legislature at the evident desire of the people of
Canada to join the Union, and instructing the congressmen of the state to co-operate in any measures of
the federal Government to promote the annexation
of the British provinces. The resolutions were opposed
by Mr. Munroe, but they were subsequently adopted
by the decisive vote of 76 to 28.[1] The preamble and
the first of the resolutions were practically identical
in phraseology with the resolutions of the Vermont
Legislature. The last two resolutions ran as follows :

> " Resolved (if the Senate concur) that the an-
> nexation of Canada and other provinces of Great
> Britain in North America, effected by negotiation
> with the British Government, and with the
> voluntary consent of the people of the said pro-
> vinces, upon equitable and honourable terms, is
> an object of incalculable importance to the people
> of the United States. It would reunite into one
> family, and make citizens of a brave, industrious,
> and intelligent people who are now our brethren
> in interest and language. It would save this
> country the expense of maintaining a line of
> customs houses and fortifications 3,500 miles in
> extent, and give to the whole continent the blessing
> of free and unmolested trade. It would secure the
> preponderance of free institutions in this Union,
> and it would unite under one republican Govern-
> ment all the people and all the territory between
> the Atlantic and the Pacific, and the Gulf of Mexico
> and the Arctic Ocean.
>
> " Resolved (if the Senate concur) that our
> Senators and Representatives in Congress be re-
> quested to co-operate in any measures which the
> general administration may adopt to promote the
> peaceful annexation of the British North American
> Provinces to this country."

[1] New York, *Journals of the House of Assembly*, 1850, pp. 206–7.

The conduct of the Government at Washington was strictly proper.   No neutral power in time of war could have observed a more scrupulous impartiality. Throughout the course of the annexation movement President Taylor carefully refrained from even an appearance of desiring to meddle in Canadian affairs. Neither by word nor action did he lend the slightest encouragement to the Canadian Annexationists.   It would have been easy for him greatly to embarrass the Canadian Government in its efforts to relieve the distress of the province.   The question of reciprocal trade was the crux of the Canadian situation, yet he endeavoured to assist the Canadian authorities in securing the passage of a Reciprocity Bill through Congress. The attitude of Congress was equally impartial, even though not as friendly to Canada.   Undoubtedly some of the Northern Congressmen would have welcomed any overtures from Canada for annexation, but the hostility of the Southern members effectually prevented any expression of opinion, or overt action, looking to the addition of more free territory.   The temptation to intervene in Canadian affairs was undoubtedly great, but the danger of Southern secession was sufficiently imminent to absorb the attention and energies of the Government and Congress at home.

The views of the press were largely coloured by political and sectional considerations.   Slavery was the all-absorbing issue which entered into the determination of every question, whether of foreign or domestic politics.   The majority of the Southern papers were favourable to the acquisition of Cuba as a slave state, but strongly opposed to the incorporation of any more free states in the Union ; the Democrat journals of the North were divided upon the question.   The pro-slavery organs of the party masked their hostility to annexation under cover of the unfitness of the Canadian people to share in the blessings of republican institutions. " But," said *The Oswego Commercial Times*, " before so multiplying the number of states of our Union, as is proposed, consisting in so large a proportion of people who are strangers to our institutions, and to the qualifications which enable our citizens to support them, it will be well to inquire what proportion of these states can be regarded as competent to carry on the government of the United States on the principles which have preserved this Union."

In some cases, the language of the editorials was most offensive to the self-respect of the Canadian people, who were represented as hopelessly committed to the accursed " bane of aristocracy," as sunk in ignorance and stupidity, and as harbouring dark designs against the democracy of the United States. " For ourselves," said *The New York Courier and Inquirer,* " we are not anxious to see any more annexations either at North or South. The Republic is already large enough, and Canada has too long been attached to monarchical forms, to relish plain republicanism." *The Steubenville Herald* warned its readers that the Canadian Tories had spent their lives in vilifying republicanism, and that their sudden conversion, owing to the loss of their aristocratic privileges, was accompanied by many suspicious circumstances. "They should now be watched, lest they are asking to be joined to us in order that they may essay to live as they have lived before."

On the other hand, many of the Whig, and a few of the Free Soil Democratic papers, were favourably inclined towards annexation, partly on political and partly on social and economic grounds. Some of these journals were inclined to look upon the British-American provinces in a patronizing way, to commiserate the colonists on their unhappy lot as British subjects, and glowingly to portray the blessings of freedom which were in store for them on their incorporation in the American Union. By annexation, it was predicted, the colonists would secure the benefits " resulting from the wholesome laws of the Republic, and partake of the comforts which freedom offered to all." They would share in the superior economic facilities, and the rising prosperity of the American nation. Peace and harmony would reign in place of racial discord and social anarchy, and " the influence of republican institutions would soon make them a contented and prosperous people." Among the Free Soil papers, there was a decided tendency to favour the annexation of the British-American provinces, in order to strengthen the anti-slavery forces in the Union.

Several of the leading Western papers came out enthusiastically for annexation. The prospect of the free navigation of the St. Lawrence especially appealed to the commercial interests of the West. The people of the West had a glorious vision of the great imperial possibilities of such a Union. " Let Canada be annexed," declared one of the Chicago papers,[1] " not because our country is not large enough for Yankee enterprise and skill, but because her people, our brethren, wish it, because nature has so designed it by the formation of the two countries, because it aids and assists a neighbouring people in gaining their proper level, and because it unites two great portions of America which never should be severed, and prevents discord and war upon our northern boundary."

A few of the metropolitan journals of the East were equally zealous for Annexation. *The Brooklyn Star* expressed the opinion that the Government should stand ready to assist Canada in her efforts to secure separation, by opening up timely negociations with the motherland ; while *The Philadelphia Ledger* coolly proceeded to determine the conditions of union and arrange the representation which the colonies should enjoy in Congress. But the more conservative journals of the North preferred to await the course of events, rather than to push forward any schemes of territorial aggrandizement. They did not wish to involve the nation in either domestic or international complications. The annexation of the North American provinces, it

[1] *The Dollar Newspaper.*

was realized, might drive the Southern states into secession, and occasion an unfortunate embroglio in England. "For our part," said *The Buffalo Commercial Advertiser*, "we do not desire to annex the Canadian provinces at the expense of the indignation of the Southern states. We trust that the contest between the North and South may first be terminated, so that annexation may take place with the consent of all Americans." But in any case, the question of annexation was one which the Canadians must first settle for themselves, and then arrange with England, before the United States should think of intervening. "It is very certain," to quote *The New York Herald*, "that the United States will never solicit the Canadians to annex themselves to this Republic, under any circumstances whatever. But while we assert this, we are willing, on the other hand, to say that, if the Canadians will at some future time procure the consent of Great Britain to be annexed to the United States, we will, when that consent shall have been obtained, and on their solicitation and earnest request, take the question into consideration ; and, if we can adjust some preliminary arrangements concerning our domestic relations, satisfactorily to the varied interests of this country, we will allow them to come in and partake of the great political blessings which we in the United States enjoy. The first thing for the people of Canada to do, however, is to obtain England's consent to dispose of themselves as they think proper."

But notwithstanding the sympathy of many of the American people with the annexation movement in Canada, no political party, or section of the Union, showed the slightest desire to interfere in the domestic concerns of the Canadian provinces. Even those Legislatures which rashly ventured to proffer welcome to the Canadian people in advance were careful to qualify their action by protestations against any intended violation of the imperial rights of Great Britain. *The New York Herald* distinctly warned the Canadian

Annexationists that, if they resorted to force in order to sever the imperial tie, they need not expect to receive any material assistance from the United States, as they did in the revolt of 1837. There was, however, a general conviction throughout the Northern states that, in the course of Providence, Canada would inevitably become a part of the great Republic, and that the United States could well afford to await the inexorable decrees of time and fate. "The true policy of the Government," said *The Toledo Blade*, " is that of passiveness. It behoves us to keep a watch upon ourselves in this regard, while tempted so strongly by our Northern neighbours to depart from it. There is no cause for our becoming anxious or excited upon the subject—when the fruit is fully ripe it will fall into our lap without any exertion on our part."

The question of annexation never became a vital political issue in the United States. The American public were too deeply concerned with domestic matters to give due consideration to the agitation of their Northern neighbours. No political party was ready to take up a question of such doubtful political expediency. The South was overwhelmingly hostile to annexation ; the North, for the most part, was lukewarm and indifferent, and at best took but an academic interest in the subject. With the cessation of the annexation campaign in Canada, the interest of the American public in the political relations of the two countries soon died out. The nation had more important matters to discuss and determine at home.

APPENDIX

ANNEXATION

An Address from the Canadians of New York and the Surrounding Districts to their Compatriots in Canada [1]

THE Canadians resident in New York and the surrounding district grasp the first opportunity which presents itself for deliberating upon their common interests, to send from the other side of the frontier an expression of the sympathies awakened among them by the Annexation Manifesto published in Montreal in the course of the last month.

The entire press of Europe and America has been pleased to recognize the cleverness and tact which have been shown in the preparation of this document : this chorus of praise frees us from the necessity of uttering a panegyric which would not add one iota to the incontrovertible force of the arguments developed in the Manifesto, nor one more feature to the distressing picture of calamities which each line there enumerates.

Compatriots of Lower Canada ! In attempting to scatter to-day the prejudices which a contrary propaganda is endeavouring to sow against the institutions and resources of the American Union, we believe we are paying a debt of gratitude towards the country which welcomes us with so much kindness, and which treats us on an equality with its own children.

Daily witnesses of an incomparable commercial activity and interested spectators of an unparalleled political organization, we flatter ourselves that our estimates formed on the spot, in the vastest centre of American civilization,

[1] Translated from *L'Avenir* of January 11, 1850. See p. 303.

will have the effect of confirming, as far as the United States are concerned, the hopes roused by the Manifesto, and of justifying the conclusions to which the ills of the present and the forebodings of the future have irresistibly led us.

We are going to state concisely the benefits, practical and of other kinds, which would arise, in our opinion, from the proposed union between the two nations.

The system of responsible government, in whose complications the Canadas are struggling, was fashioned after the pattern of the government of the mother country. Wretched copy! Awkward copyists! They wished to transfer to a distance of a thousand leagues, to the shores of America, the accumulated work of several centuries of aristocratic privilege. Hence this system has thwarted the plans of those who forced it upon us, and has become more indefinite than ever because of the reforms attempted in order to restore to it the vitality which it constantly loses.

Let us read the Act of 1840 which unites the two Canadas : let us weigh the evils which that constitution has prevented or lightened, and the advantages born under its auspices : we shall easily convince ourselves that the only anchor of safety which remains to our country is the annexation in view, which will bring with it the abundance of advantages and the brilliancy of the splendours which the star-spangled banner encloses within its folds.

Has not the Union Act created a civil list disproportionate to the revenue of the country ?

Provided for the costly maintenance of an army of officials ?

Made the right to vote and eligibility for office dependent upon certain property qualifications which render the dearest of their prerogatives inaccessible to the mass of the people ?

Set up the Imperial Government as an absolute master who rules our affairs according to his pleasure, and who, by virtue of a right which he had not claimed for himself in his former possessions in North America, appoints our Governors, who are torn between the responsibility which they owe to the Empire and that which the Provincial Cabinet exacts from them ?

Has it not, in the midst of these conflicts, stifled all the reforming impulses of the Provincial Administration, which leads a hand-to-mouth, enfeebled existence ?

Has it not imposed a Legislative Council, whose influence, if it has any, is dependent upon changes in the Ministry ?

Compare now the two systems and judge.

In the United States the governmental machine works so simply and so regularly that a child can count its pulsations.

The sea of universal suffrage bears upon its waves all candidates for popular election.

Representation is based upon the only true and just register of public opinion, on population.

The individual states, supreme within their respective boundaries, delegate to the Federal Congress their apportioned share of power and influence.

The Senate, renewed at fixed intervals, enjoys certain executive powers which revive its authority, and heighten its value.

All the powers, the executive power, the legislative power, the judicial power, from the President to the police agent, from the member of Congress to the alderman, from the President of the Supreme Court to the judge of the Court of Summons, thanks to this perpetual elective voting, rise from the people, and descend to them again.

All powers which the ballot box confers are of short duration, in order to renew by this democratic baptism the ardour which might relax, in order especially to snatch from the Governments the time, if they had the desire, to allow themselves to become corrupted, or to become corrupters.

The American citizen, at the dictate of his conscience, goes to his vote peaceably, the secrecy of the ballot having been secured for every nationality, without fearing gold intrigues and ministerial vengeance, or the collective wrath of parties animated by feelings towards one another of inveterate hatred.

Thence contentment for everybody ; thence stability within ; thence security without.

If we pass from political organization to the purely material considerations which relate to commerce, to industry, in short to all that composes national prosperity, we find the difference still more marked, doubtless because it is more apparent and more palpable.

In Canada the interests of the Government and of the citizens experience a like suffering : the St. Lawrence is deserted : our canals of imperial magnificence, far from bending under the weight of vessels, are waiting for the arms of free navigation to reopen : our watercourses and our falls flow in their picturesque uselessness : we have barely a few miles of railway : one simple telegraphic system suffices for the faintly electric activity of our business : we receive from unhappy Ireland those immigrants who are most destitute of the means necessary for ultimate success.

That, in brief, is the progress which we have made in a half-century under the government of the colonial régime.

Well, the United States during the same period have advanced like a giant from one end of the continent to the other. The sun heats the most varied climates, and vivifies all varieties of products. A stream of enterprising immigrants has turned towards the new states. Finance, terrified by the last trembling of European thrones, hastens to find here more solid ground upon which to establish her operations. Interior lines of communication by water are crowded. Telegraph lines have been multiplied in all directions. Railroads cover the country with their veins of steel. We shall soon be able, thanks to the discovery of Morse, to link together San Francisco and New York, while at the same time an immense railroad will put the two oceans side by side.

The American, while living at home, can feed himself, dress himself, buy and sell, protected from foreign dangers, while, because of poverty, the young Canadian abandons his native land, only too uncertain whether, on his return from exile, he will be able to lay his mortal remains beside the sacred bones of his ancestors. And what are we, in reality, if not poor exiles, whom our native land sends sorrowfully away, and commends to the mercy of God ?

With these historical and statistical contrasts before us, we ask you : Has a poor country, just managing to exist under colonial government, something to lose, or something to gain by the close union which we propose for it with a country rich, contented, and free ?

The considerations that we have thus far urged are the vital elements in the life of nations, but they are not the soul.

When the drawbridge of the frontiers shall have been lowered to admit American goods and American ideas, we

shall shake off two centuries of servitude, to enter, thanks
to annexation, into the great family of nations : we shall
reappear in the firmament of universal liberty, where the
prolonged domination of France and England have eclipsed
us.

Let us, therefore, without abjuring anything that patriotism holds dear, or our most sacred convictions, enlarge our
native land to the proportions of the whole continent : let
us once more attach ourselves to the life of the world by
this glorious bond : let us restore a native land to exiles
who will be proud of such a kind of naturalization ; and we
shall see the American eagle, whose wings already dip
into the two oceans, cover the continent to the pole, and
carry to the highest sky the charter of an emancipated
North America.

Inhabitants of Lower Canada (we address you in preference, because we know you better), believe in those of your
brothers who in the midst of their sorrows and their joys
do not lose sight of you for a moment : the great qualities
which have raised to the front rank of nations this people
which has grown great so quickly beside you, have been
misrepresented, in order to keep you in terror of them.

No ; you have nothing to fear for your religion, protected, as it will be, by our freedom of worship, which is
inscribed on the frontispiece of our Constitution, and is
engraven even more deeply upon the consciences of all
intelligent people.

No ; there is no danger for your language, safeguarded
by the omnipotence of universal suffrage, and, in case of
any attempt at suppression, calling forth the sympathy
and traditional respect which every descendant of Washington entertains for those who stammer the language of
Rochambeau and Lafayette.

You will draw from this alliance, we promise you, that
spirit of order and wisdom which made a state rise from
the golden sands of California, where other people were
able only to establish mines.

We shall put you in national communion with those of
your brothers who conquer, with the aid of abundant railroads, the prairies of the far west. Will you believe those
pioneers, living and unimpeachable monuments to the
gradual impoverishment of the country ?

Annexationists of both Lower and Upper Canada, we

say to you : Courage, courage, and again courage ; great causes triumph only on this condition. Persecution, whether it comes from the Government or its agents, is the first symptom of that sure success which must crown social revolutions.

Long live annexation !

Long live America, one in its national grandeur, indivisible in its republican faith !

INDEX

Address to the People of Canada, An—see Annexation Manifesto

Ami de la Religion, L', opposes annexation, 73, 132 ; hostile to Quebec manifesto, 183 ; on the Quebec election,190

Annexation manifesto, The Montreal, preparation of, 104; text of, 106 ; signers of, 114; condemned in Upper Canada, 129 ; endorsed in Eastern Townships, 154 ; second manifesto, 164 ; third manifesto, 274

Annexation manifestos issued : at Quebec, 182 ; by French-Canadians of New York, 303 ; of Troy, 308 ; of Cooperville, 310 ; at Toronto, 314

Annexation association, The Montreal, organization of, 134 ; in need of funds, 163 ; its decay, 288 ; takes part in Sherbrooke election, 291

Annexation associations : at Quebec, 182 ; in Eastern Townships, 196 ; at New York, 302 ; at Toronto, 314 ; weakness of, 357 ; disappearance of, 360

Assembly, The, standing of parties, 334 ; debate on independence, 337 ; debate on the dismissals, 338 ; debate on annexation, 339

Avenir, L', discusses advantages of annexation, 69, 70 ; approves of manifesto, 131 ; supports Clear Grits, 263 ; criticizes Earl Grey, 269 ;

accuses Lord Elgin of bribing the R. C. bishops, 300

Badgley, M.P., defends the Annexationists, 340

Baldwin, Hon. Robt., his position, 142 ; letter to P. Perry, 143 ; his action on Prince petition, 336

Bathurst Township Grand Jury opposes annexation, 237

Brattleborough Whig, The, 377

Belleville, A meeting at, 233

Bellingham, Sydney, issues prospectus of an annexation journal, 74

Benjamin, G., Orange Grand Master, 233

Benson, Jas. R., letter to W. H. Merritt, 21

Blaquière, Hon. P. B. de, 336

Bonding privilege granted by the U.S., 24

Boulton, H. J., 349

Boulton, W. H., 210

British American League, The, origin of, 53 ; address to the public, 54 ; annexationists in Montreal branch, 55 ; a branch formed at Quebec, 56 ; loyalty of branches in Upper Canada, 59 ; convention at Kingston, 61 ; discussion of annexation, 61-3 ; federal union endorsed, 64, 240 ; address adopted by convention, 65 ; conference with Colonial Association of New Brunswick, 240 ; convention at Toronto, 241 ; discussion of annexation, 243 ; meeting of Montreal branch,

Oswego Commercial Times, The, 380

Papin, Rouge leader, 199, 203, 204
Papineau, L. J., his republican views, 67 ; his political affiliations, 1, 68, 133 ; letters concerning annexation, 134, 183 ; supports Col. Prince, 337 ; supports annexation in the Assembly, 344
Parti Rouge, Le, its formation, 68 ; its policy, 69
Perry, Peter, 142, 250, 256, 260 *et seq.* ; candidate in Third Riding of York, 259
Peterborough Dispatch, The, 236, 323
Playfair, Col., 253
Preferential Trade between Canada and Great Britain, 10 *et seq.* ; results of, 12 *et seq.* ; abolition of, 13 *et seq.* ; letter of Isaac Buchanan about, 14
Prescott Telegraph, The, favours annexation, 239
Price, Hon. Jas., petition to, 223
Prince, Col., letter favouring independence, 324 ; draws up a petition, 325 ; presents a petition in favour of independence, 366 ; speeches in the Assembly, 337, 343, 345
Protest of Liberal members against the manifesto, The, 145
Protest of loyal citizens of Montreal—see Counter Manifestos
Punch in Canada, opposes annexation, 130

Quebec Board of Trade, The, protests against abolition of preferential trade, 15, 16
Quebec Chronicle, The, opposes annexation, 84 ; criticizes manifesto, 180 ; neutral in election, 189
Quebec election, The, 187 *et seq.*
Quebec Gazette, The, opposes annexation policy, 83, 191 ; neutral in election, 189

Quebec Mercury, The, opposes annexation, 84 ; criticizes dismissals, 155 ; criticizes manifesto, 181 ; supports annexation candidate, 189

Radical attitude towards Canada, The English, 44
Rebellion of 1837, 2
Rebellion Losses Bill, effect of its introduction, 9 ; signed, 9
Reciprocity with the United States, sought by Canada, 19 ; advocated by W. H. Merritt, 21 ; petition of Canadian Parliament in 1846, 36 ; Bill passed House of Representatives, 37 ; desired by American traders, 37 ; the Dix Bill, 38 ; Resolution and Bill passed by Canadian Parliament in 1849, 40 ; W. H. Merritt sent to Washington, 328 ; Hon. M. Cameron sent to Washington, 332 ; Bills introduced into Congress by Mr. McLean and Senator Douglas, 333
Redpath, John, signs first manifesto, 114 ; speech on annexation, 136 ; President of Annexation Association, 141 ; signs second manifesto, 164 ; answer to T. Wilson, 254 ; signs third manifesto, 277
Reform Party, condition of, in 1849, 50
Robertson, Hon. John, 240
Robinson, H. C., speech on Navigation Laws, 32
Roebuck, J. A., explains position of Whigs, 17 ; quoted in second manifesto, 176
Rolph, Dr. John, 256
Rose, John, speech in favour of annexation, 139 ; dismissed, 154 ; defends himself, 155
Russell, Lord John, defines opposition to responsible government, 2 ; instructions to Lord Sydenham, 3 ; permits Rebellion Losses Bill to go into operation, 75 ; discusses annexation movement, 278

ST. MARY'S COLLEGE OF MARYLAND
ST. MARY'S CITY, MARYLAND

46364